Insurance Law in Poland

Insurance Law in Poland

Third Edition

Katarzyna Malinowska
Anna Tarasiuk

This book was originally published as a monograph in the International Encyclopaedia of Laws/Insurance Law.

Founding Editor: Roger Blanpain
General Editor: Frank Hendrickx
Volume Editor: Herman Cousy

Wolters Kluwer

Published by:
Kluwer Law International B.V.
PO Box 316
2400 AH Alphen aan den Rijn
The Netherlands
E-mail: lrs-sales@wolterskluwer.com
Website: www.wolterskluwer.com/en/solutions/kluwerlawinternational

Sold and distributed by:
Wolters Kluwer Legal & Regulatory U.S.
920 Links Avenue
Landisville, PA 17538
United States of America
E-mail: customer.service@wolterskluwer.com

ISBN 978-94-035-4769-5

e-Book: ISBN 978-94-035-4779-4
web-PDF: ISBN 978-94-035-4789-3

The Authors

Katarzyna Malinowska, attorney-at-law with many years of experience in the field of business insurance. Professor at Kozminski University. She advises on insurance distribution, creation and development of insurance products and legal aspects of claims handling under insurance contracts in professional and consumer trade, both domestic and foreign. A specialist in the field of insurance distribution, including building structures for the distribution of insurance products and relations between insurers and insurance intermediaries. For many years, Katarzyna has been advising insurance brokers and cooperated on an ongoing basis with the Association of Polish Insurance and Reinsurance Brokers as well as BIPAR. She is combining her professional practice with academic work and appears as a speaker at Polish and international conferences. Author of at least several dozen publications on insurance law, including insurance distribution. Chairwoman of the Polish section of AIDA (International Insurance Law Association) in the 2018–2020 term, currently a member of the board. Vice-chair of the Risk Management Committee at the International Astronautical Federation, individual member of the International Institute on Space Law and the International Practice Group. Head of postgraduate studies in space entrepreneurship and Risk and Property Insurance, at Kozminski University. Member of the International Risk Management Institute in London.

Anna Tarasiuk, attorney at law and lecturer at the Kozminski University. She started her interests in insurance law in 1999; initially worked at CMS Cameron McKenna and then, through many years worked for Hogan Lovells, providing legal advice to the entities acting on the Polish market of financial institutions, including insurers, banks, insurance intermediaries and financial intermediaries. Currently owner of TARASIUK LEGAL Law Office. Her main interests are regulatory matters, cross-border services, distribution of insurance products and bancassurance. Anna has experience in relation to the creation adaptation to the market and legal requirements of the documentation regarding insurance products, including those that are very innovative. She has been involved in consumer protection issues on the Polish market for many years now, including payment protection insurance and these that have various collateral functions. Anna also advises on matters regarding insurance secrecy, data protection and other specific regulations of the insurance market. She is an arbiter of the Arbitration Court at the Polish Financial Supervisory Commission and a mediator at the Mediation Centre at the District Chamber of Attorneys-at-law in Warsaw. She is a lecturer at the universities (Kozminski University and the Warsaw School of Economics) and the District Chamber of Attorneys-at-law in Warsaw in relation to insurance law and financial institutions and a speaker at various conferences related to insurance matters. Anna is an author of various publications on insurance law regarding the Polish market. She was a Member of the CCBE working group on insurance matters and delegated to the Expert Group on Insurance at the European Commission.

Table of Contents

List of Abbreviations

AC	Autocasco (Insurance)
ACI	Act on Compulsory Insurances, Insurance Guarantee Fund and the Polish Motor Insurers' Bureau
AIRA	The Act on Insurance and Reinsurance Activity
AR	All Risks
BFG	Bank Guarantee Fund
CAR	Contractors All Risk
CCPC	Commercial Companies and Partnerships Code
CFS	Commission of Financial Supervision
DORA	Digital Operational Resilience Act
EAR	Erection All Risk
EBRD	European Bank for Reconstruction and Development
ECJ	European Court of Justice
EU	European Union
EUR	Euro (currency)
FPA	Free from Particular Average
GDP	Gross Domestic Product
ICT	Information and Communication Technologies
IDA	The Polish Insurance Distribution Act
IKE	*Indywidualne konta emerytalne* (Individual Pension Accounts)
IKZE	*Indywidualne konta zabezpieczenia emerytalnego* (Individual Pension Security Accounts)
IPID	Insurance Product Information Document
IPT	Insurance Premium Tax
KRS	National Court Register
MAS	Maximum Amount Sum
MTOM	Maximum Take-Off Mass
MTPL	Motor Third Party Liability
NBP	National Bank of Poland
NFZ	*Narodowy Fundusz Zdrowia* (National Health Fund)

List of Abbreviations

NNW	*Następstw Nieszczęśliwych Wypadków* (Personal Accident Insurance)
OFE	*Otwarte Fundusze Emerytalne* (Open Pension Fund)
PAYG	Pay As You Go
PCC	The Polish Civil Code
PFSA or KNF	Polish Financial Supervision Authority
PLN	Polish Zloty (currency)
PML	Probable Maximum Loss
PPEs	*Pracownicze Programy Emerytalne* (Occupational Pension Schemes)
PRL	Polish People's Republic
PSD	Payment Services Directive
PSI	Polish Investment Zone
PSR	Payment Services Regulation
PZU	Powszechny Zaklad Ubezpieczen S.A.
PZUW	Polski Zakład Ubezpieczeń Wzajemnych
RPP	Monetary Policy Council in Poland
TPL	Third Party Liability
UFG	Insurance Guarantee Fund
VAT	Value Added Tax
WA	With Average
WARTA	Towarzystwo Ubezpieczen i Reasekuracji WARTA, SA. (Insurance and Reinsurance Company WARTA, Inc.)
WSE	Warsaw Stock Exchange
WTO	World Trade Organization
YAR	York Antwerp Rules
ZUS	Zaklad Ubezpieczen Spolecznych (Polish State Insurance Agency)

General Introduction

§1. General Background Information

I. Political System

1. The Republic of Poland (Polska; official long form: Rzeczpospolita Polska) is a sovereign state situated in Central Europe. Poland is bordered to the north by the Baltic Sea and bounded to the south by the Sudetes and Carpathian mountain ranges. It shares international borders with seven countries: Germany to the west; the Czech Republic and Slovakia to the south; Ukraine and Belarus to the east; and Lithuania and the Kaliningrad Oblast of the Russian Federation to the north. Poland encompasses an area of 312,685 square kilometres, ranking as the ninth-largest country in Europe. The population is approximately 37,552,000, making Poland the eighth most populous country on the continent. The official language is Polish, and the national currency is the Złoty (PLN), which is further subdivided into 100 groszy.

2. Poland is a parliamentary republic. According to the provisions of the 1997 Constitution, the Republic of Poland is a democratic constitutional state whose system is based on the principle of the separation and balance of powers. The Constitution recognises the inherent, inalienable and inviolable dignity of the individual as the source of rights and freedoms. The fulfilment of these values and principles requires the existence of a democratically elected Parliament, which makes laws and controls the activities of the executive. The executive consists of the President as Head of State, the Prime Minister as Head of Government and the Council of Ministers. All ministers are proposed by the Prime Minister, appointed by the President and approved by the Sejm.

3. The President serves as the head of state and is elected by general ballot for a term of five years. The current President, Mr Andrzej Duda, was first sworn into office in 2015 and was re-elected in 2020.

4. The Prime Minister acts as the head of government and is responsible for appointing ministers, subject to presidential approval and parliamentary confirmation. The executive branch is responsible for the administration of national policies.

5. Poland's Parliament, or National Assembly, is bicameral, comprising the Sejm (Lower Chamber) and the Senate (Upper Chamber). The Sejm consists of 460 deputies, while the Senate is composed of 100 senators. Both chambers are elected by direct, general ballot for four-year terms.

6. Poland's legal system adheres to the continental legal tradition. Its common courts include district courts, provincial courts, and courts of appeal. Judicial orders are enforceable upon issuance unless a court suspends enforcement by decision. Such decisions are appealable. Enforcement proceedings commence based on a court decision, which must be marked ex officio with a statement of enforceability upon the request of a party. Poland prioritises political and economic integration with the European Union (EU), which it joined on 1 May 2004.Strengthening cooperation with neighbouring countries is a cornerstone of Polish foreign policy.

7. In conclusion, the Republic of Poland is a state with a robust legal framework, democratic governance and a judiciary rooted in continental traditions. Its Constitution emphasises the dignity of the individual and establishes a system of government that reflects the separation and balance of powers. These principles are underpinned by Poland's commitment to the rule of law, its active participation in the EU and its efforts to promote regional cooperation.

II. Commerce and Industry

8. Poland is the EU's sixth largest economy, after the Netherlands, Spain, Italy, France and Germany.[1] Poland has a stable economy with an established macroeconomic position. The unique conditions for doing business and starting a business are supported by a repeatedly proven resilience to economic crises. Since the transition to a market economy, Poland has maintained strong Gross Domestic Product (GDP) growth above the EU average. Rising wages and consumption make it an attractive consumer market. Key sectors attracting investment include automotive, electronics, business process outsourcing and renewable energy. With its strategic location, business-friendly environment and promising growth prospects, Poland offers excellent opportunities for global investors seeking access to European markets. Since the mid-1990s, the Polish economy has been growing at a fairly rapid pace, averaging 4% over the past thirty years. Even after 2008, Poland did not fall into recession. In 2019, the economy grew by 4.5%. 2020 was the first year since the transition when the economy contracted by 2.8%. In 2024, the Polish economy emerged from the slowdown suffered during the COVID-19 pandemic. Compared to other EU countries, the COVID-19 pandemic affected Polish GDP growth to a lesser extent and the Polish economy recovered quickly in 2021. Despite the war in Ukraine, Poland remains a safe and stable investment environment and a member

1. Zagraniczne Inwestycje Bezpośrednie w Polsce, raport SGH 2024, accessed 23 Dec. 2024 https://gazeta.sgh.waw.pl/sites/gazeta.sgh.waw.pl/files/zalaczniki-2024/ZIB_ARCH.pdf. Doing Business in Poland, Investor's guide, Poland 2024, https://www.paih.gov.pl/wp-content/uploads/2024/11/Doing-Business-in-Poland-Investors-guide-2024.pdf, accessed 23 Dec. 2024.

of key strategic alliances such as NATO. For 2024, all major rating agencies have maintained their ratings for Poland, unchanged from last year, with a very stable outlook.

9. GDP growth is forecast to be around 2.6% in 2024 and 4.1% in 2025. Inflation will be 3.6% and 4.6% respectively in these years. The unemployment rate will remain one of the lowest in the EU. At the end of 2024, the registered unemployment rate is around 5.3%. Wage growth also remains in double digits in 2024, averaging 12.3%. Over the last twenty-five years, the Polish economy doubled in size, as measured in terms of real GDP. In terms of GDP per capita (at PPP), Poland narrowed the gap by nearly half, moving from 32% to 60% of the Western European average (EU-15).1 Annual GDP growth between 1991 to 2008 amounts to 4.6%.[2]

10. Poland has established itself as a dynamic and attractive destination for investment, characterised by economic stability, a strategic geographic location, and a highly skilled workforce. As one of the fastest-growing economies within the EU, Poland provides numerous opportunities across a wide range of sectors. The nation's robust infrastructure, investment-friendly policies, and proactive governmental initiatives create an environment conducive to the growth and success of both domestic and international business ventures. Poland continues to attract significant volumes of direct investment, which serves as a key driver of its economic development. Despite challenges such as inflationary pressures and rising interest rates, the country has demonstrated economic resilience, as evidenced by sustained mergers and acquisitions activity within the emerging European market. According to Emerging Europe, Poland has been identified as the leader in transactional activity among thirteen emerging economies in the region.

11. The strategic concept of nearshoring has become an integral element of corporate planning as companies strive to develop resilient, sustainable, and competitive supply chains in response to a rapidly changing global landscape. In this context, Poland has emerged as a highly attractive destination, ranking 4th globally according to the report concerning the nearshoring, developed by Maersk and Reuters Events.[3] This ranking reflects the increasing trend among businesses to relocate production facilities from distant locations to countries that are geographically closer to key markets, with Poland being a favoured choice for such transitions:[4]

1. Poland is a leader in the business services sector in CEE and offers a number of attractive advantages for investors planning to establish new SSC and BPO centres. It is one of the most important and fastest-growing sectors in Poland. With over 1,800 centres employing more than 430,000 people, the country remains the largest in the region. The Polish Investment Zone (PSI) is also an

---

2. McKinsey, Poland 2025: Europe's New Growth Engine.
3. Reuters Events, A.P. Moller-Maersk 2023, A generational shift in sourcing strategy: A global and European deep dive into near-sourcing, nearshoring and reshoring in the post-pandemic world.
4. KPMG Report 2024.

investment incentive scheme that divides the country into seven macro-regions covering a total of sixteen voivodeships. Within the PSI, companies can benefit from tax breaks and other investment incentives, the value of which depends on the location of the investment and its impact on regional development.

2. Poland has a number of economic sectors with high development potential, such as aerospace, household appliances, electronics, Information and Communication Technologies (ICT), electromobility, business services, food, pharmaceuticals and meditech.

12. According to the Polish Information and Foreign Investment Agency (www.paih.gov.pl), the Polish economy can be briefly described as:

- robust and resilient to external shocks – mainly due to the country's large domestic market and diversified export structure;
- providing a safe environment for economic activity and long-term planning (stable prices, continuous GDP growth);
- very low risk of financial crisis;
- driven by a large number of agile small and medium-sized enterprises (over 3,000,000 registered units).

13. In 2023, the European Bank for Reconstruction and Development (EBRD) significantly increased its financial commitments to the Republic of Poland, allocating a total of EUR 1.3 billion. This allocation reflects a 31% increase compared to the EUR 990 million disbursed in the preceding year. Poland ranked as the third-largest recipient of EBRD funding during this period, following Ukraine, which received over EUR 2 billion, and Türkiye, which secured nearly EUR 2.5 billion. A substantial portion of the EBRD's investments in Poland – comprising 75% of the total – was allocated to green finance initiatives. This level of investment notably exceeds the EBRD's established minimum target of 50% for green financing within its new investments. The increased financial commitment and prioritisation of green finance underscore the EBRD's strong commitment to fostering sustainable development and facilitating economic transformation within Poland.[5]

14. As regards commerce and industry in Poland, there is quite an extensive number of regulations influencing business life in Poland to a great extent. The regulations can be divided into three categories: (i) applicable to business activity; (ii) applicable to consumer protection; (iii) applicable to specific business activity, such as insurance activity. ESG regulations affect many parts of the Polish economy and the introduction of more restrictive regulations regarding greenhouse gas emissions may affect the costs of doing business, especially in sectors generating high emission levels. The country is set to receive significant funds from the EU that will

5. https://www.ebrd.com/news/2024/ebrd-invests-record-13-billion-in-poland.html, accessed 23 Dec. 2024.

represent a potential influx of capital directed towards ESG-compliant projects. Foreign investors in Poland are subject to transparent regulations based on EU laws, ensuring the protection of their investments.

15. Additionally, companies operating in Poland must comply with data protection laws and environmental regulations, which promote sustainable development and data security. The Polish tax authorities hold the power to undertake a tax audit in the five years after a tax liability arises and to reassess the amount of that tax liability. Understanding and adhering to these tax regulations is crucial for foreign businesses operating in Poland to ensure compliance and avoid legal issues.[6] The main regulation concerning business activity is the Act of 6 March 2018 on Entrepreneurs (Journal of Laws 2018, item 646 as amended). It implements Directive 2006/123/WE of the European Parliament and of the Council of 12 December 2006 on services in the internal market (Journal of Laws of 27 December 2006, L 376) and regulates the basic principles of conducting business in Poland. It defines the rules for commencing, conducting and terminating a business activity on the territory of the Republic of Poland, including the rights and obligations of entrepreneurs and the duties of public authorities in this respect. The act defines an entrepreneur as a natural person, a legal entity or an organisational unit that is not a legal entity and whose legal capacity has been conferred by a separate legal act, who carries out an economic activity.

16. The above-mentioned act relates to the conduct of economic activities in Poland by entrepreneurs with their registered office in Poland, while the principles of the commencement, performance and termination of economic activities by foreign entities are set out in separate regulations. These separate regulations mainly consist of the Act of 6 March 2018 on the Principles of Participation of Foreign Entrepreneurs and Other Foreign Persons in Economic Turnover on the Territory of the Republic of Poland (Journal of Laws 2018, item 649, as amended). The Act regulates the commencement and pursuit of economic activities by foreign persons on the territory of the Republic of Poland, the temporary offering or provision of services on the territory of the Republic of Poland by foreign entrepreneurs and establishes the principles of establishing branches and representative offices in the Republic of Poland by foreign entrepreneurs. It also defines the rules of international cooperation of competent authorities in the field of service provision. Pursuant to the Act, foreign entities may commence and conduct business activities in Poland, and entrepreneurs may open branches and representative offices and offer and provide services on the territory of Poland in accordance with the provisions of the Act.

17. Protection of Competition and Consumer Rights Act of 16 February 2007 (uniform text: JL 2021, item 275). It reflects the basic principles of European standards in the field of consumer protection. It covers aspects of protection of individual consumer rights as well as regulation of free market competition (e.g., merger control). It is not the only law that refers to consumer protection. Several

6. KPMG Report 2024.

others refer to consumer rights from the point of view of contractual relations, including the Act of 30 May 2014 on Consumer Rights (JL 2020, item 287). The Act contains legal regulations on the obligations of the entrepreneur concluding a contract with the consumer, rules and procedures for concluding a distance and off-premises contract with the consumer, rules on withdrawing from the contract and the regulation of contracts concluded at a distance or off-premises, as well as rules and procedures for concluding a distance contract with the consumer concerning financial services.

18. The most important Polish regulation governing the conduct of commercial activities is the Code on Commercial Companies and Partnerships of 15 September 2000, which regulates the general manner in which business may be conducted in an organised form of companies or partnerships. In addition to harmonising Polish company law with European Community directives, the Code brought Polish company law into line with modern business practices. Polish company law continues to follow the continental civil law tradition, in particular German law, as opposed to the common law tradition of the United Kingdom and the United States of America. Polish company law is primarily concerned with the relationship between a company and its shareholders, between companies and their creditors and between shareholders. It is not concerned with protecting the interests of the company's managers or employees.

19. Other regulations that have a direct impact on the conduct of business in Poland are quite extensive. With regard to starting a business, it is important to note the Act of 20 August 1997 on the National Court Register (uniform text: Journal of Laws 2021, item 112, as amended), which regulates the manner in which organisational units (including companies and partnerships) are registered and the maintenance of the register, which is updated and available to the public free of charge (ekrs.ms.gov.pl).

In view of the dynamic development of technology and digitisation, Polish regulations are undergoing dynamic changes in order to adapt business activities to the requirements of maximum security of market participants. In the near future, changes in regulations for the financial sector are also planned – some of them are at the stage of draft legislation, and some have already been passed and will soon come into force. The upcoming changes may have a significant impact on the functioning of the financial market, so it is worth taking a look at them today in order to plan appropriate adaptation measures. Among the most important can be mentioned:

20. PSD3 regulatory package.

Significant changes in open banking and payment services are planned in the near future, resulting from the EU's work on the PSD3 package. The purpose of the proposed regulations is to strengthen and modernise the European payments market. The PSD3 package includes several pieces of legislation that together will comprehensively regulate the payment services sector, including primarily, the Payment Services Directive (PSD3), which will be the core legislation of the PSD3 Package and will replace the PSD2 Directive currently in force. It will aim to adapt regulations to new technological challenges and increase the security and competitiveness of the payments market. In addition, the Payment Services Regulation (PSR) should be mentioned. The PSR Regulation will supplement the provisions of the PSD3 Directive, introducing detailed regulations on operational and technical issues, as well as access to payment services. In addition, new rules on access to account information will be introduced. In addition to this, the Open Banking Data Access – Open Banking (FIDA) Regulation should be kept in mind. The FIDA Regulation will also be complementary to the PSD3 Directive. It will introduce new rules for sharing customer banking data with third parties. The proposed PSD3 package is aimed at increasing the level of security for payment market participants and allowing new entrants into the market, which may contribute to its further liberalisation and innovation. This raises the question of the future shape of the market in the context of these changes. At present, it is difficult to clearly predict the final consequences, as work on the PSD3 package is ongoing and the final shape of the legislation has not yet been determined. It is expected that the final version of the new regulations will be presented by the end of this year, and their implementation could take place by 2026. We will monitor the progress of the legislative work and provide an update on the status of the project.

21. New Consumer Credit Directive (CCD2)

Another important area of special attention for regulators is the protection of consumer rights. In this regard, the EU has updated its consumer credit legislation by enacting the so-called New Consumer Credit Directive (CCD2). The CCD2 Directive establishes a new legal framework for consumer credit agreements, adapting them to the realities of today's digital transformation. The changes introduced are aimed at strengthening borrower protection and include, in particular, an expanded scope of application, clear pre-contractual information, thorough creditworthiness testing, and advertising guidelines. The CCD2 directive aims to unify certain legal areas regulating consumer credit providers, with a particular focus on the regulation of information obligations at various stages of the credit process, including pre-sales (advertising). The upcoming changes should be viewed positively and seen as important for the Polish market, where consumers often choose to assert their rights by challenging contract provisions in the courts. Of course, the final shape of the regulations will depend on how the national legislator implements the EU regulations. Poland is obliged to implement the CCD2 Directive by 20 November 2025, and the new regulations are expected to take effect from 20 November 2026. Admittedly, project work on implementation has not yet begun. We invite you to follow our pages, where we will keep you updated on legislative initiatives in this regard.

22. Amendment of Recommendation G

On the domestic front, an important change comes from the Polish Financial Supervision Authority's (PFSA). Amendment to Recommendation G dated February 2024 sets out the principles for interest rate risk management in banks. The refresh of the supervisory authority's guidelines is a result of changes made to generally applicable laws and guidelines (including the EBA Guidelines) setting out criteria for identifying, assessing, managing and mitigating risks arising from potential changes in interest rates, as well as assessing and monitoring credit spread risk arising from an institution's banking book activities, the Regulation on the Criteria and Manner of Conducting a Supervisory Examination and Assessment in Banks, the Regulation on the Risk Management System and Internal Control System and Remuneration Policy in Banks, as well as the current market situation.

The revised Recommendation G is a set of good practices dedicated to the banking sector, which relate to managing interest rate risk and maintaining the financial result (including certain covenants) at a level that does not threaten the security of the bank. In the recommendation issued, the FSC took into account the current conditions in terms of products generating such risk and techniques for its appropriate management. Banks should adapt their activities to the FSC's updated guidelines by 31 December 2024.

23. New technologies under the microscope: the Artificial Intelligence Act (AI Act) and Digital Operational Resilience Act (DORA)

In addition to strictly regulatory issues, in the era of new technology development, the EU has also taken steps intended to regulate the use of artificial intelligence (AI Act) and the security of networks and information systems in the financial sector (DORA). The primary objective of the AI Act, which came into force on 1 August 2024, is to harmonise the EU internal market for the development and use of artificial intelligence-based systems. The new regulation is intended to promote trustworthy and human-centred artificial intelligence, consequently stimulating innovation and employment in Member States.

The DORA Regulation, however, aims to introduce harmonised and high ICT standards in the financial sector. The new regulation thus establishes uniform requirements for network and information system security in the financial sector and for providers of key ICT services to the sector.

III. Supervising Financial Institutions

24. Financial institutions can be defined in several ways. The most common is to define financial institutions by the type of activity that is strictly regulated and supervised. Thus, a financial institution is usually a depository institution, a custodian institution, an investment company or a specified insurance company. The type of financial institutions is also recognised by the supervisory powers of the Polish public authorities and includes such sectors of the financial market as banking, insurance, pension, capital, cooperative banks and payment services.

25. Supervision of financial institutions is entrusted to the 'PFSA', or 'KNF'. The KNF is responsible for the supervision of the banking sector, the capital market, the insurance and pension markets, the supervision of payment institutions and payment service offices, electronic money institutions and the cooperative credit union sector. Details of the KNF can be found at https://www.knf.gov.pl/en/.

26. In addition, the guarantee schemes for the financial market should be mentioned. For this purpose, two main institutions governing the guarantee schemes in Poland will be explained. These are the Bank Guarantee Fund (BFG) and the Insurance Guarantee Fund (UFG).

27. The BFG was established on the basis of the Act of 10 June 2016 on the BFG, Deposit Guarantee System and Resolution (i.e., Journal of Laws 2022, item 793, as amended). The said Act transposed into the national legal order the provisions of Directive 2014/49/EC of the European Parliament and of the Council of 16 April 2014 on deposit guarantee schemes and Directive 2014/59/EC of the European Parliament and of the Council of 15 May 2014 establishing a framework for the recovery and resolution of credit institutions and investment firms. Details of the BFG are available at www.bfg.pl.

28. UFG was established on the basis of the Act of 22 May 2003 on Compulsory Insurance, the Insurance Guarantee Fund and the Polish Motor Insurers' Bureau (ACI). The UFG is responsible for paying compensation and benefits to injured parties in traffic accidents and collisions caused by uninsured motor vehicle owners and uninsured farmers. Each of these groups is required to have valid third party liability (TPL) insurance. UFG is also responsible for making payments to injured parties in traffic accidents when the liable party has not been identified. Details of the UFG can be found at https://www.ufg.pl.

29. Other examples of important public players in the Polish financial market are:

- Korporacja Kredytów Eksportowych S.A., which deals with trade insurance and trade finance. They provide credit insurance, as well as guarantees or factoring, which currently provide liquidity and funds for the growth of Polish companies. Details can be found at www.kuke.com.pl (English version available).
- Warsaw Stock Exchange (WSE) in Warsaw, the largest financial instruments exchange in Central and Eastern Europe. Details are available at www.gpw.pl.
- Krajowy Depozyt Papierów Wartościowych, being a central infrastructure institution responsible for the management and supervision of the Depository, Clearing and Settlement System (kdpw_stream) to enable the trading of financial instruments in Poland. Details are available at www.kdpw.pl.
- The Central Offer Table is an unofficial public securities market established on 12 February 1996 as a joint-stock company. Its main shareholder is the WSE. CeTO is a part of the regulated secondary public OTC market. The OTC market is intended for companies that do not meet the restrictive requirements of the stock market.
- Towarowa Giełda Energii (Commodity Exchanges, TGE) is the only licensed commodity exchange in Poland operating under the Act on Commodity Exchanges and holding a permit to operate a regulated market. TGE is supervised by the PFSA with regard to trading on the markets operated by the Exchange, including the markets for electricity, natural gas, property rights, CO_2

emission rights and, from 2020, agricultural and food commodities. More details can be found at www.tge.pl (English version available).

IV. Currency and Monetary System

30. The National Bank of Poland (NBP) is responsible for monetary, credit and exchange rate policies, as well as banking supervision and regulation. The NBP is an independent central bank.

31. In 1997, the amended NBP Act established a Council for Monetary Policy in Poland (RPP). The RPP's task is to draw up annual monetary policy guidelines. In 1995, the Law on the Bank Deposit Guarantee Fund came into force. It requires all banking institutions to establish a deposit insurance system. In 1997, together with a new package of banking laws – the amended Banking Act and the NBP Act – the Parliament adopted the Mortgage Bonds and Mortgage Banks Act.

32. The Polish currency is the zloty (PLN). The zloty is divided into 100 groszy.

33. The primary statutory objective of monetary policy is to maintain price stability while supporting sustainable economic growth and financial stability. The Monetary Policy Council achieves this through an inflation-targeting strategy. Since 2004, the policy objective has been to maintain inflation, as measured by the annual change in the consumer price index, at 2.5%, with a symmetric tolerance margin of +/- 1 percentage point over the medium term. Temporary deviations from this target may occur due to macroeconomic and financial shocks.

34. The main instrument of monetary policy is the NBP interest rates, complemented by instruments such as open market operations, the required reserve system and standing facilities. As stated in the monetary policy guidelines, monetary policy parameters, including interest rates, are adjusted in response to economic conditions with the aim of maintaining price stability in the long term while supporting sustainable growth and financial stability. The Council's strategy allows for flexibility in the use of instruments, adapting them to the nature of economic and market disturbances.

V. Insurance Business: General Organisation and Special Features

35. The market model of insurance has been developing in Poland since 1990. The Polish insurance market is currently the largest among the countries of Central and Eastern Europe. Although the size of this market (measured by gross written premium) more than doubled as from 2009, it is still significantly behind Western European countries. In terms of size, the Polish insurance market is also inferior to those countries in Western Europe that have a significantly smaller population than

Poland, such as Austria, Belgium, Denmark, Finland, the Netherlands, Switzerland and Sweden.

36. According to the publication 'Insurance in Numbers 2023' issued by the Polish Insurance Chamber (PIU), the insurance sector in Poland showed significant economic integration and financial stability at the end of 2023. Domestic insurance companies' investments in securities totalled PLN 96.4 billion, contributing to a total asset base of PLN 218.1 billion. Gross written premiums amounted to PLN 78.9 billion, of which 29% was life and 71% non-life, while claims and benefits paid reached PLN 44.2 billion. Key figures for motor insurance included 28,063,871 active motor liability policies and 7,390,729 motor own damage policies, with average claims costs of PLN 9,980 and PLN 9,356 respectively. Agricultural insurance included 1,422,588 building insurance policies and 1,493,379 farmers' liability insurance policies. The health insurance segment grew to 4.8 million insured persons, generating gross premiums of PLN 1.7 billion. The contribution of bancassurance to gross life premiums reached 15.9%, or PLN 5.97 billion. Financially, the sector achieved technical results of PLN 4.1 billion (life insurance) and PLN 2.9 billion (non-life insurance), with net financial results of PLN 3.3 billion and PLN 6.2 billion respectively. The investments of the life and non-life insurance segments amounted to PLN 84.1 billion and PLN 102.6 billion respectively, supported by equity of PLN 11.9 billion and PLN 37.0 billion, respectively.

37. The market structure in 2023 included twenty-nine life insurance companies, eighteen non-life insurance companies, seven mutual insurance companies and two reinsurance companies, which provided a solid framework for operational sustainability and economic contribution.[7]

38. The insurance penetration rate, which shows the ratio of gross premiums written to GDP, remains below the European average in Poland. Insurance premium penetration – is EUR 377 per person compared to EUR 329 average for CEE-14, which corresponds to 2.7% of GDP with the regional average of 2.5%, while the average for Europe is 4.8%. Analysing the penetration of insurance in relation to GDP per capita, it can be expected that the Polish insurance sector will develop along with the economic development of Poland (GDP growth), the wealth of society (increase in disposable income of households) and increasing insurance awareness of Poles, similar to Western European countries.

39. The situation in the Polish insurance market is also driven by Poland's public health system, which is highly inefficient, with costs rising faster than premiums. As a result, more and more patients are forced to co-finance health services in order to receive proper treatment, the report said. In addition, the demographic trends will make the situation in public health care even more complicated, as the number of recipients of health services is expected to steadily grow, while the number of people

7. https://www.knf.gov.pl/en/ accessed 23 Dec. 2024.

contributing to the system will shrink. Despite huge potential medical insurance market is still at a very early stage of development, mainly due to the lack of appropriate regulations which could allow public health institutions to absorb additional private funds.

40. The insurance market went quite well through the pandemic period. Premium volumes and values rose. Although insurers' profitability has decreased during that time, it was still relatively high compared to other countries and other sectors in the Polish economy. In the life insurance market, there has recently been a change in the trend towards growth after many years of decline.

41. Regarding the importance of the insurance market in Poland, several extensive surveys have been conducted recently. According to a survey by the Polish Chamber of Insurance, as many as 72% of Poles trust insurers. That is more than many other financial institutions. Poles understand that insurance is an important financial instrument that helps protect what is most precious to us. Eighty-three per cent of those surveyed by the Polish Chamber of Insurance felt that insurance is needed when something bad happens. This percentage is higher – accounting for 89% – among those who have liquidated a claim in the past. So we are increasingly aware of the value of financial security in case of random events, especially those related to loss of life and health.

42. In 2021, domestic insurance companies paid out PLN 41.3 billion in claims and benefits. This means more than PLN 113 million in payouts per day. Per capita in Poland, that is PLN 1,086 per person per year, of which PLN 485 are life insurance benefits. In 2021, insurance companies settled a total of 7.5 million claims from insurance property and other personal insurance. This means they helped more than 20,000 cases every day. The importance of insurance to the economy is described not only by the numbers related to claims and benefits. The impact of the industry on Poland's GDP in 2021 was 2.25%, which means PLN 58.9 billion of added value to the economy. It is worth emphasising that while the share of insurance in the GDP of EU countries combined has declined in the last ten years, Poland has seen an increase in GDP generated by insurance companies over this period. Insurers create 221,500 full-time jobs. For every full-time job created in the insurance industry, there are seven full-time jobs in other sectors of the economy indirectly and inductively related to insurance. Insurers are also taxpayers and important investors. In 2021, insurance companies paid PLN 1.2 billion in income tax and PLN 650 million in asset tax. These are funds that went into the economy to support the development of education, transport, culture and security. Insurers invested nearly PLN 56 billion in government bonds issued in the domestic market. That's one-third of their investments and as much as the investments of all households combined. Insurance companies are the second-largest commercial domestic investor in the government bond market.

§2. Historical Background of Insurance and Insurance Legislation

Early History (Before 1772)

43. The prototype of insurance in Poland was a kind of mutual society ('Porządki ogniowe', later 'Kasy ogniowe') founded in Poznań in 1544, whose aim was to protect its members against fire. In Poland, as elsewhere, marine insurance was the forerunner of property insurance for risks on land. The origins of the insurance contract are to be found in the practices adopted by the marine insurance provisions of the Wilkierz Gdańsk of 1761.

Partition (1772–1919)

44. A real development of non-marine insurance owes its impetus to the policy of Prussia, which occupied the western provinces of Poland from the end of the eighteenth century. A royal decree of 1803 established an insurance office in Poznan to provide mutual fire insurance for buildings. After the unification of Poland in 1871, there was a tendency to establish several new public insurance offices for separate branches of insurance. In 1873, a group of liberal Polish patriots in Poznañ raised the necessary capital to finance a new joint-stock insurance company 'Vesta', which would have only Polish shareholders and offer insurance to Poles. The project was part of the general programme to protect the Polish community from the growing pressure of economic Germanisation. The Prussian system of mutuals was so successful that it was applied to the central provinces occupied by Russia (from 1815 – the so-called Congress Kingdom with the Russian Tsar as king). Such an association was established in Warsaw as early as 1804.

45. Austria brought its part of Poland under loose control as an integral part of the Austrian state. In 1860, a mutual company called 'Florianka' was established in Krakow. It was a private company that provided both life and non-life insurance. This type of activity spread to central Poland (1873). Needless to say, all forms of private activity were controlled by the occupying powers and foreign (to Poland) capital.

Polish Resurrection (1919–1939)

46. When Poland regained its independence in 1918, the existing systems continued to operate but were adapted to the needs of modern society. A public insurance company based in the Polish capital, PZUW (the Common Polish Mutual Insurance Company), was established in 1927, and a reinsurance company 'WARTA' was established even earlier, in 1920. However, private companies engaged in voluntary insurance (which grew in the years before the Second World War) were still owned by German, French and/or Italian capital.

World War II

47. During the Second World War, Germany directly annexed part of Polish territory and made it an integral part of the German state. In this territory, only the

PZUW was allowed to continue its activities. The memory of German-occupied Poland was organised into a separate Government General of Occupied Polish Territories. In this territory, all existing insurance companies were allowed to continue their activities. The Soviet Union directly annexed the territories it occupied and made them an integral part of the Soviet state. All Polish insurance companies were excluded from this territory and insurance operations there were placed under the control of the Soviet administration through Soviet institutions.

Polish People's Republic (PRL)

48. The post-war development of insurance under the regime of the Polish People's Republic (PRL) can be divided into four phases: from 1945 to 1952, from 1952 to 1958, from 1958 to 1984 and from 1984 to 1989.

49. The first stage begins with two decrees which had a double effect: nationalisation of all industry and adaptation of the insurance sector to the socialist concept of a planned economy. With the exception of PZUW, all joint-stock and mutual companies were dissolved. However, PZUW was given a monopoly for all branches of insurance as a 'public utility', and WARTA was entrusted with reinsurance. It was believed that the new public insurance system should provide the same level of protection as the private insurers had provided before the war in order to rebuild the war-ravaged country. The doctrine that state industry should act as its own insurer was abandoned by an early decree of the Minister of Industry because industrial premises were to be subject to compulsory fire insurance. All units of the socialist economy were also advised to insure themselves against losses due to burglary, civil liability and other risks normally encountered in various industries.

50. The second stage, which was centred on the 1952 Law on State Insurance, saw the further development of socialism. The PZUW was transformed from a traditional mutual insurance company into a state insurance company – Państwowy Zakład Ubezpieczeń.

51. A general trend in the 1950s was to reduce compulsory insurance of government property (while maintaining the possibility of facultative insurance) and to increase the scope of compulsory insurance of private property, especially in the agricultural sector. Several risks subject to compulsory insurance were reduced and more emphasis was placed on voluntary insurance. As a result, there was a shift from administrative to contractual insurance and a more business-like approach to the management of the insurance industry.

52. The third stage was marked by the 1958 Law on Property and Personal Insurance. The PZU became a 'state insurance company', which could solicit business and use agents (people who worked on behalf of the PZU and for a commission). In order to carry out preventive tasks, the PZU was authorised to appropriate a certain proportion of the premiums collected and the profits made. In order to ensure social control, the 'Insurance Council' was set up to represent the insured and interested state organisations. At the same time, the rules governing reinsurance were liberalised. PZU could now reinsure abroad with the approval of the Minister of Finance. On 1 January 1960, 'WARTA' was given a wider scope of activity and was authorised to underwrite risks arising from shipping and foreign trade.

53. The fourth stage was inspired by the 1984 Act on Insurance of Property and Persons. According to its provisions, PZU was an independent, self-financing economic entity, separate from a mere state enterprise, and 'WARTA' retained its original character of a limited liability company, although the State was its sole shareholder. At that time, the state monopoly in the insurance business was formally abolished, but PZU and 'WARTA' retained their monopolistic positions.

54. The Act on Insurance Activities, adopted by the Polish Parliament on 28 July 1990, was a historic piece of primary legislation that set out the general conditions and procedures for taking up and conducting business in both non-life and personal insurance. In the years 1990–2010, numerous amendments were introduced, mainly aimed at adapting the Polish legal system in this area to the requirements of the EU. The changes concerned the regulation of insurance companies (in principle, authorisation of insurance companies, minimum capital and solvency standards), rules on annual financial reports and consolidated results of insurance companies, and the establishment of the State Office for Insurance Supervision. Shortly before Poland's accession to the EU, a package of laws was adopted to align the insurance market regulations with the acquis communautaire. Since then, Polish insurance legislation has continuously followed the development of legislation in the EU.

55. The most recent regulations concerning the Polish insurance market, the conduct of insurance business and insurance distribution reflect the requirements of the relevant EU directives, including Solvency II and the Insurance Distribution Directive.

§3. Sources of Insurance Law

56. The sources of insurance law are quite diverse, mainly because, as explained in the introduction, this law contains legal provisions that are part of different basic branches of law, i.e., they are contained in different normative acts. These sources are also differentiated in terms of the hierarchy of normative acts in which the provisions of insurance law are contained: codes, statutes, implementing decrees of the Minister of Finance, as well as supplementary instructions. It should also be mentioned that, although it is not a legal act, 'soft law' plays an important role in insurance, including the recommendations and standpoints of the KNF.

I. Legislation

57. The most general normative act defining the basic conditions for the organisation and functioning of commercial insurance in Poland is the Act of 11 September

2015 on Insurance and Reinsurance Activities – Journal of Laws, item 1844. According to Article 1 of the Act, its provisions determine the general conditions and rules for undertaking and carrying out activities in the field of insurance of persons and property. In view of its provisions, the State still enjoys ius operandi, being responsible for complex relations: the organisation of the insurance establishment, the allocation of the insurance establishment and the allocation of its funds' regulations of activities and premises. It is much more than state supervision in its modern version.

58. The following list of laws enacted by the Parliament or binding directly as an EU law can be considered the most important legislation regulating the insurance market:

- Law of 11 September 2015 on insurance and reinsurance activity.
- Law of 22 May 2003 on compulsory insurance, the Insurance Guarantee Fund and the Polish Motor Insurers' Bureau.
- Act of 15 December 2017 on insurance distribution.
- Act of 15 April 2005 on supplementary supervision of credit institutions, insurance companies, reinsurance companies and investment companies that are part of a financial conglomerate.
- Act of 29 September 1994 on accounting.
- Act of 6 March 2018. Law on entrepreneurs.
- Act of 14 June 1960 Code of administrative procedure.
- Act of 15 September 2000. Commercial Companies Code.
- Act of 23 April 1964 Civil Code.
- The Act of 16 November 2006 on stamp duty.
- The Act of 14 February 1991 on the Law on Notaries Public.
- Commission Delegated Regulation (EU) 2015/35 of 10 October 2014 supplementing Directive 2009/138/EC of the European Parliament and of the Council on the taking-up and pursuit of the business of insurance and reinsurance (Solvency II).
- Commission Delegated Regulation (EU) 2016/467 of 30 September 2015 amending Regulation (EU) 2015/35 with regard to the calculation of regulatory capital requirements for several categories of assets held by insurance and reinsurance undertakings.

59. Recent key developments in the area of insurance law include several regulations derived from European law, as well as those imposed by the Polish supervisory authorities on their own initiative. These include:

- KNF Recommendation on Bancassurance (26 June 2023). The KNF has issued recommendations aimed at raising standards within the bancassurance sector and promoting stable market growth. Central to these recommendations is ensuring that customers receive substantial value from insurance products offered through bancassurance channels. The guidelines address critical aspects of the bancassurance framework, including management and board governance, risk mitigation strategies, accounting practices, customer relationships and internal control systems. These recommendations underscore the imperative of compliance and consumer protection in the conduct of bancassurance activities.

- KNF Recommendation on Life Insurance with Investment Elements (15 September 2023). Replacing the previous 2016 guidance, the new KNF Recommendations provide insurance companies with enhanced guidance on assessing the suitability of life insurance products with an investment component. The guidelines are designed to align with recent legislative changes, emphasise consumer protection and promote higher quality and transparency in the product distribution process. By increasing regulatory clarity, the recommendations aim to strengthen market confidence and customer satisfaction.
- Law of 16 August 2023: Amendments to the financial market regulations. Enacted to refine the functioning of financial market institutions, the law introduces a series of amendments to strengthen supervision, protect consumers and minority shareholders, and remove barriers to market access. Key provisions include: (1) Ensuring that life insurance policyholders with insurance capital funds receive protection similar to that afforded to participants in unit trusts; (2) Clarifying the obligations of insurance companies and the UFG with regard to compensation payments when the guaranteed sum is exhausted, in particular with regard to foreign insurers; (3) Establish rules for an IT database managed by the UFG to improve operational transparency and efficiency. Taken together, these amendments promote consumer rights, digitalise supervisory functions and strengthen market stability.
- Amendments to the Commercial Companies Code (13 October 2022). Recent amendments to the Commercial Companies Code expand the powers of corporate bodies and introduce new liability rules for members of governing bodies within corporate groups. These changes have a direct impact on the structure and offering of indemnity insurance products, in particular Directors & Officers (D&O) insurance, by redefining liability standards and risk profiles for directors and officers.
- Criminal Code Revision (1 October 2023). The Criminal Code Revision introduces new offences with implications for the insurance sector. In particular, uninsured drivers who fail to compensate accident victims now face up to five years of imprisonment. If the UFG pays the compensation, the offender will be subject to a recourse claim requiring reimbursement of costs plus interest.

60. Together, these legislative and regulatory developments aim to improve transparency, consumer protection and market integrity in the Polish insurance and financial sectors. Insurers need to adapt to these changes by reviewing distribution strategies and recalibrating product offerings, particularly in the bancassurance and indemnity insurance markets, to meet heightened regulatory expectations and protect consumer interests.

II. Governmental Regulations

61. Most of the legal acts indicated in point I are supplemented with the number of executive ordinances.

62. Executive regulations concerning insurance activity and financial management of the insurers are as follows:

- Regulation of the Minister of Finance dated 12 April 2016 on specific accounting principles for insurance and reinsurance companies.
- Ordinance of the Minister of Development and Finance of 13 October 2016 on documents attached to notices of intent to acquire or take up shares or rights over shares of a domestic insurance or domestic reinsurance company or to become the parent of such a company.
- The Ordinance of the Minister of Finance, Funds and Regional Policy concerning the membership fee for the Polish Chamber of Insurance of 3 December 2020 (Journal of Laws of 2020, item 2223).
- Regulation of the Minister of Health on information to be provided to insurance companies by healthcare providers and the national health fund (*Narodowy Fundusz Zdrowia*, NFZ) of 28 April 2020 (Journal of Laws 2020, item 784).
- Regulation of the Minister for Development and Finance on the Audit of the report on the solvency and financial condition of insurance and reinsurance undertakings by an audit firm of 4 December 2017 (Journal of Laws of 2017, item 2284).
- Regulation of the Minister for Development and Finance on statistics on co-insurance of 14 December 2016 (Journal of Laws of 2016, item 2121, uniform text: Journal of Laws of 2022, item 1222).
- Regulation of the Minister of Development and Finance on the regulations of the examination committee for actuaries, the remuneration of its members and examination fees of 12 December 2016 (Journal of Laws 2016, item 2068).
- Regulation of the Minister of Development and Finance on the actuarial examination of 9 December 2016 (Journal of Laws 2016, item 2182; uniform text: Journal of Laws of 2021, item 1350).
- Regulation of the Minister for Development and Finance on documents to be attached to the notifications of an intention to acquire or take up shares or rights arising from shares in a domestic insurance or reinsurance undertaking or to become the parent undertaking of such an undertaking of 13 October 2016 (Journal of Laws of 2016, item 1772).
- Regulation of the Minister of Development and Finance on documents relating to the conclusion and performance of insurance contracts drawn up in electronic form of 5 October 2016 (Journal of Laws of 2016, item 1693).
- Regulation of the Minister of Finance on the annual and half-annual reports of the insurance capital fund of 25 May 2016 (Journal of Laws of 2016, item 789).
- Regulation of the Minister of Finance on supplementary financial and statistical reports of insurance and reinsurance undertakings of 29 April 2016 (Journal of Laws of 2016, item 634; uniform text: Journal of Laws of 2018, item 392).

- Regulation of the Minister of Finance on data collected by the Polish Chamber of Insurance in relation to insurance statistics of 18 March 2016 (Journal of Laws of 2016, item 378).
- Regulation of the Minister of Finance on the form and manner in which insurance and reinsurance undertakings compile data and information for supervisory purposes of 22 February 2016 (Journal of Laws of 2016, item 236; uniform text: Journal of Laws of 2020, item 1003).
- Regulation of the Minister of Finance on the minimum data to be included in the questionnaire on the needs of the policyholder or the insured person of 2 February 2016 (Journal of Laws of 2016, item 167).
- Regulation of the Minister of Finance on the detailed manner of calculation of the basic solvency capital requirement according to the standard formula of 23 December 2015 (Journal of Laws of 2015, item 2321).
- Regulation of the Minister of Finance on information to be included in model contracts used by an insurance undertaking of 16 December 2015 (Journal of Laws of 2015, item 2189).

63. Except for the governmental regulations, there are a number of soft law acts issued by the PFSA, examples of which are presented below:

- Recommendation U on good bancassurance practices, adopted in June 2023.
- Recommendations on motor vehicle insurance claim settlement, adopted in July 2022.
- Recommendations regarding the process of determining and paying compensation for non-pecuniary damage from contracts of third-party insurance of vehicle owners adopted in June 2016.
- Recommendations for insurance companies on assessing the suitability of life insurance with an investment component, adopted in September 2023.
- Recommendations for insurance companies regarding product management system adopted in March 2016.

III. Private International Law

64. The Polish approach to the choice of law is somewhat mechanical – first, a matter is categorised as 'procedural' or 'substantive'. The substantive issue concerns the law applicable to a given matter. The procedural issue concerns the forum (the court having jurisdiction to resolve the dispute). As an example of substantive choice of law rules, if the matter is categorised as contractual, it will be reflected in a proper law of contract (as insurance law).

65. In general, the Polish legislator allows the parties to a contract to freely determine the application of foreign law. The only restriction is a general public policy clause, which states that foreign law that contradicts the fundamental principles of the legal system in force in Poland shall not be applied. The insurance contract is one of the areas of insurance law where the freedom to choose the applicable law is limited. The restrictions are in line with EU law and are basically consumer-oriented.

66. It is provided that if Polish law provides for compulsory insurance, the insurance contract concerning such compulsory insurance shall be governed by Polish law. If a law of an EOG Member State provides for compulsory insurance and designates its own law, the law of that state shall apply to such insurance.

67. The above rules are special provisions of a general rule, according to which the law applicable to contractual relations is determined by the Regulation of the European Parliament and of the Council No. 593/2008 of 17 June 2008 concerning the law applicable to contractual relations (Rome I) (O.J. EU L 177 of 4.7.2008). The law applicable to obligations arising out of acts other than contracts, i.e., non-contractual obligations, is laid down in Council Regulation (EC) No. 864/2007 of 11 July 2007 ('Rome II') (O.J. EU L 199 of 31.7.2007).

IV. Jurisdiction

68. As regards jurisdiction, it should be noted that Poland is bound by Council Regulation (EC) No. 44/2001 of 22 December 2001 on jurisdiction and the recognition and enforcement of judgments in civil and commercial matters. This means that in insurance matters alternative rules of jurisdiction apply. The policyholder or any other person entitled to bring an action against the insurer may do so either in the country where the insurer has its registered office or in the country where the policyholder or the other person entitled to bring an action has his domicile or registered office. In the case of liability insurance, the insurer can also be sued in the country where the accident occurred.

69. Such favourable jurisdiction rules are only binding for claims against the insurer. The insurer can generally only be sued in the court of the policyholder's domicile or seat (with some minor exceptions).

70. Similar rules in favour of the policyholder, the insured and other parties entitled to bring a claim against the insurer are binding if the dispute is local in nature. This issue is discussed in more detail in section 4 below.

§4. Dispute Settlement and Arbitration

71. The Act on Insurance and Reinsurance Activity (AIRA) contains mandatory rules which state that in addition to the ordinary courts with jurisdiction for the insurer's registered office, a person entitled to a sum of money from the insurer may bring an action before a court with jurisdiction for the registered office or domicile of the claimant. This rule cannot be changed by an insurance contract.

72. Polish law provides for various ways of settling disputes amicably. For example, the law provides for the operation of a mediation and arbitration court by the Insurance Ombudsman, the purpose of which is to resolve disputes between policyholders (or other persons entitled under insurance contracts) and insurers. However, participation in such arbitration is voluntary, and no party is obliged to agree to have the dispute resolved by the arbitration court.

73. Similarly, disputes between insurers may be resolved by the Arbitration Court of the Polish Chamber of Insurance in accordance with the rules adopted by the Chamber. In addition, a new Act on the Handling of Complaints by Financial Service Providers and on the Financial Ombudsman of 5 August 2015 (Journal of Laws of 2015, item 1348) entered into force, on the basis of which new procedures for amicable settlement of disputes between insureds and insurers have been introduced.

§5. Consumer Protection

I. General

74. The consumer law is widely regulated in Poland, having its backgrounds in the Polish Constitution, according to which 'The public authorities protect consumers, users and lessees against activities threatening their health, privacy and safety and against unfair market practices. The scope of this protection is regulated by statutory law' (Article 76).

75. General provisions of the consumers can be found in various statutory laws, including the Act of Polish Civil Code (PCC) and the Act of 16 February 2007 on the protection of competition and consumers. Both acts refer to the same definition of a consumer being '*a natural person who makes a legal transaction with an entrepreneur which is outside his business or professional activity*' (Article 22(1) of the Civil Code).

76. The Act of 30 May 2014 on consumers' rights governs the rights of the consumers, including the obligations of the entrepreneur concluding a contract with a consumer; the rules and procedures for the conclusion of distance and off-premises contracts with the consumer; the rules and procedure for exercising the consumer's right of withdrawal from a distance or off-premises contract; the rules and procedures for the conclusion of a distance contract with a consumer concerning financial services; the rules and procedures for the exercise of the rights of a consumer who is a party to a contract obliging to transfer ownership of goods to the consumer; the rules and procedures for exercising the rights of a consumer who is a party to a contract for the supply of digital content or digital service and, as from January 2024 also governs the rules concerning the payment by the consumer through a payment account.

77. The provisions of the said Act do not apply to agreements concerning financial services, in particular: banking transactions, consumer credit agreements, insurance contracts, agreements for the purchase or repurchase of units of an open-ended investment fund or a specialised open-ended investment fund and the purchase or subscription for investment certificates of a closed-ended investment fund, payment services, with the exception of agreements concerning financial services concluded at a distance, to which only limited regulations apply (provisions of Chapters 1 and 5), and agreements concerning financial services concluded away from business premises (provisions of Article 7ab of the Act apply).

78. One of the most important consumer protection regulations on the Polish market is also the Act of 23 August 2007 on counteracting the unfair market practices. It defines the unfair market practices in business and professional activities and the rules for counteracting such practices in the interest of consumers and in the public interest.

79. There are also various regulations concerning specific branches of law or activity of the consumers, including the Act of 27 July 2002 on special conditions of consumer sales and on the amendment to the Civil Code, the Act of 20 July 2001 on consumer credit, the Act or 23 September 2016 on out-of-court settlement on consumer's disputes, the Banking Law or the Act on tourist services.

80. It should also be noted that the protection of consumers against unfair terms of contracts has been substantially strengthened in such a way that certain contractual clauses can be claimed ineffective if they are proven to be unfair (abusive). The respective provisions are included in the Civil Code.

81. On 10 November 2024, new provisions of the Electronic Communications Law came into force, significantly raising standards for the protection of consumer rights in the telecommunications services sector. The new regulations were introduced to simplify the use of telecommunications services and increase customers' control over their contracts. The regulations also indirectly affect the insurance market to the extent that insurance products are offered to customers (regardless of their status as consumers) electronically or by telephone. The new regulations introduce uniform rules, according to which any marketing contact – whether to individuals, companies or public institutions – will require the explicit, documented consent of the recipient. This means that any business wishing to conduct cold mailing or cold calling activities will have to meet specific requirements.

II. Insurance

82. Notwithstanding the general provisions governing the status of consumers and their protection in Poland, some additional provisions apply to consumers in relation to insurance contracts, which extend the application of the definition of a consumer and the protection afforded by the legislation to a wider range of natural persons.

83. Currently, the Civil Code provides that consumer protection is also granted to the policyholder who is a natural person, even if the conclusion of the insurance contract is directly related to the policyholder's business activity. Consumer protection has also been granted not only to the policyholder in the above circumstances but also to a person on whose behalf an insurance contract is concluded if such insurance is not related to a business activity of the insured.

84. There are a number of other legal provisions that provide for a wide range of protections, but these do not refer directly to a consumer, but to either a policyholder or the insured. For example, according to the AIRA, 'provisions of the insurance contract, general conditions of insurance and other contractual documents that are ambiguous shall be interpreted in favour of the policyholder, the insured or the beneficiary of the insurance contract'.

85. The current legal status regarding insurance consumer protection is considered to be in line with EU regulations in this respect.

§6. Compulsory Insurances

86. Compulsory insurance in Poland is regulated by the Act of 22 May 2003 on Compulsory Insurance, the UFG and the Polish Motor Insurers' Bureau (the 'ACI'). The ACI regulates the general conditions and rules for the conclusion and performance of compulsory insurance contracts, as well as the methods of monitoring the fulfilment of the obligation to insure and the consequences of failure to fulfil the obligation. It also regulates the functions and principles of operation of the UFG and the Polish Motor Insurers' Bureau.

87. In addition, compulsory insurance is regulated by the Civil Code with regard to matters not covered by the ACI. In addition, it should be mentioned that compulsory insurance has its sources in laws regulating specific types of activities, e.g., the Real Estate Management Act, the Legal Professions Act, the Health Care Institutions Act, etc., which are supplemented by executive acts – regulations to the above-mentioned 'branch' laws and which regulate the guaranteed amount and the basic scope of insurance. The ACI provides for three main types of compulsory insurance. They are the following:

- civil liability insurance of motor vehicle owners in respect of the use of motor vehicles (Motor Third Party Liability (MTPL));
- insurance of farm buildings against fire and/or other accidents (fire insurance for farmer's buildings);
- insurance of civil liability of farmers in relation to the operation of the farm (farmer's third-party liability).

88. Apart from the above, compulsory insurance may result from international conventions ratified by the Republic of Poland. Such compulsory insurance based on international conventions concerns the liability of the Insured for damage caused in the course of performing actions and professional activities or running a business or as a result of defects in products as defined in the act introducing the given obligation or in international conventions ratified by the Republic of Poland. Examples of such insurances are liability insurance of air carriers and aircraft operators for passengers, baggage and cargo, liability insurance of air carriers and aircraft operators resulting either from the Chicago Convention or from EU directives (*see* Part II for details).

89. The number of compulsory insurances in Poland is constantly increasing due to the new professions covered by the insurance obligation. The exact number of compulsory insurances in Poland is therefore difficult to determine, as there are different concepts of what insurance should be considered compulsory. These concepts are based on the assumption that a compulsory insurance is only a property or liability insurance that is required by law and whose basic characteristics are described by such law. Insurance that does not meet these requirements can only be classified as mandatory, but not as compulsory. Nevertheless, according to the latest calculations of the Polish Chamber of Insurance, the total number of insurances that are compulsory in some way is approximately 220, of which 120 are based on the provisions of Polish law and 100 are based on international legal instruments.

90. The most important include:

- insurance of civil liability for nuclear damage provided by the Atomic Law Act;
- insurance of third-party liability of healthcare institutions;
- insurance of third-party liability of tax advisors;
- insurance of third-party liability of debt collectors;
- insurance of third-party liability of insurance brokers;
- insurance of third-party liability of tourist agencies;
- insurance of third-party liability of public events' organisers;
- insurance of third-party liability of public notaries;
- insurance of third-party liability of legal advisors;
- insurance of third-party liability of advocates (barristers);
- insurance of third-party liability of warehouses;
- insurance of third-party liability of property appraisers;
- insurance of third-party liability of real estate managers;
- insurance of third-party liability of real estate agents.

91. A policyholder may conclude a compulsory insurance contract with a selected insurer that performs insurance activities within the scope of compulsory insurance. However, an insurer who has a licence to conduct insurance activities within the scope of compulsory insurance may not refuse to conclude a compulsory insurance contract. The higher risk of the customer can only be compensated by a higher premium. The same applies to misrepresentation or concealment of the risk, i.e., the insurer may not refuse the application, but may only set a higher premium in accordance with the actual level of risk. If the policyholder does not inform the insurer about the circumstances of which he/she is aware and about which the insurer has inquired before concluding the compulsory insurance contract, and which result in a significant change in the probability of an insured event, the insurer is entitled to demand the corresponding change in the insurance premium, taking into account the increase in the probability of an insured event due to the circumstances that were not communicated to the insurer. If the insurer concludes a compulsory insurance contract despite the lack of answers to certain questions, the omitted circumstances are considered insignificant.[8]

92. With regard to compulsory insurance, the Minister of Finance has determined the form and scope of the policy confirming the conclusion of a compulsory insurance contract, taking into account the type of insurance.

93. Tariffs and premium amounts for compulsory insurance are set by insurers and are not subject to approval by the supervisory authority. However, each insurer is obliged to provide the supervisory authority with information on the tariffs of compulsory insurance premiums and the reasons for setting them. In particular, this information must include an analysis of the loss ratio and the cost of servicing the policy, which justifies the introduction of any changes to the tariffs.

94. Some compulsory insurances (e.g., Motor Third-Party Liability) are subject to automatic (tacit) renewal unless the policyholder decides otherwise up to one day before the expiry of the previous insurance period. If the insurance premium is paid in instalments, the non-payment by the Insured or the Policyholder of an instalment of the premium within the time limit set by the Insurer shall not result in the cancellation of the insurance cover. Compulsory insurance is also subject to a tacit conclusion, i.e., if the insurer has received an offer to conclude a compulsory insurance contract, the absence of a reply within fourteen days is deemed to be an acceptance of the offer.

95. Compulsory insurance has its own specificities and principles that differ from voluntary insurance contracts. These differences are particularly evident in the case of third-party liability insurance. A rule of compulsory civil liability insurance is that it covers the liability of the policyholder in relation to a legal obligation to insure against damage caused by unlawful acts or as a result of failure to perform or improper performance of an obligation. In addition, a contract of compulsory civil liability insurance covers damage caused intentionally, which is not allowed in voluntary insurance.

96. The ACI also provides for specific time limits for the payment of compensation. Apart from a general rule of payment within thirty days from the date on which the injured party or a person entitled to claim has made a claim, and a further fourteen days from the date on which all the circumstances necessary to determine the insurer's liability or the amount of compensation have been established, in the case of compulsory insurance, the insurer should pay compensation no later than

8. M. Orlicki, Ubezpieczenia Obowiązkowe, 2011.

ninety days from the date on which the claim has been made, unless the determination of the insurer's liability or the amount of compensation depends on criminal and/or civil proceedings being in progress.

97. If it is not possible to pay the compensation within the first deadline, the Insurer will inform the rightful claimant in writing of the reasons for the total or partial non-payment of his claim, as well as of an estimated date, of its final position with regard to the rightful claimant's claims, and will pay the undisputed part of the compensation.

98. If the compensation is not due or is due in a different amount than that determined in the submitted claim, the insurer should notify the claimant in writing in due time, stating the circumstances and legal grounds justifying the total or partial refusal to pay the compensation, as well as the reasons for denying the credibility of the evidence presented by the claimant. The notification should include an appropriate instruction on the possibility of vindicating the claim by means of legal proceedings.

99. If the compulsory insurance has not been taken out by an obligated party, the injured party may apply to the UFG, which is competent to pay compensation in accordance with the conditions laid down in the ACI (Chapter 7).

100. The insurance cover, within the limit of the guarantee sum (or sum insured), includes, in addition to the compensation of the injured party, the costs incurred in order to prevent the damage, as well as the indispensable costs of legal representation in civil proceedings.

101. The ACI specifies the main obligations of the insured. The most important of these obligations are: (1) to take all necessary measures to ensure the safety of the place of the event and to mitigate the consequences of the event, as well as to provide medical assistance to injured persons and, within the limits of their possibilities, to secure the property of injured persons; (2) to prevent, if possible, an increase in the extent of the damage; (3) to immediately notify the police of the event and, in particular, of the event resulting in personal injuries. The other obligations include the obligation of the insured: (1) to provide the other participants in the event with all necessary information about the insurer, including the insurance policy; (2) to immediately notify the insurer of the event, providing all necessary information.

102. The Insurer may have recourse against the Insured in certain circumstances. The insurer is entitled to recourse if the damage was caused by wilful misconduct or gross negligence (the latter also applies to professional indemnity insurance), if the insured failed to fulfil his obligations and this affected the damage or the extent of liability, or if the insured was under the influence of alcohol, drugs, etc. The insurer is not obliged to prove the facts justifying the recourse claim. The insurer bears the burden of proving the facts justifying the recourse claim.

103. In the case of compulsory liability insurance, the injured party may file a claim directly with the UFG or the Polish Motor Insurers' Bureau if the perpetrator has not been identified or is not insured.

104. Claims relating to compulsory insurance contracts may be brought before the court competent for the place of residence or seat of the injured party. If the legal action concerns a damage covered by compulsory insurance, it is obligatory to inform the insurer of the existence of such an action.

105. The satisfaction or acceptance of a claim by an insured person covered by compulsory civil liability insurance does not have any legal consequences if the insurer (or the UFG or the Polish Motor Insurers Bureau) did not express its acceptance of the claim beforehand.

106. When assessing the effects of compulsory insurance, it should be noted that it very often leads to standardisation of the offered product, which may result in minimisation of the scope of coverage and lack of adjustment to actual needs. In addition, the introduction of different rules for compulsory and voluntary insurance creates a dualism of legislation.

Part I. The Insurer

Chapter 1. The Insurer: General Information

107. Insurance activities in Poland are conducted on the basis of the AIRA of 11 September 2015, the Commercial Companies Code, the Civil Code and other legislation, including legislation of an executive nature. In addition to the AIRA, insurance legislation includes the ACI, the Insurance Distribution Act, the Insurance Supervision Act and the Act on the Handling of Complaints by Financial Service Providers and on the Financial Ombudsman of 5 August 2015.

108. Insurers always provide insurance protection on the basis of insurance contracts concluded with policyholders. Insurance contracts are generally of a voluntary nature, subject to the provisions of the ACI, which regulate compulsory types of insurance.

109. Domestic insurers (with their registered office in Poland) may operate in the form of a joint-stock company, a mutual insurance company or a European company in accordance with the provisions of Council Regulation (EC) No. 2157/2001 of 8 October 2001 on the Statute for a European company (SE). The general provisions on the conduct of insurance business are similar and apply to all types of domestic insurers.

110. Foreign insurers established outside the EU may conduct insurance activities in Poland through a main branch (without establishing a subsidiary). Foreign insurers with their registered office in one of the EU Member States may operate in Poland on the basis of the single licence principle, either by establishing a branch (Freedom of Establishment, FoE) or by using the Freedom of Services (FoS) regime.

111. The main condition for carrying out insurance activities in Poland is the possession of an insurance licence issued by the competent insurance supervisory authority. The AIRA provides for certain requirements and conditions necessary for obtaining an insurance licence and maintaining the licence during the activity of the insurance company. The AIRA generally implements the requirements of Solvency II, including organisational, capital, personnel and ownership matters.

112. In Poland, a dualistic management system has been adopted for joint-stock companies and mutual insurance companies (the European company can have a dualistic or monistic system). This means that the management board manages the company, while the supervisory board exercises ex-post control.

113. The AIRA imposes certain requirements on persons appointed as key persons, including members of the board of directors and the supervisory board, as well as persons supervising key functions.

114. With regard to the board of directors, the following main requirements apply:

- the management board of a domestic insurer, with the exception of a mutual insurance company, must consist of at least two members and should include a chairman;
- at least two members of the management board of the domestic insurer, including the chairman of the management board and the member responsible for risk management, must have a certified knowledge of Polish;
- at least two members of the management board of the domestic insurer, including a chairman of the management board and a member responsible for risk management, must have the professional experience necessary for the management of the insurance undertaking;
- the appointment of two members of the management board, including the president of the domestic insurer, requires the approval of the PFSA (subject to compliance with the statutory conditions) unless the appointment relates to persons who have performed a function of a member of the management board during the previous term of office. If the PFSA refuses to give its approval, the appointment of the domestic insurer's board member has no legal effect (including in respect of any acts performed by such person) and the mandate expires.

115. A person who is a member of the management body of an insurance undertaking should meet the following requirements:

- has full legal capacity;
- has a higher education degree obtained in the Republic of Poland or a higher education degree obtained in another country in accordance with the relevant regulations of that country;
- has not been convicted of an intentional crime or an intentional fiscal offence by a final court decision;
- is able to guarantee the proper conduct of the business of the insurance undertaking.

116. A member of the Board of Directors of an insurance company may not be a member of the Board of Directors of: an investment fund company or an ASI manager within the meaning of the Investment Fund Act operating on the basis of a licence, an entity performing brokerage activities or other activities in the field of trading in financial instruments within the meaning of the Act of 29 July 2005 on trading in financial instruments, a universal pension company, a bank or a reinsurance undertaking.

117. Similar but less stringent requirements apply to the members of the insurer's supervisory board. The members should have full legal capacity, should not have been convicted of an intentional criminal offence or an intentional fiscal offence by a final court judgment, and should give a guarantee that they will properly conduct the business of the insurer.

118. Similar requirements apply to persons supervising key functions. They should meet the following requirements:

- have full legal capacity;
- have a higher education degree obtained in the Republic of Poland or a higher education degree obtained in another country in accordance with the relevant regulations of that country;
- has not been convicted of an intentional crime or an intentional fiscal offence by a final court decision;
- has the necessary professional experience to perform the key function to be supervised;
- is able to guarantee the proper performance of his duties.

§1. Joint Stock Company

119. A joint-stock company is a company governed by the Commercial Companies and Partnerships Code (the CCPC). It should be noted, however, that the provisions of the AIRA take precedence over the provisions of the CCPC with respect to joint-stock companies engaged in insurance activities.

120. As a rule, there are at least several main aspects that are regulated in a very specific manner, including capital requirements, governing bodies, organisation, prudential requirements and ownership (shareholders).

121. The share capital of a domestic insurance company may not be less than the absolute amount of the minimum capital requirement required for the classes of insurance listed in the Annex to the AIRA in respect of which the domestic insurance company is authorised to conduct insurance business.

122. The share capital shall be covered by a cash contribution and shall be paid up in full before the national insurance undertaking and the national reinsurance undertaking are registered in the KRS.

123. Contributions to the share capital shall not come from illegal or undisclosed sources and shall not relate to the financing of terrorism.

124. The statutes of a domestic insurance company and the articles of association of a national reinsurance undertaking are subject to supervisory approval prior to registration. In addition, the PFSA's approval is required for certain amendments to the articles of association of a public limited company in the course of carrying on insurance business.

125. Shares in an insurance undertaking, with the exception of shares dematerialised in accordance with the provisions of the Law of 29 July 2005 on trading in financial instruments, may only be registered shares. The disposal of registered shares requires the approval of the PFSA by way of a resolution, if it takes place within twelve months from the date of registration of the domestic insurance company in the KRS. Any disposal of such shares without the approval of the PFSA shall be null and void.

126. Another limitation introduced by the legislator is the restriction on trading in shares or rights to shares of insurance companies. Entities intending to purchase or acquire, directly or indirectly, through subsidiaries or by way of agreements, shares or rights in shares of a domestic insurer in a number that ensures reaching or exceeding 1/10, 1/5, 1/3, 1/2 of the votes at the general meeting or in the share capital, respectively, are obliged to notify the PFSA. Such a notification is also required whenever measures are taken with a view to acquiring control of the insurer/reinsurer (acquisition of a dominant position in the sense of securing a majority of votes at a general meeting of the insurer) by means other than the acquisition of shares or the subscription of shares in the increased share capital. The notification must be accompanied by detailed information and documentation.

127. The PFSA may, within sixty working days of the date of submission of the notification with all the required documents, raise an objection to the acquisition or subscription of shares or rights arising from shares by way of a decision. An objection may be raised in particular if there is a need to ensure proper and prudent management of the insurer, taking into account the financial situation of the entity notifying the above intention.

128. The obligation of notification concerns also the shareholders disposing of the shares if in consequence of such sale their share in a number of votes at a general meeting or in a share capital dropped respectively below 1/10, 1/5, 1/3, 1/25. The notification should be made within fourteen days before the intended disposal, at the latest.

An insurer conducting insurance activities in the form of a joint-stock company may be recognised by the PFSA as a 'small joint-stock company' (Article 101 AIRA) if the following conditions are jointly met:

- the company's annual gross written premium income does not exceed the equivalent in PLN of PLN 5 million;
- the total gross technical provisions of the undertaking for solvency purposes do not exceed the equivalent in PLN of EUR 25 million;
- the total gross technical provisions of the group for solvency purposes do not exceed the equivalent in PLN of EUR 25 million – if the undertaking is part of a group;

- the undertaking does not conduct insurance or reinsurance of civil liability, credit and insurance guarantee business, except as an ancillary activity;
- the company's annual gross written premium from active reinsurance does not exceed the PLN equivalent of EUR 0.5 million and 10% of the total gross written premium;
- the company's gross technical provisions for solvency purposes from reinsurance acceptances do not exceed the PLN equivalent of EUR 2.5 million and 10% of the total gross technical provisions for solvency purposes.

If either of the above amounts is exceeded in three consecutive business years, the insurer loses the status of a small joint-stock company and must adjust its activities to the full requirements of the AIRA as of the following fourth business year. The supervisory authority must be informed accordingly.

The provisions concerning the capital requirements are not applicable to the small joint stock insurance company.

§2. Mutual Insurance Undertaking

129. Carrying out insurance activities in the form of a mutual insurance undertaking was intended for certain professional groups, societies with the same interests, professions and common goods. A mutual insurance undertaking acquires legal personality when it is registered in the KRS. The share capital of a mutual insurance undertaking must be covered by cash payments within thirty days from the date of its registration.

130. A mutual insurance undertaking carries out its activity by providing insurance to its members on a reciprocal basis. As a general rule, membership of a mutual insurance company should be linked to the conclusion of an insurance contract and the loss of membership should be linked to the expiry of the insurance contract. However, a mutual's articles of association may contain provisions allowing it to insure persons who are not its members, but the number of such persons must be limited so that the contributions paid by such persons do not exceed 10% of the total contributions collected by the mutual. A mutual insurance undertaking with a limited scope of activity may be recognised as a small mutual insurance undertaking if it meets all of the following conditions:

- the mutual's business is limited because of the small number of its members and the small number or small sums insured or the small geographical area in which it operates;
- the mutual insures only its members;
- the members of the mutual insurance undertaking are a group defined in the memorandum and articles of association:
  i. natural persons exercising a specific profession or activity and members of their families;
  ii. legal persons whose object relates to the profession or activity referred to in point (i), with the exception of commercial companies;

- the annual gross premiums written in the last three financial years, and in the case of an association carrying on its business for a shorter period – since the beginning of its business, does not exceed the PLN equivalent of EUR 5 million, determined in accordance with Article 272(6) of the AIRA, and the mutual association submits a reliable forecast that the above value will not be exceeded in the next five financial years;
- the mutual insurance company does not carry out the activity of liability insurance, credit insurance or insurance guarantee unless they constitute additional risks.

131. A small mutual enjoys certain privileges in terms of capitalisation but is also subject to certain restrictions. For example, it cannot engage in inward reinsurance. If the amount is exceeded in three consecutive turnover years, the insurer loses its status as a small mutual and must adapt its activity to the full requirements of the AIRA as of the following fourth turnover year. The PFSA must be informed accordingly.

132. The capital requirements for mutuals are similar to those for limited companies. However, there are some differences. The share capital should be fully paid up in cash within thirty days of the date of registration of the society. A mutual's articles of association may provide for repayment of the share capital only from annual surpluses and within a period of establishing a reserve capital to persons who have contributed the share capital; the articles of association may also provide for exemption from the obligation to increase the share capital for certain persons. The share capital may be reduced by the nominal value of the shares or by the redemption of part of the shares.

133. A mutual insurance undertaking may be converted into a joint-stock company. The provisions of the CPC concerning the establishment of a joint stock company apply to the conversion of such a company. A decision of the general meeting to convert a mutual insurance undertaking into a joint-stock company must be approved by the PFSA, which is subject to the fulfilment of certain requirements, including, in addition to the formal requirements, the obligation to protect the interests of insured persons, beneficiaries or other persons entitled under insurance contracts.

134. A mutual is managed by a board of directors, the rules of which are laid down in the AIRA. In addition to the board of directors, there is a supervisory board and a general meeting of the company. All the rules for the functioning of the organs of the company are regulated in the AIRA.

135. In 2024, there will be seven mutual insurance companies on the Polish market (one in the life insurance market and six in the non-life insurance market). They cover professional groups such as notaries and farmers. Mutual insurance companies do not play a significant role in the Polish insurance market. They are often used as a vehicle to create captive insurers in some industries, such as oil refining (PKN Orlen). The latest data can be found on the website of the PFSA.

§3. Main Branch

136. Under the AIRA, foreign insurers having their registered office outside the territory of the EU may undertake and carry out insurance activity in Poland through their main branch offices on a reciprocal basis. The requirement of reciprocity does not apply to countries being members of the World Trade Organization (WTO).

137. A foreign insurer/reinsurer pursuing an insurance activity in Poland through the main branch should apply the Polish law within the scope of the activity of the main branch.

138. A vital condition to commencing insurance activity by a main branch office is obtaining a permit from the supervisory body for a foreign insurance company to conduct insurance activity in Poland (*see* Chapter 2 section 2 below). The AIRA requires that a main branch be managed by a manager. The right to represent the main branch is granted to the manager and one of its deputies or to two deputies of the manager acting jointly.

139. The AIRA provides for some requirements that must be fulfilled by a person appointed as a director of the main branch or at least one of the deputies, such as the knowledge of the Polish language, higher education degree, clean criminal records, full legal capacity and being fit and proper for the function.

140. Moreover, a foreign insurer is subject to unlimited liability for obligations of its main branch.

141. A main branch operates on the basis of its statutes, which are drawn up by a foreign insurer in the form of a notarial deed. The statutes of a main branch and amendments thereto shall be subject to the approval of the PFSA. The statutes of the main branch shall, in particular, determine the organisational structure of the main branch, the rules for the establishment of regional units and the principles of their representation, the types of technical provisions established by this main branch and the methods of their establishment, as well as the rules for settling accounts with the foreign insurer.

142. The main branch of a foreign insurer from a non-EU Member State must be registered in the KRS and may commence its activities from the date of registration. The foreign insurer should commence its insurance activities through a main branch within twelve months from the date of obtaining a licence to conduct insurance activities in Poland through a main branch.

143. The requirements for the main branch's financial management in Poland are rather strict, which makes this form of insurance activity uncommon.

§4. Single Licence

144. An insurer with its registered office in a Member State of the EU may conduct insurance activities in Poland provided that it has obtained a licence to conduct such activities in its home Member State of the EU (single licence rule) and has completed the relevant notification procedure with the host Member State of the EU. The activity of such an insurer is subject to supervision by a competent authority of the EU Member State in which it has its registered office (home country supervision rule).

145. A foreign insurer operating in Poland on the basis of a single licence rule is obliged to apply Polish law in relation to its activities in Poland and within the framework of the 'general good' provisions (mainly relating to business and consumer protection rules) unless an international agreement to which Poland is a party stipulates otherwise. The foreign insurer is fully liable for all obligations arising from the performance of insurance activities on the territory of Poland. There are two main ways of conducting insurance business in Poland: through a branch (freedom of establishment) or without a branch, in accordance with the rules of freedom to provide services.

146. The financial supervision of the activity of the foreign insurer is performed exclusively by the supervisory body of the EU Member State where the insurer has its registered office. The supervision in the other areas of activity may also be performed to a certain extent by the PFSA.

147. The foreign insurer which intends to perform insurance activity within branch II, group 10 (with the exclusion of the carrier's liability) on the basis of freedom of services, shall inform the supervisory body about the data of the claims representatives as well as declare being a member of the Polish MTLP Insurers Bureau.

§5. Insurance Self-Government: Polish Chamber of Insurance

148. All insurers operating in Poland (both Polish and foreign) are members of the Polish Chamber of Insurance (PIU). Membership of the PIU is obligatory for all insurers and commences upon commencement of insurance activity and ends upon liquidation of the insurer. Reinsurers may be members on a voluntary basis.

149. The main tasks of the PIU are to represent the interests of insurers and to solve problems of the insurance market in Poland. This includes, in particular, expressing opinions on legislative acts relating to insurance, representing the common interests of PIU members and taking actions to protect these interests, such as influencing fair competition and ethical rules. The activities of the PIU are financed by insurers – members of the Chamber.

Chapter 2. Access to Business (Permit: Requirements and Procedures)

150. The conditions for taking up insurance activities are set out in Chapter 6 of the AIRA for domestic insurers, in Chapter 7 for foreign insurers with their registered office in a non-EU country and in Chapter 8 for foreign insurers with their registered office in an EU Member State.

151. Commencement of insurance activities as a mutual insurance undertaking, a joint-stock company, a European company or a main branch of a foreign company (with its registered office outside the EU) requires a licence issued by the PFSA. Insurers from EU Member States may operate in Poland under the single licence regime, subject to a notification procedure.

152. The licence is issued for life or non-life insurance activities. An insurance company may not conduct both life and non-life insurance activities at the same time. The licence is issued for one or more insurance groups or one or more types of insurance as defined in the AIRA.

§1. Joint Stock Company, a European Company and a Mutual Insurance Undertaking

153. As far as the procedure of establishing an insurance company is concerned, the following steps should be undertaken:

- collecting all necessary documents and preparation of all information as required by the AIRA for a permit to conduct insurance activity in Poland;
- submitting a signed application together with other necessary documents to the PFSA;
- adopting the statute;
- obtaining a permit from the PFSA;
- contributing a share capital and payment to the organisational fund;
- registering the insurer in the KRS.

154. A licence is granted after the PFSA has examined an application from the founder(s).

155. An application should include, *inter alia*, information on: (1) a name, a seat, a territorial and objective scope of an activity of the insurer; (2) details on an amount of the share capital; (3) details on founders of the insurer; (4) an organisational form of activity (joint-stock company or mutual insurance company); (5) personal data and information on persons who are to be members of the Board of Directors (persons with professional experience necessary for the management of the insurer, having higher/university education) and a Supervisory Board, as well as an actuary and an accountant.

156. An application must be accompanied by certain documents, the most important of which are: (1) a business plan (scheme of operations) for a period of the first three financial years of activity, together with a simulation calculation; (2) a declaration by the founders (evidence) on the possession of unencumbered assets in an amount corresponding to a fixed share capital (initial capital) and an organisational fund, and on the use of such funds for the specified purposes; (3) financial statements of the founders for the last three years; (4) a calculation of solvency and capital requirements and the value of own funds; (5) corporate documents of the founders, bank statements, tax statements, etc.; (6) a draft of the articles of association and a draft of the memorandum and articles of association; (7) Curriculum vitae and documents proving the experience and qualifications of the members of the management board, supervisory board and actuary of the future insurer; (8) Declaration as to whether the insurer/reinsurer is to be a subsidiary of another insurer/reinsurer or whether there are any other interdependencies.

157. When considering an application to conduct insurance activities, the PFSA may also require the founders to provide additional information, if necessary, on the ownership structure, financial situation and previous activities.

158. After considering all documents and information relating to a prospective insurer and its founders, the PFSA may refuse to issue a licence in circumstances specified in the AIRA. The main circumstances justifying refusal include situations where: (1) persons designated for positions of members of the management or supervisory board do not have the experience and qualifications necessary to manage the insurer, or have been convicted of intentional crimes (the latter also applies to founders of an insurance company); (2) there is no guarantee that the founders will conduct insurance activities properly; (3) the applications do not provide evidence that the insurer has the required capital as mentioned above, or the founders use significant assets derived from illegal or undisclosed sources; (4) a business plan does not ensure the insurance company's ability to meet its obligations on a permanent basis.

159. In addition, a licence to conduct insurance activities within the scope of section II Class 10 of the Annex to the Act (compulsory motor vehicle insurance), except for carrier's liability insurance, cannot be obtained if a domestic insurance company does not submit a list of claims representatives.

160. After obtaining a licence, the insurer is obliged to commence insurance activity within twelve months from the date of obtaining the licence, i.e., the first insurance contract must be concluded by the insurer within this period.

161. Any change in the territorial scope or material scope of activity of a domestic insurer requires the approval of the PFSA.

162. The AIRA also sets out the conditions under which a licence to conduct insurance business must or may be withdrawn by the supervisory authority. The withdrawal of the licence may concern one or more classes of insurance. The mandatory conditions for the withdrawal of the licence include: (1) failure to comply with the minimum capital requirements and failure to obtain the supervisory authority's approval of the short-term financing plan; or (2) failure to comply with the short-term financing plan within three months; (3) failure to have a claims representative in Poland (for insurance of class II, group 10).

163. The main circumstances in which the PFSA may decide to withdraw the licence are: (1) the insurer no longer fulfils the conditions for obtaining the licence; (2) the insurer conducts business in breach of the law, the articles of association or the business plan, or fails to ensure the ability to fulfil its obligations; (3) the insurer fails to implement a plan for restoring a sound financial position or a short-term financing plan in a timely manner; (4) the insurer ceases to conduct insurance business for a period exceeding six months; (5) the insurer fails to commence conducting insurance business within twelve months of obtaining the licence. The licence may also be withdrawn at the insurer's own request.

164. If the licence is withdrawn, the insurer may not conclude insurance contracts, may not prolong insurance contracts already concluded, and may not increase the sums insured in insurance contracts already concluded. Furthermore, the Insurer may not conclude inward reinsurance contracts or inward retrocession contracts, and already concluded inward reinsurance contracts and inward retrocession contracts may not be prolonged and will not be prolonged; furthermore, the Insurer may not accept new cessions under concluded inward reinsurance contracts and inward retrocession contracts and may not increase the liability under concluded inward reinsurance contracts and inward retrocession contracts.

§2. Main Branch of Foreign Insurance Companies

165. The main branch of a foreign insurance company is a form of activity of a non-EU insurer on the territory of Poland. An essential condition for commencing the insurance activity of a main branch is obtaining a permit from the domestic supervisory authority.

166. A licence may be issued to an interested party only if a foreign insurance company has been granted a licence to conduct insurance activities in the applied scope and operates in the form of a joint-stock company or a mutual insurance undertaking on the territory of the country in which its head office is located. The obligation to operate in one of the above-mentioned forms does not apply to foreign insurers whose registered office is located in countries that are members of the World Trade Organisation.

167. A foreign insurer is granted a licence to conduct insurance business if it pays a deposit to guarantee the future obligations of the insurance company. The deposit is equal to 25% of the minimum amount of the capital provided for the class of insurance in which the foreign insurer intends to operate through its main branch.

The deposit is valid for the entire period of the main branch's activity in Poland. The deposit, together with the interest, is included in the own funds and is placed in a separate interest-bearing account with a bank having its registered office in Poland. The deposit, together with interest, is returned to the foreign insurer after all claims arising from insurance contracts concluded by the head office have been settled. It is also important to note that the deposit is not subject to execution. Satisfaction of the deposit can only take place in the course of liquidation of the main branch, with the consent of the supervisory authority, which is given by way of a decision.

168. The minimum capital requirement for the main branch is 50% of that applicable to insurers.

169. If a foreign insurer conducts business through branches in more than one EU country, it may apply to the supervisory authority for a common calculation of financial requirements (such as the solvency margin) for all EU Member States in which it conducts business, as well as for the possibility of recognising a deposit and financial resources covering insurance technical provisions placed in another EU country.

170. An application by a foreign insurer for permission to conduct insurance activities through a main branch should include the name and registered office of the foreign insurer and the country in which the insurer is domiciled. The application should also contain the name and registered office of the foreign insurer and the country in which the insurer is established; the registered office and scope of activity of the main branch; and the names of the persons proposed for the posts of head of the main branch, deputy directors, actuary, person responsible for keeping the accounts, etc.

171. The application must be accompanied by a number of documents, including: (1) the foreign insurer's articles of association; information on the amount of the foreign insurer's qualifying capital; (2) drafts of the general insurance conditions under which the licence is to be granted; (3) the calculation of the solvency margin and the calculation of the value of the foreign insurer's own funds; (4) draft articles of association of the branch; (5) certificate of the insurance supervisory authority of the state in which the foreign insurer has its registered office confirming that the insurer has a licence to conduct insurance business and that it has its own funds and information on the insurer's financial situation; (6) financial report for the last three years of the foreign insurer's activity; (7) information on the amount of the organisational fund intended for the establishment of the branch's administration and the organisation of its regional units; (8) documents and information concerning the director of the main branch, deputy directors and actuary.

172. A foreign insurer may not obtain a licence to conduct or expand insurance activities in Poland if any of the circumstances listed in the AIRA apply. The most important of these circumstances are: (1) the application does not meet the requirements specified in the AIRA; (2) the persons proposed for the position of the director of the main branch and their deputies do not meet the requirements specified in the AIRA; (3) the foreign insurer does not provide a guarantee for the proper conduct of the insurance activity in Poland; (4) the foreign insurer does not possess funds in the amount of at least the organisational fund and the own funds of the head office as specified in the scheme of operations; (5) the foreign insurer does not possess funds in the amount of at least the organisational fund and the own funds of the main branch as specified in the scheme of operations; (6) the foreign insurer does not have the necessary funds to ensure the coverage of the main branch's technical provisions; (7) the foreign insurer uses material assets derived from illegal or undisclosed sources or related to the financing of terrorism; (8) the business plan does not ensure the ability to meet the obligations of the main branch; (9) the pursuit of the activity threatens the state's defence, security or public order and safety.

§3. Sanctions

173. Article 430 of the AIRA provides that anyone who conducts an insurance activity without the required authorisation or in contravention of the provisions of the AIRA is liable to a fine or imprisonment for up to two years.

174. The AIRA provides for several other actions that are punishable, such as failing to notify the supervisory authority or providing false information, concluding insurance contracts without the authorisation of the insurer, failing to notify bankruptcy when the conditions are met, and disclosing an insurance secret. Sanctions usually include a fine, restriction of liberty or imprisonment for between one and five years.

Chapter 3. Supervision

175. The specific nature of the insurance industry requires the supervisory authorities to protect the interests of the insured and to prevent a situation in which the insurer is unable to meet its obligations to the insured. Insurance supervision is exercised over domestic insurers and the main branches of foreign insurers operating in Poland. In accordance with the single licence rule, supervision of insurers with their registered office in an EU Member State is exercised by a home supervisor, while supervision by the PFSA is subsidiary and relates mainly to corporate and consumer matters.

176. Insurance supervision is carried out by the PFSA, which provides comprehensive supervision of the entire financial market in Poland. The PFSA is a central state administrative authority and is supervised by the Prime Minister.

§1. General

177. The rules of insurance supervision are laid down in the AIRA. According to this law, the functions of the supervisory authority generally include:

- taking measures to ensure the proper functioning of the insurance market and the protection of the interests of policyholders, insureds, beneficiaries or persons entitled under insurance contracts;
- ensuring that the activities of insurers and reinsurers comply with the provisions of the law, in particular with regard to financial matters within the scope of solvency requirements, rules for establishing technical provisions for solvency and accounting purposes, assets, amount of own funds;
- assessing the insurer's and reinsurer's ability to manage risks effectively under the management system;
- issuing permits for the conduct of insurance activities;
- issuing permits for the performance of brokerage activities;
- to inspect the activities of insurers and brokers;
- performing other activities specified in the Act, such as approving portfolio transfers.

178. In practice, the supervisory activities consist of the control of the activity and the financial standing of the insurers. Such control may be carried out at any time but should be completed no later than one month from the date of commencement of the control and must be carried out during normal working hours. As the nature of insurance supervision under Polish law is financial, prospective and based on a risk management approach, the controls carried out by the Authority focus on the financial and legal aspects of the activity. Therefore, the control includes an assessment of the compliance of the insurer's activities with the law, the articles of association, the business plan, the interests of policyholders, insureds, beneficiaries or persons entitled under insurance contracts, as well as the insurer's financial situation.

179. Within the framework of an on-site inspection, the supervisory authority may, at any time, conduct an on-site inspection of the activities and financial condition of entities that perform insurance operations for and on behalf of the insurer within the scope of these operations (control of outsourcing activities).

180. AIRA has also implemented the EU rules on supplementary supervision of insurance and reinsurance holdings. The Polish regulation is in line with the EU regulations and concerns the supervision of a parent insurer or a subsidiary of the parent insurer from a country that is not a member of the EU, or a subsidiary of the parent insurer engaged in mixed insurance activities.

181. In the case of an insurance holding company whose member is a domestic insurer and a foreign insurer having its seat in a Member State of the EU, the supervisory authority shall cooperate closely with the supervisory authorities of the Member States of the EU. The supervisory body may, at the request of the supervisory authority of any Member State of the EU, carry out a control of the domestic insurer forming part of the insurance holding company or ensure the possibility of carrying out such control by representatives of the supervisory authority of the Member State of the EU. Likewise, the supervisory authority may, in accordance with these agreements, require representatives of the supervisory authority to carry out a control of the foreign insurer or to ensure a possibility to carry out such a control. A competent authority of the Member State of the EU in which the domestic insurer in question conducts insurance activities through a branch may take part in the supervision of the branch of the domestic insurer carried out by the Polish supervisory authority if it so requests. The same possibilities are granted to the PFSA.

I. Supervisory Instruments

182. The supervisory remedies that may be applied by the supervisory authority include:

- issuing recommendations and decisions on irregularities in the activities of the insurer and reinsurer;
- requiring the insurer to provide information and explanations concerning the activity of the insurer and its management, to the extent necessary for the performance of its supervisory functions;
- order the insurer to provide periodical data specified by the supervisory authority;
- appoint a trustee or board of trustees;
- other remedies, including those listed below.

183. The PFSA may make recommendations to an insurer in order to:

1. ensure that the activities of the insurer comply with the provisions of the law, the articles of association or the business plan;
2. ensure the continued ability of the insurer to meet its obligations;

3. prevent damage to the interests of policyholders, insured persons, reinsured persons, beneficiaries or other persons entitled under insurance and reinsurance contracts;
4. increase the amount of technical provisions;
5. eliminating irregularities detected in the course of supervisory activities;
6. change and strengthen the management process;
7. reduce the risk in the insurer's or reinsurer's business.

184. If the insurer does not implement the recommendations voluntarily, the PFSA may, by decision, require the insurer to implement the recommendations. If an insurer fails to comply with such a decision, the supervisory authority may, by way of decision:

- impose on members of the management board or their deputies fines of up to three times their gross monthly remuneration, calculated on the basis of their remuneration for the previous twelve months, but not exceeding PLN 100,000;
- impose on insurers fines of up to 0.5% of the gross premiums written in the previous year, up to PLN 100,000;
- suspend members of management boards from their functions until a motion for their removal is considered at the next meeting of the body authorised to remove them;
- request the competent body of the insurer or other authorised entity to remove a member of the Management Board or to revoke a power of attorney.

185. The above remedies may also be imposed in case of:

1. the insurer/reinsurer operates in breach of the law, the articles of association, the insurance and reinsurance contracts or the business plan;
2. failure to comply with the obligation to have financial statements audited by an auditor;
3. failure to comply with the obligation to provide documents, information or explanations, to carry out audits required by the supervisory authority or to comply with other obligations imposed by the supervisory authority;
4. failure to convene a general meeting or to place certain matters on the agenda of a general meeting;
5. failure to recalculate the solvency capital requirement for the group of insurers or reinsurers.

186. The PFSA may order an insurer to terminate, within a specified period of time, a contract on the basis of which insurance or reinsurance activities have been entrusted to another entity, if it finds that the activities in question are being carried out in violation of the law, have a negative impact on the performance of insurance activities by the insurer in accordance with legal provisions, on the prudent and stable management of the insurer, or on the interests of policyholders, insureds, reinsureds, beneficiaries or persons entitled under insurance/reinsurance contracts.

187. Insurers/reinsurers shall notify the supervisory authority of the date of a general meeting within seven days prior to the date of the meeting and, in the case of an extraordinary general meeting, immediately upon learning of a decision of the general meeting. The supervisory authority may delegate its representative to attend the general meeting of the insurer. A representative of the supervisory authority may speak on any matter at the general meeting, but shall not have the right to vote.

188. The PFSA may also instruct the bodies of an insurer to convene a general meeting of that insurer on a specified date or to include specific items on the agenda of the next general meeting. If a general meeting is not convened within fourteen days of the day on which the above-mentioned order is served, the supervisory authority shall convene a general meeting of the insurer or include specific items on the agenda of the next general meeting.

§2. Solvency Control

189. If irregularities are found in an audit of the annual accounts carried out on behalf of the insurer/reinsurer, the supervisory authority may require that the insurer/reinsurer commission an audit of the correctness and reliability of all the annual accounts drawn up by that insurer/reinsurer and an audit of its accounting records in order to verify the financial management and solvency of that insurer/reinsurer. The audit may not be reassigned to the auditor who carried out the audit of the report in which irregularities were found.

190. The provisions of the AIRA provide for certain measures that may be applied by the PFSA in the event that the financial situation of the insurer/reinsurer is endangered. In particular, the following remedies may be applied:

1. if the solvency capital requirement is not met or there is a risk that it will not be met within the next three months, the supervisor may require the insurer to submit a recovery plan;
2. if the minimum capital requirement is not met or there is a risk that it will not be met within the next three months, the supervisory authority may require the insurer to submit a realistic short-term financing plan for approval by the supervisory authority.

191. In the above situations, the supervisory authority may prohibit the insurer from freely disposing of its assets or restrict the scope of its activities, set a deadline for the insurer to submit the above-mentioned plans or a date by which the insurer should restore its corrected financial situation or solvency, prohibit the insurer from continuing to pay dividends.

192. In the event of non-compliance with the minimum capital requirement, the supervisory authority may oblige the insurer to maintain its own funds at a level higher than the required solvency margin requirement throughout the period covered by a recovery plan and/or to calculate the insurer's own funds on the basis of a lower value than that which would result from the valuation rules adopted by the insurer/reinsurer for the elements used in its calculation, in particular if significant changes in the market value of those elements have been observed within the last financial year.

193. The PFSA may take a decision to appoint a trustee to supervise the insurer's implementation of the restoration of sound financial condition within the framework of the capital requirement, a recovery plan or a short-term financing scheme. In addition, the PFSA may appoint a board of trustees. The appointment of a board of trustees has serious consequences for the insurer, i.e., the mandates of the members of the board of directors expire, existing proxies and powers of attorney expire and the rights and obligations of other bodies of the insurer are suspended for the duration of the receivership. The Board of Trustees has the right to take decisions in all matters reserved by law and the articles of association for the Board of Directors, the Supervisory Board and the general meeting of the insurer.

194. The PFSA may order the compulsory liquidation of the insurer if: (1) the insurer is operating in breach of the law, the articles of association or a business plan and does not ensure the ability to fulfil its obligations; (2) the insurer does not implement a plan for restoring a sound financial position or a short-term financing plan in a timely manner; (3) a general meeting of the insurer does not adopt a resolution on covering a financial loss or such financial loss is not covered within the time and in the manner provided for in such resolution; (4) a board of trustees has not restored the proper financial relations of that insurer within the time limit set; (5) the insurer does not pay benefits under insurance contracts or pays them late or in part; or (6) a licence to conduct insurance business has been withdrawn in respect of the entire business.

§3. Supervision on Tariffs and Insurance Conditions

195. With regard to the supervision of tariffs and insurance conditions, the supervisory authority is prohibited from regularly approving or controlling tariffs or general insurance conditions. It may, however, request the submission of insurance conditions and tariffs in the course of supervisory procedures.

Chapter 4. Technical Provisions and Investments

§1. Technical Provisions

196. Technical provisions are intended to meet current and future liabilities that may arise from written insurance contracts.

197. Every insurer is required to establish the following technical provisions:

- a provision for unearned premiums;
- a provision for unexpired risks;
- a provision for outstanding claims, including a provision for the present value of future profits;
- a risk equalisation provision;
- a life assurance provision;
- a life assurance provision where an investment risk is borne by the policyholder;
- a provision for bonuses and rebates;
- a provision for the refund of premiums to members;
- other technical provisions provided for in the articles of association.

198. The insurer may also set up other funds, such as a prevention fund (up to 1% of premiums written).

199. The value of technical provisions is calculated for solvency purposes. It should be equal to the value of an amount that the insurer/reinsurer would have to pay to the other insurer/reinsurer by transferring all its obligations under insurance and reinsurance contracts. The value of technical provisions for solvency purposes should be calculated in a prudent, reliable and objective manner. The calculations should be made in accordance with data available in the market and general data on actuarial risks.

200. In practice, the choice of method for calculating technical provisions depends on a number of factors, such as the level of detail and availability of statistical and accounting information on premium income, claims and benefits paid, the number of claims in each line of business and their volatility over time, the duration of insurance contracts and the average payout of claims and benefits. The methods used to calculate technical provisions shall be set out in an insurer's accounting records. The calculation of technical provisions in an insurance undertaking operating in classes I of the Annex to AIRA (i.e., life insurance) may be carried out only by an actuary.

§2. Investments Restrictions

201. The insurer should invest its funds in such a way as to ensure maximum security and profitability while maintaining solvency. If an insurer's investment policy could jeopardise its solvency, the supervisory authority may impose restrictions on its investment instruments. In addition, the AIRA provides for objective criteria for the investment of funds. Most of the restrictions do not apply to unit-linked insurance, but in the case of insurance where no guaranteed benefit is provided, the technical provisions should reflect as closely as possible the units or relevant assets of the insurer; in the case of unit-linked insurance, the insurer should employ an investment advisor for the management of the insurance capital fund or enter into an agreement with a specialised entity for this purpose.

202. The AIRA sets out detailed requirements for the investment of funds held by insurers and reinsurers. First, the insurer/reinsurer must invest the funds in accordance with the principle of the prudent investor. This means that the funds may only be invested in assets and financial instruments with an identifiable and measurable risk that can be monitored, managed and reported and that can be appropriately taken into account in the assessment of solvency requirements.

203. The remaining types of eligible investments are subject to restrictions specifically provided for in the Act on Insurance Activities, while the restrictions are fully in line with the EU Directives.

Chapter 5. Accountancy

§1. Accounting and Reporting Regulations

204. Accounting in Poland is regulated by the Accounting Act of 29 September 1994. In the case of insurers, in addition to the general regulations, an implementing act has been issued, which sets out special rules. A large part of the accounting regulations specific to insurers and reinsurers is contained in the implementing regulations of the AIRA.

205. Regarding the financial reports to be prepared by insurers, it should be noted that in addition to the usual annual financial reports, insurers are required to prepare additional reports. According to the AIRA, the insurer should prepare a report on solvency and financial condition. The insurer must also submit additional statistical reports to the supervisory authority, as well as reports on proceedings before the financial ombudsman. Life insurers must also prepare reports on unit-linked insurance (annual and semi-annual). Additional reporting requirements concern groups of insurers and reinsurers with respect to the concentration of certain types of risks and significant transactions within the group.

206. Other reporting requirements relate to co-insurance. Co-insuring insurers or co-insuring main branches are obliged to compile statistical data on the scope of co-insurance and to submit them to the supervisory authority.

207. The specific requirements regarding the content and the deadline for the preparation of the statements are laid down in the implementing provisions of the AIRA.

§2. Finances of Insurers and Insurance Funds

208. In terms of financial requirements for insurers, the most important is the solvency capital requirement, the calculation of which has changed significantly under Solvency II.

209. The insurer is required to calculate the minimum capital requirement in accordance with the following principles:

1. it must be calculated in a clear and simple manner and in such a way as to ensure that the calculation can be audited; and
2. it shall correspond to an amount of eligible basic own funds below which policyholders and beneficiaries would be exposed to an unacceptable level of risk if insurance and reinsurance undertakings were allowed to continue their activities.

Chapter 6. Mergers and Transfer of Portfolio

§1. Mergers of the Insurers

210. Insurers may merge if they operate under the same legal form (joint stock companies, mutuals or European companies). Apart from the provisions of the AIRA, issues relating to mergers and acquisitions of insurers are regulated by the Competition and Consumer Protection Act in the context of merger control, and by the Commercial Companies Code in the case of mergers of joint-stock companies (although the latter provisions may also apply to mutual companies).

211. The merger of insurers requires an agreement on the merger plan, which should be in writing. A merger plan should include (apart from the matters regulated by the Commercial Companies Code): (1) the classes of risks in respect of which the insurer taking over the other or a newly established insurer will operate; (2) the names of the persons who will be members of the bodies, the person responsible for keeping the accounts and the actuary of the insurer taking over the other or a newly established insurer. A merger plan should include a number of documents, including evidence of the possession of assets to cover technical provisions, evidence of the possession of an available solvency margin to cover the required solvency margin, and the annual accounts of the insurer taking over the other or of a newly formed insurer.

212. The PFSA may, within twenty-one days of the notification of the merger plan, raise an objection to the proposed merger by way of a decision if the documents submitted indicate that, after the merger, the newly established insurer will not have an available solvency margin in the amount of the required solvency margin or will not possess assets covering technical provisions, and the interests of policyholders, insured persons, beneficiaries or persons entitled under insurance contracts have not been duly protected. The objection raised by the supervisory authority shall render the draft terms of the merger ineffective.

§2. Transfer of Insurance Portfolio

213. The insurer may enter into an agreement with another insurer to transfer all or some of its insurance contracts ('portfolio transfer'). The portfolio transfer agreement must be approved by the PFSA.

214. A transfer of insurance portfolio may take place provided that the insurer taking over the insurance portfolio and the insurer transferring the insurance portfolio have an available solvency margin of at least the required solvency margin and assets covering technical provisions after the contract is concluded. The supervisory authority may exempt the transferring or acquiring insurer from the above condition if the contract is intended to protect the interests of policyholders, insured persons, beneficiaries or persons entitled under insurance contracts in a situation that threatens the solvency of the transferring insurer.

215. After approving the transfer of the insurance portfolio, the PFSA shall, at the expense of the insurers concerned, announce the transfer of the insurance portfolio in a Polish daily newspaper with nationwide circulation and invite policyholders to submit objections within three months from the day of the announcement. Policyholders who have submitted an objection shall have the right to terminate the transferred insurance contracts as of the last day of the aforementioned period following the day of the announcement of the transfer of the insurance portfolio.

216. Merging insurance undertakings shall jointly apply for approval of the transfer of the insurance portfolio. The supervisory authority shall issue a decision approving the transfer of the insurance portfolio if the transferring insurers and the insurer taking over the insurance portfolio meet the financial conditions and the interests of policyholders, insured persons, beneficiaries or persons entitled under insurance contracts are duly protected.

217. The transfer of the assets of the transferring insurer to the acquiring insurer shall be accompanied by the transfer of the insurance portfolio in the amount of the technical provisions established for the insurance portfolio transferred. Only in cases justified by the protection of the interests of policyholders, insured persons, beneficiaries and persons entitled under insurance contracts may the supervisory authority, at the request of the insurer concerned, determine the value of the assets to be transferred together with the insurance portfolio or approve a transfer of the insurance portfolio without a transfer of financial resources.

Part II. The Insurance Contract

Chapter 1. Generalities

218. The insurance contract in Poland is regulated in a separate title of the Civil Code of 1964 (Title XVII, Articles 805–834). Since then, the provisions governing the insurance contract have been amended several times, adapting the form of the insurance contract to the progress of jurisprudence and strengthening the rights of policyholders. The latter changes have also been influenced by the tendencies of the European *acquis communautaire*. The last major changes to the provisions of insurance contract law were introduced in 2010, but it should be noted that the rights and obligations of the parties may depend on other provisions of the Civil Code, for example, on the limitation of claims and others. The provisions regulating liability in tort and for breach of contract, which are contained in the general part of the Civil Code dealing with obligations, have a significant impact on liability insurance.

219. In addition to the provisions of the Civil Code, the form of the insurance contract is also influenced by various provisions contained in the general provisions of the Insurance and Reinsurance Act. They concern the insurance terms and conditions, the content of life insurance contracts, as well as the obligation to provide information to the policyholder and in cases where the insurance contract is concluded for the benefit of a third party. An important element of the rules contained in the AIRA are the obligations of the insurance company in the claims settlement process. In 2018, the Act on Insurance Distribution entered into force. Although it does not directly regulate the insurance contract, it has an undeniable impact on its performance and interpretation, especially with regard to the policyholder's interests at the stage of concluding the insurance contract.

220. The contract of marine insurance is excluded from the general regulation of the Civil Code on insurance and became part of the Maritime Code, first in 1961 and then in 2001 with the adoption of the new Maritime Code. The contract of marine insurance, being a professional contract (and usually an insurance of large risks), is based on the British law of marine insurance. In general, consumer protection rules do not exist to the same extent as in the case of land insurance. It should be noted that, in practice, marine insurance contracts contain transnational elements and are subject not to Polish law but to international law and practice.

221. Neither the Civil Code nor the Maritime Code covers a reinsurance contract. In the absence of statutory regulation and case law, it is necessary to extract legal rules from various branches of the law that are to some extent applicable to reinsurance. Thus, any discussion of the legal nature of the reinsurance relationship must take into account all the terms and conditions agreed by the parties. As with marine insurance, reinsurance contracts are often governed by foreign law [*see also* Part VIII on Reinsurance].

222. The parties to an insurance contract are the insurer and the policyholder. However, there may be other entities involved in the insurance relationship that are not parties to the contract, such as a beneficiary (in life insurance) and an injured party (in liability insurance).

223. Insurance contracts may be concluded, on the one hand, by any entity with general legal capacity and, on the other hand, by a licensed insurer who is entitled to conduct insurance activities on the territory of Poland on the basis of a licence issued by the supervisory authority [*see* Part I above]. With regard to consumer protection, the provisions on insurance contracts extend a higher level of protection to entrepreneurs – natural persons, even if they conclude insurance contracts in connection with their business activities.

224. The provisions of the Civil Code on insurance contracts are divided into three sections. Section I regulates general issues and applies to all types of insurance. Section II deals with indemnity insurance, including liability insurance, and section III deals with personal insurance, i.e., all types of insurance that are fixed sum insurance, including life insurance and accident insurance.

225. It is widely accepted that the insurance contract in Poland is a bilaterally binding, payable agreement, unilaterally qualified (in such a way that the insurer has to be a licensed/qualified entity), bailable and undoubtedly consensual. However, the development of domestic law has led to a lively discussion about its other characteristics, namely: a consumer characteristic and the dichotomy of arbitrariness versus reciprocity.[9]

226. The provisions of the general conditions of insurance or the provisions of insurance contracts that are contrary to the provisions of this title are null and void unless other provisions provide for exceptions (Article 807 of the Civil Code. As this provision represents a significant restriction on contractual freedom, there is much debate in the case law as to the correct interpretation of this provision. As a rule, the regulation of insurance contracts is in principle mandatory and the only exceptions are provided for in this title of Book III of the Civil Code (e.g., Article 814 §1, Article 815 §2 sentence 1 of the Civil Code). The main reason for this is the adhesiveness and mass of the legal relations of insurance, which leads the legislator to do the same as in the regulation of consumer law. In view of the explicit sanction of nullity contained therein, it will only be applied if there is a strict conflict with the content of the cogent standard contained in Articles 805–834 of the Civil Code. The correct application of the provision of Article 807 §1 of the Civil Code, and the

9. Fuchs, Malinowska & Maśniak, Kontrakty na rynku Ubezpieczeń, Wolters Kluwer 2020.

application of the sanction of nullity provided for therein, requires an explicit indication, without any doubt, as to which provision of Title XXVII of the Civil Code on insurance contracts remains a specific provision of the insurance contract or a specific provision in conflict. The question arises as to whether there is any possibility of derogating from the mandatory provisions of the Civil Code on insurance contracts without incurring the automatic sanction of nullity. According to the prevailing doctrine, it is acceptable if the interests of the policyholder are protected, i.e., by invoking an interest of the policyholder.

Chapter 2. Insurable Risk

§1. Subject-Matter Insured

227. An essential task at this stage is to formulate the first definition of the insurance contract. According to Article 805 of the Civil Code, by an insurance contract, the insurer, acting within its business activity, undertakes to carry out specified duty if an event defined in the contract occurs (the even insured), while the policyholder undertakes to pay premium. The amount recoverable under an insurance contract is measured by the extent of the pecuniary loss being specified as indemnity for a loss sustained by a person entitled to a claim in connection with an event envisaged in the contract (property insurance) or a payment of an agreed sum of money, pension or other contribution when an insurance event occurs (in personal insurance).

228. According to the above definition of the insurance contract, the policyholder (insured) agrees to pay premium in return for protection granted by the insurer during a period of insurance. It is suggested, that the amount of premium depends on the insurer's estimation of the degree of risk that an insured subject incurs a loss and on the amount of indemnity he will have to pay. Rules setting a basis for risk calculation can be derived not only from the Civil Code but also from the AIRA. There are specific provisions concerning insurance tariffs and relevant statistics as a basis for calculating insurance premiums. It has been explicitly stated that insurance premiums should be calculated on the basis of the risk analysis, in the amount ensuring at least coverage of the insurer's obligations from insurance contracts and costs of insurance activity (prohibition of dumping premiums). Rules of calculating insurance premium should be included in the insurance terms and conditions provided to the policyholder. The rules laid down in the Act on Insurance Activity forbid differentiating insurance premium and benefits with respect to gender criterion, as well as with respect to maternity and pregnancy criteria.

229. The Civil Code underlines a distinction between indemnity and non-indemnity insurance since Article 805 creates not only a definition of the contract but also states which category of payment is typical for a non-life insurance (a specified indemnity for damage caused by an event envisaged in the contract) and personal insurance (an agreed sum of money, an annuity or other performance in the event of the happening in lifetime of the insured due to an event envisaged in the contract). Not only the type of payment but also other rules are different for indemnity and non-indemnity insurance. Specific exclusions of coverage and rules for terminating the contract concluding the contract for the interest of a third party are regulated in section III, devoted to Personal insurance.

230. With regard to marine insurance contracts, Article 262 of the Maritime Code defines the insurance contract as a contract of indemnity. In accordance with the provisions of the Maritime Code, the insurer undertakes, in return for an insurance premium, to pay compensation in the event of a marine accident. Specific terms of the marine insurance contract impose certain limitations on the types of events that may cause losses for which the insurer will pay indemnity (*see* Chapter 4). Additional exclusions apply to certain types of loss (*see* Chapter 5 of the Maritime Code).

231. The causation requirement is the most common condition for a legitimate claim. There should be a causal link between the insured perils and a loss in order for insurance cover to exist. However, it should be emphasised that, apart from compulsory insurance, a type of causal link can be freely regulated in an insurance contract. It can only be limited to a direct causal link to the exclusion of all consequential losses. In compulsory insurance, the causal link is subject to the general rules of law, which provide for an 'adequate' causal link, including all consequential losses if they are a normal (adequate) result of an insured event.

232. The term 'insured event' is not defined in the Civil Code. However, the doctrine has formulated a concept according to which it is 'a fortuitous event provided for in the insurance contract, the occurrence of which transforms the policyholder's expectation of a cash payment from the insurance company into an insurance claim, i.e., a specific subjective right of a property nature'. An insured event is a fortuitous event that is covered by an insurance transaction and that, in accordance with the provisions of the terms and conditions of a given insurance policy, results in an obligation on the part of the insurance company. In this sense, it should be noted that the occurrence of a fortuitous event, which is defined as an insured event on the basis of Article 805 §1 of the Civil Code, has consequences which, in the context of property insurance, include a designation in the form of a loss.

233. The concept of an insured event is also interpreted by the courts with the help of the concept of a 'fortuitous event' (as provided by the AIRA for the purpose of defining the insurance activity), which is 'beyond the control of the policyholder, future and uncertain'. However, the doctrine draws attention to the fact that such a definition is too narrow, as there are some events that go beyond the above definition but are still allowed to be covered by the Civil Code itself. This concerns, for example, the possibility of covering past events (retroactive coverage), as well as the coverage of suicide, which is an intentional event. This inconsistency can also be observed in the context of liability insurance, the purpose of which is to protect the victim rather than the insured, but where some protective measures for insurers have been introduced, enabling them to recover claims paid to the injured party from the policyholder (*see* Part IV). The problem, however, caused by the above notion of accidental event is that insurance undertakings in Poland are allowed to provide insurance cover only in respect of accidental events as defined above. A change in the above definition seems imminent.[10]

234. Pursuant to Article 806 of the Civil Code, an insurance contract is null and void if, at the time of its conclusion, the possibility of the occurrence of an insured event is excluded. In the context of the temporal aspect of the insurance, it must be

10. Fuchs, Malinowska & Maśniak, Kontrakty na rynku Ubezpieczeń, Wolters Kluwer 2020.

assumed that the contract is void if the occurrence of the accident is impossible, regardless of the stage at which this impossibility occurs. However, the regulations provide for an exception to the above principle. The parties may agree to cover a period prior to the conclusion of the contract, but the contract will not be valid if, at the time of the conclusion of the contract, one of the parties knew, or by exercising due diligence could have known, that the event had already occurred or that the possibility of it occurring had ceased (Article 806, paragraph 2 of the Civil Code). In such a case, the insurance contract remains valid with the modification that for the period prior to the conclusion of the contract, the insurer is not obliged to pay compensation or other benefits and the insured is not obliged to pay premiums for this period.

235. It should be emphasised that the possibility or impossibility of an accident occurring should be analysed on the basis of objective criteria and not on the basis of potential legal – e.g., powers held, i.e., *ius contrahendi*, or de facto – to acquire (by the contracting parties) to the insurance contract.

236. The Civil Code does not list the types of risks or events that are excluded from insurance coverage. In practice, many risks or events are never covered by insurance. A number of risks and events are never covered by insurance and the provisions of the Civil Code are basically neutral in this respect unless the exclusion is an abusive clause or contrary to Articles 826 and 827 Civil Code (*see* Chapter 5). These are mainly wear and tear and inherent vice. They are simply not fortuitous and therefore cannot be covered as uncertain risks.

§2. Insurable Interest

237. The theory of insurable interest, together with the concepts of risk, need and damage, is considered to be one of the main concepts of insurance contract law. This is because loss is the negation of the existence of the interest covered by the risk and, therefore, the denial of enrichment under the contract. The existence of an insurable interest is considered a condition for the validity of the insurance contract.

238. The concept of insurable interest was developed by Polish jurisprudence before it was introduced into the Civil Code in 2007. Since then, Article 821 states that the object of insurance can be any material interest that is not contrary to the law and can be valued in monetary terms. It is believed that it is the insurance interest that distinguishes an insurance contract from betting and gambling and emphasises its protective and guarantee function. Moreover, the insurance interest justifies the insurance principle of indemnity and introduces a prohibition of enrichment under an insurance contract.

239. Nevertheless, case law still has an important influence on the understanding of an insurable interest provision. This can be seen in the many court cases concerning theft insurance in the 1990s, in which the courts have analysed the nature of the relationship between the policyholder and the insured property, extending it from the narrow understanding adopted by the insurers (who only accepted possession as a legitimate insurable interest) to a broader meaning that includes possession and its loss as a source of compensable damage:

> 'The policyholder is entitled to compensation even if he is a bona fide possessor and not the owner of the vehicle'. SN III CZP 1/93 OSNC 10/93, p. 170.
>
> 'The fact that the insured is not the owner of the insured vehicle does not mean that the insurance contract is invalid, provided that the insured is not acting in bad faith. It is important that the insured considered himself as the owner of the insured vehicle and that he intended to conclude the insurance contract in this capacity. Conclusion of an insurance contract on the basis of a valid registration card, without checking other documents of the insured vehicle and without further investigation of its ownership status, seems to be part of the risk of the insurer's activity, and refusal to pay compensation to the insured transfers this risk to the insured'. S.A. Łódź of 26 February 1992; I Acr 25/92 OSA 10.92 p. 70.
>
> If the insurance conditions do not exclude the possibility of insuring assets that are in the possession of the policyholder but are not his property, and there is no reason to believe that the policyholder has concealed this fact, the insurance contract is legally binding. SN II CK35/05.
>
> 'The insurer is liable for the damage caused by the theft of the car if the policyholder was convinced that he was the owner of the car at the moment of concluding the insurance contract and at the moment of the theft. For the insurer's liability to arise, it is irrelevant that it later transpired that the policyholder was only the possessor of the vehicle and had not yet acquired ownership of it'. SN IV CKN 1131/00, LEX nr 80263.

240. There is still considerable difficulty in determining what is covered by these types of insurance products, which insure insured property against fire, theft, etc. It is up to the individual contract to decide what kind of right to the object is covered by the insurance contract. In general, insurance contracts protect all rights over property (usufruct, easement, pledge, mortgage, the right of a member of a cooperative to an apartment, etc.). However, the question of possession remains controversial, as it is only a fact protected by law and not a right. Nevertheless, a possession is usually considered to be protected by insurance, regardless of whether a possessor has a right to it or even whether he is in good faith.

241. In the case of property insurance, an insurable interest must exist at the time of the loss. It is not necessary for the interest to exist at the time the insurance contract is entered into.

242. Insurable interest problems do not generally arise in liability insurance. An insured risk is itself an interest, called 'liability to third parties', which is a future potential legal situation. The only concern that may arise is in relation to motor liability insurance. In order to avoid disputes, a possessor is treated in the same way as an owner of the vehicle and the fact of possession is a determining factor.

243. A concept of insurable interest has also been expressly defined in the Maritime Code. According to the definition in Article 293 §1, the insurer undertakes, by virtue of a contract of marine insurance, to pay compensation for losses arising from maritime adventure. Although it is a basic principle of insurance that an insured must have an insurable interest in an object damaged, it has become common practice in marine insurance to conclude contracts which waive the requirement of proof of insurable interest. Policies issued under such a contract – P.P.I. (policy proof of interest) or F.P.A. (full interest admitted) – are used in practice.[11]

244. Although the Civil Code only mentions the insurable interest in relation to property and liability insurance, in the case of personal insurance, Article 829 of the Civil Code (which can be considered an expression of the insurable interest) states that the insurance may relate in particular to: (1) in the case of life insurance – the death of the insured person or his reaching a certain age; (2) in the case of accident insurance – bodily injury, impairment of health or death as a result of an accident. In this respect, there are provisions limiting the possibility of insuring the life of a third party without the consent of the person whose life is to be insured. In the case of a life insurance policy taken out for the account of a third party, the insurance cover does not commence until the day following that on which the insured person declares to the policyholder that he wishes to make use of the reservation in favour of the insurance. The declaration should also include the amount of the sum insured. Any modification of the agreement to the detriment of the Insured or a beneficiary requires the consent of the Insured. Similarly, a change of beneficiary always requires the consent of the insured.

§3. Non-insurable Risk and Exclusion of Coverage

245. The law defines the general characteristics of the insurable risk, which correspond to the object of the insurer's activity, which is regulated by the Insurance and Reinsurance Activity Act. The core of the insurance activity is the coverage of the consequences of fortuitous events, which are defined as an event that is independent of the will of the policyholder or insured, a future and uncertain event, the occurrence of which causes damage to personal or property rights or increases the needs of the policyholder's or insured's property. All events that do not fulfil these characteristics are not insurable. This principle is expressed in the provisions of the Civil Code on the insurance contract, which excludes the coverage of risks that are not future and that depend on the will of the policyholder.

246. To this end, Article 827 of the Civil Code provides that the insurer is not obliged to indemnify if the policyholder caused the damage intentionally. In the case of gross negligence, no indemnity is due unless the payment of all or part of the indemnity is in accordance with the principles of social coexistence in the circumstances. However, this rule has been the subject of much controversy in the light of the wording of the insurance terms and conditions, which provide for the exclusion

11. Brodecki, '*Insurance Contract Law in Poland*', 19.

of cover even in the event of the ordinary negligence of some of the obligations of the policyholder/insured which led to the occurrence of the insured event.

247. For this reason, for the correct application of this article, jurisprudence is of key importance, which qualifies the behaviour of the policyholder or insured with regard to the legitimacy of the refusal to pay the claim. According to the regulations, which are also confirmed by the jurisprudence of the Supreme Court, Article 827 §1 of the Civil Code is an absolutely binding norm. This means that, on the one hand, neither the insurance contract nor the general conditions of insurance may provide for more extensive exclusions of coverage and, on the other hand, Article 827 §1 of the Civil Code, as a mandatory provision, may not be interpreted in a more extensive manner. In this respect, it is important to note that Polish law does not recognise the common law concept of warranty. Therefore, the breach of the policyholder's obligations is interpreted in the light of Article 827 of the Civil Code.

248. At the same time, it should be noted that in the case of third-party liability insurance, different assumptions can be made regarding the exclusion of coverage. Thus, even in the case of voluntary civil liability insurance, changes may be made to the principles derived from Article 827 §1 of the Civil Code. At the same time, it follows from the above that these modifications may not only take the form of an extension of the liability of the insurer in question with regard to the risk intentionally caused by the policyholder but may also cause a limitation, i.e., a modification to the detriment of the policyholder.

Chapter 3. Formation of the Insurance Contract

§1. Concluding the Insurance Contract

249. Modern insurance contracts are concluded using all the methods used in Poland for concluding any other type of contract, i.e., by means of an offer, negotiations and an offer.

250. An offer expresses the willingness of the offeror to conclude a contractual agreement on a specific subject. According to Article 66 of the Civil Code, it is a declaration of intent that specifies the essential terms of the contract. Not all types of statements made by one of the parties are considered to be an offer; for example, announcements, advertisements, price lists and other information addressed to the public or to specific persons are not considered to be an offer but an invitation to negotiate.

251. An offer must be definite and certain. If an essential element is missing, or if an offer is indefinite or vague, an attempt to accept it does not create a contract. If an offer states that it is open until a certain date, the offer expires on that date if it has not yet been accepted (Article 66 §1 of the Civil Code). This is particularly the case if the offeror declares that the offer is null and void after the expiry of the specified period. If the offer does not specify a time limit, it lapses after a reasonable time has elapsed. It follows from Article 66 §2 that what constitutes a reasonable delay depends on the nature of the transaction.

252. An insurance form normally filled in by the policyholder (as provided for in Article 810 of the Civil Code) is treated as an offer made by the policyholder (if the policyholder is qualified as an offeror). Once an insurance application expresses the willingness to enter into a contractual relationship with the insurer as the offeree, the insurer may accept the offer. No particular form of acceptance of the offer by the insurer is required, although it should be clear that the offer has been accepted. In practice, evidence of acceptance is the insurance policy issued by the insurer as confirmation of the cover granted. Implicit acceptance is not possible in the case of voluntary insurance, but only in the case of compulsory insurance.

253. A contract is deemed to be concluded at the moment of acceptance of an offer. In the case of insurance contracts, a contract is deemed to have been concluded at the moment of delivery of an insurance document (policy) containing the *essentialia negotii* (basic provisions of the contract, such as the parties, the insured event, the sum insured and the premium):[12]

> According to the provisions of the Civil Code, the insurance contract is concluded when the insured makes an offer and the insurer accepts it. No specific form is required for the validity of such a contract. The documents referred to

12. Z. Brodecki, '*Dobrowolne ubezpieczenia od odpowiedzialnoCci cywilnej*', 15 et al.

in Article 809 of the Civil Code only constitute proof (confirmation) of the conclusion of the contract, which is subject to the general rules of interpretation (Articles 74 and 74 of the Civil Code). A presumption of Article 809 §2, concerning the moment of conclusion of the contract, may be of some importance only if the parties have not agreed on the moment of conclusion of the contract. This moment may precede the delivery of the insurance documents to the insured. S.A. Łódź of 14 March 1996 I Acr 62/95 'Prawo Gospodarcze' 8/96 p. 63.

254. The Code also regulates the conditions of acceptance of the insurance application with some deviations. While according to the general rules of contract law the acceptance of an offer with some changes is considered a new offer, a special procedure is required in the case of an insurance contract. If, in response to a submitted offer (insurance application), the insurer delivers to the policyholder a policy containing provisions that deviate from the content of the offer to the detriment of the policyholder, the insurer is obliged to draw the policyholder's attention to this fact in writing upon delivery of the policy and to give the policyholder at least seven days to object. If the Insured fails to comply with this obligation, the changes made to the detriment of the Insured shall be null and void and the insurance contract shall be concluded in accordance with the terms of the offer. If no objection is made, the insurance contract will take effect in accordance with the contents of the policy on the day following the expiry of the objection period.

255. With regard to the other two methods of concluding insurance contracts (tendering and negotiation), it appears that they are used for specific and large-value contracts concluded with corporate policyholders (e.g., in the case of group insurance taken out by an employer for the benefit of its employees), as well as in situations involving public funds or where the policyholder is a public entity (in the latter case, a tendering procedure is mandatory under the Public Procurement Act of 29 January 2004).

256. At the stage of concluding insurance contracts, certain requirements are imposed on the insurer. They mainly concern the obligation to provide the policyholder with certain information (as provided for in Article 13a of the Insurance Act): (1) the law applicable to the insurance contract, if the parties are free to choose the applicable law; (2) the applicable law proposed by the insurer, if the parties are free to choose the applicable law; (3) the procedure for settling complaints submitted by the policyholder or beneficiary, as well as the designation of a body competent to settle them.

257. The law implementing the Insurance Distribution Directive, i.e., the Insurance Distribution Act, which entered into force on 15 December 2017, introduced significant changes to the information requirements. According to the Act, the process of concluding an insurance contract includes the obligation to assess the needs and requirements of the client (including the policyholder and the insured, if different), the obligation to disclose the type of remuneration for the distributor, as well as to provide the policyholder with a number of insurance documents, such as the Insurance Product Information Document (IPID).

258. Prior to the conclusion of a contract, whether or not it is subject to advice and whether or not the insurance product is part of a package, the distributor should make an analysis of the needs and requirements of the customer and should offer only such insurance as meets the needs and requirements of the customer. Offering a product that does not meet the needs and requirements is considered an unfair market practice under the Consumer Protection Act. However, the requirement to carry out a needs and wants test is not limited to consumer insurance and applies to all types of insurance and all types of policyholders (including large-risk insurance – albeit with some restrictions on the form of the information).[13]

259. Specific obligations regarding information and advice on IBIPs are contained in the Insurance Activity Act and are addressed only to insurers, which means that they are also effectively fulfilled by agents, but brokers are not bound by them. Before concluding an IBIP, the insurer must obtain from the policyholder (or, in the case of group insurance, before the insured gives his or her consent to the insurance), in the form of a questionnaire, information on his or her needs, knowledge and experience in the field of life insurance, as well as on his or her financial situation, so that the insurer can assess which insurance contract is appropriate to the policyholder's needs.

260. The minimum information to be included in the questionnaire shall be determined by the Minister. On the basis of an analysis of the information provided by the policyholder, the insurer shall submit to the policyholder insurance proposals which are appropriate to the policyholder's needs, together with a statement of reasons which shall include, in particular, an identification of the policyholder's needs and an explanation of how the proposals submitted meet those needs. If the analysis of the information shows that the policyholder's needs do not correspond to his experience, knowledge of life insurance or financial situation, or that there is a lack of adequate cover for the policyholder's needs, the insurer shall warn the policyholder in an appropriate manner that the result of the analysis or the offer made by the insurance undertaking precludes the offer of adequate cover. The policyholder must acknowledge receipt of this information in writing and provide a written statement that he has read the warning. In such a case, the insurance contract may only be concluded at the written request of the policyholder. In the case of group insurance, the Insurer will provide the Insured with a recommendation, together with a justification, prior to the Insured's agreement to be covered by IBIP, which will include, in particular, an identification of the Insured's needs and an explanation of how the cover provided by the insurance contract meets those needs.

261. The distributor should provide the customer with relevant information about the insurance product in an understandable form to enable the customer to

---

13. D. Maśniak, Commentary to the Art. 7 in: Dystrybucja Ubezpieczeń, Komentarz, Wolters Kluwer 2020.

make an informed decision, taking into account the complexity of the insurance product and the type of customer. In the case of non-life insurance, the information takes the form of an IPID (not applicable to large-risk insurance) and in the case of life insurance, the document is called a KID (key information document).

262. There are additional obligations regarding the conclusion of unit-linked insurance. Before concluding such an insurance contract, the insurer collects from the policyholder, in the form of a questionnaire, information on his needs, knowledge and experience in the field of life insurance and his financial situation, so that the insurance company can assess which insurance contract is suitable for the policyholder's needs. In the case of an insurance contract concluded for the account of a third party, the insurer shall obtain information in the form of a questionnaire about the insured person before the insured person gives his consent to be covered by the insurance contract concluded by the policyholder, so that the insurer can assess whether the insurance contract is appropriate to the insured person's needs.

263. On the basis of an analysis of the information, the insurer shall submit to the policyholder insurance proposals that are appropriate to the policyholder's needs, together with a statement of reasons, which shall include, in particular, the identification of the policyholder's needs and an explanation of how the proposals submitted meet those needs. If the analysis of the information shows that the policyholder's needs do not correspond to his experience and knowledge in the field of life insurance or to his financial situation, or that there is no insurance, the insurance undertaking shall, where appropriate, communicate this information to the policyholder, with a warning that the result of the analysis or the offer made by the insurer prevents it from offering appropriate insurance. The policyholder shall acknowledge receipt of this information in writing and provide a written statement that he has read the warning. In this case, the insurance contract can only be concluded at the written request of the policyholder.

264. The insurer should provide the insured with a recommendation and justification for the use of the insured prior to the insured's consent to the insurance cover. The justification should include, in particular, an identification of the insured person's needs and an explanation of how the cover provided under the insurance contract meets those needs.

§2. General Insurance Terms and Conditions

265. The standardisation of an insurance contract is a worldwide phenomenon, although it has a significant impact on the real freedom of contract and the balance between the parties. The legislator's usual response to this situation is to introduce strict procedures for the application of standard terms, in order to ensure that the freedom of will of the weaker party does not remain a fiction. The relevant provisions concern the way in which standard terms are incorporated into the contract, the content of the standard terms and the rights of the consumer to withdraw from the contract. Polish law fully reflects the legal restrictions introduced by the EU regarding the use of standard contract terms, especially in consumer contracts. All of these rules apply to the Insurance Contract Act, with some additional specific rules included in the Insurance Act (the Civil Code and the laws regulating insurance activities and distribution).

266. The standardisation of insurance contracts is reflected in general insurance conditions, which are used as a model for concluding insurance contracts. Specific regulation of insurance terms and conditions is provided by the Law on Insurance Activity. Article 15 states that insurance terms and conditions and the insurance contract should be formulated in an unambiguous, clear and transparent manner. Any unclear provisions shall be interpreted in favour of the policyholder, insured, beneficiary or any other person entitled to claim under the insurance contracts. General insurance conditions and other model contracts should be made available on the insurer's website.

267. The law regulates in detail the content of general insurance conditions for a specific type of compulsory insurance. The parties are obliged to comply with their provisions unless it is expressly stated that amendments or additions to them are permitted (e.g., with regard to rates and tariffs, where there are some options for both parties to the contract).

268. Standard insurance conditions should contain specific contents required by the Law on Insurance Activity in Article 16, such as: (1) rights and obligations of the parties to the insurance contract; (2) the scope of coverage; (3) the method of determining the amount of damage – for property insurance; (4) the method of determining the amount of indemnity or other benefit, if the insurance conditions provide for deviations from the rules established by law; (5) the method of determining and paying the insurance premium, if the insurance conditions provide for indexation of the premium; (6) the method of determining the amount of indemnity or other benefit, if the insurance conditions provide for indexation of the premium; (7) the method of determining the amount of indemnity or other benefit, if the insurance conditions provide for indexation of the premium; (8) the method of determining the amount of indemnity or other benefit, if the insurance conditions provide for indexation of the premium; (9) the method of determining the amount of indemnity; or (10) the procedure and conditions for amending an insurance contract concluded for an indefinite period; (11) the reasons, manner and date of terminating the insurance contract, if the insurance conditions provide for such a possibility, as well as the reasons for it; (12) the manner and date of withdrawing from a group insurance contract; (13) the date and manner of withdrawing from the insurance contract.

269. In addition, the text of the insurance conditions should be preceded by the information/index indicating which provisions of the conditions govern: (1) conditions for payment of indemnification and other benefits or surrender value insurance; (2) limitations and exclusions of the insurer's liability; (3) costs and other charges deducted from insurance premiums, insurance capital fund assets or surrender units of insurance capital funds; (4) the surrender value of the insurance in certain periods of coverage during which the right to surrender value payment does not exist. In the practice established on the market and in accordance with the legislation in force (ministerial decree), the index is placed on the first page of the insurance conditions in the form of a table.

270. In the case of an insurance contract concluded on behalf of another person, in particular in the case of group insurance, the insurance company provides information on the insurance conditions through the policyholder. It shall be provided before the conclusion of such an insurance contract, in writing or, if the person concerned agrees, on another durable medium.

271. Additional requirements concerning the content of an insurance contract are regulated in Article 20 of the Law on Insurance Activity in relation to life insurance. They are based on the Life Insurance Directive 2002/83/WE. For insurance specified in Chapter I of the Annex to the Act, the insurer shall include in the insurance contract: (1) the amount of the premiums corresponding to the individual basic and additional benefits, if the contract divides the benefits into basic and additional benefits; (2) the rules for determining the benefits due under the contract, in particular the method of calculating and awarding bonuses, rebates and profit-sharing to the policyholder, the determination of the technical interest rate, the surrender value and the amount of the sum assured when the insurance contract is converted into a non-contributory one, where this is guaranteed, the determination of the expenses and other charges levied by the insurance undertaking on the payment of the benefits; (3) a description of those factors in the methods of calculating technical provisions which may affect a change in the insurance undertaking's benefit or surrender value; (4) an indication of the provisions governing the taxation of insurance benefits; (5) an indication of where the solvency and technical reports of financial insurance undertakings are published.

272. In the case of insurance referred to in section I of the Annex to the Act, before the parties agree to change the terms of the contract or to change the law, the insurer must provide the policyholder with the contract-specific information in writing or, if the policyholder agrees, on another durable medium, together with an indication of the impact of these changes on the value of the benefits to which he is entitled under the concluded contract.

273. The policyholder will be informed on a durable medium, at least once a year, of the amount of benefits payable under the concluded insurance policy, if the amount of benefits changes during the term of the insurance policy, as well as of the surrender value of the insurance policy, if the insurance policy entitles the policyholder to surrender it. If the insurance contract provides for a benefit that is determined on the basis of the sum insured expressed as a fixed amount, the insurer shall inform the policyholder of any change in the sum insured. Where the insurer has undertaken to provide the assessment referred to in Article 22(2)(7) at specified intervals, the above information shall also include an assessment of the adequacy of the life assurance contract, if linked to an insurance holding company, to the needs of the policyholder.

274. The policyholder shall be informed on a durable medium or in writing at least once a year of the value of the premium if the insurance contract includes for accounting purposes a share in the investment return on technical provisions. In the case of an insurance contract concluded for the account of a third party, in particular group insurance, the policyholder shall provide the insured person or, if the insured person so agrees, another person, with the information referred to above in writing on a durable medium. This information must be given to the insured person before he consents to any change in the conditions of the contract or in the law applicable to the contract, or immediately after it has been communicated to him by the insurer.

275. The insurer shall provide the information to the policyholder for the first time not earlier than ten months and not later than fourteen months after the conclusion of the insurance contract. Prior to the conclusion of the group insurance contract, the Insurer shall provide the interested party with information on the conditions of the insurance. Such information shall include: (1) the data of the insurer, the address of its registered office; (2) the type of remuneration received by the distributor; (3) the possibility of filing a complaint and out-of-court settlement of disputes.

276. With regard to the interpretation of general conditions, their rules have been established by the courts, which have a protective attitude towards the rights of the insured.

> 'Negative consequences of badly written general conditions, i.e. the possibility of their different interpretation, should be borne by the insurer as a professional and by the author of the conditions'. S.A. I Acr 37/96 OSA 9/96 p. 43.
>
> 'The interpretation of the provisions of the insurance contract, including the provisions of the insurance conditions, should take into account the purpose of the contract and the interests of the policyholder, insured or beneficiary'. SN I CSK 64/08, LEX no. 457853.
>
> 'If there is any doubt about certain provisions of the insurance conditions, they must be interpreted in favour of the insured. It would be contrary to the rules of social coexistence to burden the insured with the negative consequences of their incorrect and negligent wording'. SN V CK 35/03, LEX no. 196761.

§3. Form of the Insurance Contract

277. Polish law recognises various forms of contract. However, the basic rule is that the form of a contract is subject to contractual freedom, i.e., the parties may choose to conclude a contract only orally, or to give a transaction a simple written form or a specific written form (e.g., a notarial deed). However, for certain contracts, the Civil Code provides for an obligation to observe a certain form (e.g., simple written form, written form with certified signatures, full notarial deed). Consequently, there are three types of legal consequences of failure to comply with the form prescribed for a particular contract. Each of them is related to other consequences – *ad solemnitatem* (on pain of invalidity), *ad probationem* (for evidence purposes) and *ad eventum* (to cause certain specific legal consequences).

278. Polish law does not provide for a mandatory form for an insurance contract. Consequently, an insurance contract is valid whether it is in written or oral form, but it should be confirmed by the insurer with a policy, certificate or other insurance document. Since no consequences are attached to an insurance document, this means that confirmation of an insurance contract by issuing a policy should be for evidentiary purposes only and does not affect the validity of the contract itself.

279. The provisions of the Civil Code do not provide for a written form requirement for the submission of an offer to conclude an insurance contract to the insurer, nor for the acceptance of the offer. SN II CSK 181/06, LEX No. 260147, Palestra 2007/1-2/289.

280. Nevertheless, it should be noted that several insurance documents to be provided by the insurer prior to the conclusion of the insurance contract must be in a certain form. The Insurance Distribution Act and some regulations on insurance activities provide for the obligation to deliver the documents in paper form and, if the policyholder or insured agrees, also in the form of a durable medium.

281. In addition, the insurer is obliged to provide the policyholder with a written explanation of the difference between the content of the contract and the insurance conditions before concluding the contract. If the insurer fails to do so, it may not invoke the difference to the detriment of the policyholder. This provision does not apply to insurance contracts concluded by way of negotiation.

§4. Insurance Documents

282. As stated above, the conclusion of an insurance contract should be confirmed by the insurer by means of a policy, certificate or other insurance document (Article 809 §1 of the Civil Code). This document has only the function of an instrument evidencing the conclusion of the contract. The fact of the conclusion of the insurance contract, as well as its terms, may be proved in any other way.

283. If an insurance policy contains provisions that deviate to the detriment of the Insured from the content of an offer made by the Insured or from the general terms and conditions of insurance, the Insurer is obliged to draw the attention of the Insured to this fact in writing when delivering this document and to give the Insured a period of at least several days in which to object. If the insurer fails to comply with this obligation, any amendment to the detriment of the policyholder shall be null and void. In the absence of an objection, the contract is deemed to be concluded in accordance with the contents of the policy on the day following the expiry of the objection period (Article 811 of the Civil Code).

284. In practice, insurance companies use many forms of insurance policies, depending on the type of insurance contract. The most common on the market are group policies, general policies, unit policies, etc. This issue is not regulated by law and is a matter of commercial practice.

285. The legal regulations on the insurance contract contained in the Civil Code do not provide for the content of the insurance policy. However, the content of the policy has been regulated in the provisions on cross-border insurance activities.

286. The content of an insurance policy has been regulated in Article 215 of the Act on Insurance Activity with regard to insurance documents issued in Poland by foreign insurers acting through a branch or on the basis of the principle of freedom of services. It is stipulated that an insurance policy or other document confirming the conclusion of an insurance contract by a branch or otherwise than by a branch in accordance with the principle of freedom to provide services must contain the following information: (1) the address and registered office of the insurer or the address of the branch of the insurer providing the insurance cover; (2) the place of conclusion of the insurance contract; (3) the court of jurisdiction in the event of a dispute between the parties to the insurance contract; (4) the date of conclusion of the insurance contract and the period of its validity; (5) the subject of the insurance contract; (6) the name of the insurer; (7) the address and registered office of the branch of the insurer providing the insurance cover; (8) identification of the parties to the insurance contract; (9) amount of the insurance premium; (10) identification of the general terms and conditions of the insurance contract on the basis of which the insurance contract has been concluded and the fact that they have been delivered to the policyholder.

287. The mandatory content of the insurance policy (or other documents confirming the conclusion of the insurance contract) has also been provided with regard to compulsory insurance. This issue is regulated by the Regulation of the Minister of Finance of 13 July 2012 on the nature and scope of the document confirming the conclusion of a compulsory insurance contract. The basic information required concerns the identification of the parties to the insurance contract, the subject of the insurance, the number and series of the insurance contract, the insurance period, the sum insured or the guarantee sum, and the amount of the insurance premium. Specific requirements in this respect concern motor vehicle insurance and compulsory agricultural insurance.

288. The content of the policy is also provided for in the Regulation of the Minister of Finance on the Accounting of Insurers of 28 December 2009, paragraph 7, according to which, for accounting purposes, an insurance policy should include at least the parties to the insurance contract, the extent of the insurer's liability, the insurance period, the amount of the sum insured or guarantee and the amount of the premium due.

289. The Maritime Code regulates issues relating to an insurance policy in a specific way. First of all, there are some mandatory elements of the insurance policy. An insurance policy must state the insurer's details, the subject of the insurance, the risks covered by the insurance contract, the period or voyage for which the contract is concluded, the sum insured, the place and date of issue of the policy, and the insurer's signature.

290. The policy may be issued in the name of the policyholder or in the name of the bearer (Article 295 of the Maritime Code). The nature of the policy in maritime insurance is different from that in non-marine insurance. It mainly concerns the rights included in an insurance policy. According to Article 296, the fact of holding an insurance policy is decisive for the identification of the entity entitled to make a claim against the insurer. It is particularly important in the case of insurance taken out for the benefit of a third party. As long as an insurance policy is held by the policyholder, a third party cannot make its own claims against the insurer. A right of action is transferred with the possession of an insurance policy. In non-marine insurance, the fact of possession of a policy document is not decisive in determining the person entitled to make a claim.

291. A special provision of the marine insurance contract stipulates that the insurer is obliged to issue, at the request of the insured, a policy stating the conclusion of the contract. Before issuing the policy, the insurer is obliged to issue to the insured, at his request, a provisional document stating the conclusion of the contract (Article 294 of the Maritime Code).

§5. Indemnity Value and the Insurance Sum

292. A notion of the indemnity value refers to property insurance and is a basis for the calculation of the premium and sum insured, which then affects the amount of the indemnity paid by the insurer in case an event insured occurs. Indemnity value generally means value of the property insured and it should in principle refer to the sum insured. In case of a deviation for minus and plus, there will appear over or under insurance (*see* Chapter 5 below).

293. The compensation value and its relation to the sum insured is also expressed in the Civil Code, which establishes a rule that the insurance payment cannot be higher than the amount of the damage unless an insurance contract provides otherwise. The freedom of the parties in this respect concerns two basic issues: it can be agreed in the insurance contract that the payment would exceed the value of the damage, or that the damage is defined not as the market value (which is the case in the absence of other rules) but as the replacement value.

294. The rules of marine insurance are very specific in this respect. The relevant provisions of the Maritime Code suggest that there is an important link between 'insurable value and sum insured'. It would be difficult to understand the provisions of the Maritime Code relating to marine insurance without knowing the relationship between these two issues and something about 'valued' and 'unvalued' policies.

295. A valued policy is one which specifies the agreed value of the insured property. It can usually be identified by the use of the term 'valued at' in front of the stated value. The value stated in the policy is conclusive as to the insurable value between the insurer and the insured, whether or not it is the true value. Article 301 of the Maritime Code clearly provides that if the parties have specified the insurable value (taxed value) in the insurance contract, that value is conclusive as the measure of the insurance indemnity.

296. An overriding point is that the insured cannot recover more than the maximum amount expressly stated in a policy. This is usually referred to as the 'sum insured', which represents a monetary value of the insurance contract that has been taken into account by the law in the context of the maximum indemnity of the insurer. Article 824 §1 of the Civil Code clearly states that the sum insured stated in the contract is the upper limit of the insurer's liability, unless otherwise agreed.

297. There is also the question of risk modification, which seems to be important in a period of economic change. Article 824 §§2 and 3 of the Civil Code reflect the idea of the fluctuation of the insurance value during the term of the contract. If, after the conclusion of the contract, the value of the insured property has decreased, the Insured may request an appropriate reduction in the sum insured. The Insurer may also unilaterally reduce the sum insured for the same reason, informing the Insured at the same time. The reduction of the sum insured will entail a corresponding reduction of the premium from the first day of the month in which the Insured requested the reduction of the sum insured or in which the Insurer notified the Insured of the unilateral reduction of the sum insured.

298. However, there is no provision in the Code for an increase in value, in which case it is up to the insured to increase the sum insured by notifying the insurer. The insurer is not entitled to do this on its own initiative. If the sum insured is increased, the change will be recorded and the premium will be increased from the first day of the month in which the increase takes place. Problems that may arise from an inaccurate figure in the sense of being below or above the actual value of the insured property. In the case of goods, the measure of what the Insured has lost is prima facie the market value of the property lost at the time and place of the loss, in other words, its second-hand or resale value. For this reason, it is the sum that it will cost him to obtain equivalent goods. The Civil Code only provides some basic rules on the aggravation of risk. According to Article 816 of the Civil Code, if a circumstance is discovered that causes a significant change in the probability of an insured event, either party may request a corresponding change in the amount of the premium, starting from the time when the circumstance occurred, but not earlier than the beginning of the current insurance period. If such a request is made, the other party may terminate the contract with immediate effect within fourteen days. This provision does not apply to life insurance.

299. In the case of civil liability insurance, neither the value of the damage nor the sum insured can be easily determined in advance. In order to deal with this situation, there is the guarantee sum, which sets a limit on the insurer's liability. In the case of general civil liability insurance, the limit is set at a certain amount by law. In the field of compulsory TPL motor insurance, the limit of indemnity corresponds to the values imposed by the EU directives.

300. The issue of the sum insured and the insurable value is much more precisely regulated in the Maritime Code. For example, the Code defines the insurable value as the usual value of the object insured, while the sum insured is the total amount of the cover and the limit of the insurer's liability as stated in the policy. When an object is insured for its full value, both the sum insured and the insurable value are identical. In practice, all hull and cargo policies have an agreed value, but the Maritime Code must provide for the possibility of an unvalued policy being used.

301. In the absence of an agreed value, an insurance contract should specify a sum for which an object of insurance has been insured. This rule, as defined in Article 302 §1 of the Maritime Code, is supplemented by principles concerning both over-insurance and under-insurance.

302. An insured sum should not exceed an insured value and, if it does, a contract is not valid in respect of the amount by which an insured sum exceeds an insured value (Article 302 §§2 and 3 of the Maritime Code). However, if the sum insured in a contract is less than the insurable value, the insurer is liable for losses in proportion to the sum insured to the insurable value (Article 266 §4 of the Maritime Code).

§6. Over and under Insurance

303. Indemnity value generally means value of the property insured and it should in principle refer to the sum insured. The sum insured is a limit of the insurance cover under the contract. In cases where indemnity value is higher than the sum insured (which is called under-insurance), the obligation of the insurer may be reduced proportionally. However, if the indemnity value is higher than the sum insured, the insurer will anyway be liable only up to the insurance sum.

304. The consequence of taking too high a sum insured in relation to the value of the vehicle is so-called over-insured. Due to the fact that the compensation in accordance with the rule resulting from Article 824^1 §1 of the Civil Code cannot basically exceed the amount of the loss suffered by the injured party (understood as the value of the subject matter insured), setting a higher sum insured does not bring any benefit to the Insured. However, it entails a necessity of paying a higher premium, which is calculated by the insurer-la on the basis of the sum insured and is not, in case of a loss, reflected in the amount of the compensation paid. For this reason, the consequences of over-insurance are usually negative for the insured. In such a case the only hypothetically beneficial consequence related to over-insurance may be the fact that in case the value of the vehicle would increase after the conclusion of the insurance contract, the compensation in the case of a total loss would have a chance to cover the whole loss (value of the vehicle) and would not be limited by the amount of the sum insured. However, this is a purely theoretical case, as in practice the value of the vehicle actually always decreases over time.

305. The reverse situation, i.e., where the insurable value is higher than the sum insured, i.e., under – insurance has not been regulated by the Polish insurance law. The rules applicable in this respect result from the long-lasting practice. A negative effect of accepting a sum insured lower than the value of the vehicle may be a so-called pro-rata liability system, whereby the amount of compensation paid is proportionately reduced to the extent that the sum insured remained in line with the value of the vehicle at the time the insurance contract was concluded. In the event of complete nullification of the insurance interest, the insurer is simply liable to the amount insured and is free from liability for the part of the loss which exceeds the amount insured.

306. In contrast to the negative consequences of over-insurance, which occur automatically in the case of determining too high a sum insured (overpayment of premium), the negative consequences of under-insurance occur only if the provisions of the general insurance terms so provide. If the general terms do not provide for any consequences of assuming a sum insured lower than the value of the insured property, the so-called first-risk liability system applies. Under this liability regime, the compensation paid in the case of partial damages shall not be proportionally reduced. However, it should be noted that the limit of the insurer's liability remains the sum insured. Accepting too low a sum may, therefore, result in the entire damage suffered by the injured party not being compensated for.

§7. Subrogation

307. The insurer's right of subrogation has a fundamental correlation with the principle of indemnity. It applies to all non-life insurance contracts which are contracts of indemnity and in particular to contracts of property and liability insurance.

308. Right of subrogation has been provided in Article 828 of the Civil Code, according to which, if not otherwise agreed, claims of the policyholder against a third person liable for damage pass by force of law to the insurer up to the amount of the indemnity paid by the insurer. If only a part of the damage was covered by the insurer, the policyholder is entitled to priority of satisfaction with respect to the remaining part of the claim of the insurer. Right of subrogation is excluded in case of claims against persons with whom the policyholder lives in a common household unless a damage has been caused intentionally by such a person.

309. There are certain important features of the subrogation that result from the jurisprudence and market practice. For example, it should be noted that despite the original source in the insurance contract, subrogation claims to which the insurer is entitled are not covered by the rules of limitation of claims applicable to the insurance contract's disposition. The doctrine and case law consistently recognise that these claims are subject to limitation under the general rules in such conditions in which the claim of the policyholder against a third party responsible for damage, acquired by the insurer is time-barred. Therefore, the Insurer, when entering in place of the policyholder, acquires a claim to a third party with such a limited limitation period which – after deducting the period which has elapsed until then – remained with the policyholder on the day of payment of compensation to claim from that person the remuneration of the loss caused to him/her.

310. The insurer is entitled to claim compensation only if the claim for damages was previously held by the injured party against a third party responsible for the damage, which unfortunately in practice is a relatively often neglected factor. Insurers focus, in the case of claiming under Article 828 of the Civil Code, only on proving the fact that the compensation has been paid to the beneficiary and its amount. It is also worth noting that in accordance with the position of doctrine and jurisprudence, the claim to which the insurer is entitled is exclusively of a monetary nature. Since a claim acquired by an insurer is essentially the same as that to which the injured party was entitled against the person suffering civil liability for the damage, in an action for recourse, that person shall be entitled against the insurer to all objections it had against the injured insured.

311. The upper limit of the liability of the perpetrator towards the insurer is what the insurer would be obliged to provide directly to the injured party on the basis of civil law provisions. Therefore, where the compensation paid by the insurer to the victim under the insurance contract does not exceed this upper limit, the perpetrator cannot effectively plead guilty to misinterpretation of the provisions of the insurance contract by the insurer and overstating the compensation due to the victim. If in light of Article 828 §1 of the Civil Code, payment of insurance compensation is a premise for the insurer to acquire the claim, then its fulfilment is determined by the mere fact of payment of compensation in performance of the insurance agreement. Therefore, the perpetrator of the loss could refer to the invalidity of the insurance agreement or lack of payment of the indemnity in order to obtain the fulfilment of this condition. Not being a party to the insurance contract, the perpetrator cannot effectively raise a charge of erroneous overstatement of insurance compensation, if it does not exceed the upper limit of its liability in the process of recourse. In another ruling, the Supreme Court additionally stated that there are no grounds to differentiate the scope of third-party liability under Article 828 §1 of the Civil Code, depending on what is the basis for the liability of the perpetrator of loss. In yet another judgment, the common court stated that 'the insurer always has only as many rights as the injured party is entitled to'. (Wyrok SN z 30.06.2005 r., IV CK 784/04, LEX nr 183613, Wyrok SW w Siedlcach z 25.02.1993 r., I Cr 68/93, LEX nr 1726000).[14]

> Subrogation rules regulated in Article 828 §1 in relation to Article 518 of the Civil Code, exclude possibility of the insurer accepting a claim of the insured towards a person responsible for the damage in the extent greater than the compensation paid, as the relevant part of Article 828 has an obligatory binding character. S.A. Gdańsk dated 29 April 1991, I Acr 118/91 OSA 3/91 p. 18.

14. Fuchs, Malinowska, Maśniak, Kontrakty na rynku Ubezpieczeń, Wolters Kluwer 2020

Chapter 4. Obligations of the Policyholder

§1. Risk Declaration

312. The rules according to which the insurance contract is called a contract of *uberrimae fidei* (of utmost good faith) are clearly visible throughout the entire insurance period, starting from the conclusion of the contract until the occurrence of the insured event.

313. The insurance contract is based on the information provided by the policyholder. In the process of risk assessment, the insurer can only rely on the policyholder for all necessary information. In view of the above, it seems that the most important obligation of the policyholder is to provide the insurer with all the information required in the application form. The information provided by the policyholder should be truthful and accurate, as the insurer is unlikely to be able to verify the information provided. Pursuant to Article 815 of the Civil Code, if the insurer concludes a contract despite the policyholder's failure to answer certain questions, the omitted circumstances are considered immaterial.

314. The Civil Code provides for a system of 'questionnaires', as opposed to the Anglo-Saxon system of 'spontaneous declarations'. This means that the insurer is obliged to ask the questions and the policyholder is obliged to answer them accurately. The policyholder is not required to proactively disclose the circumstances that he/she considers relevant to the risk assessment.

315. The sanction for breach of the duty of disclosure, provided for in Article 815 §3 of the Civil Code, is the possibility of releasing the insurer from liability unless the non-disclosure does not affect the probability of the insured event. In the case of intentional misrepresentation, it is presumed that the non-disclosure is related to the occurrence of the insured event.

316. The obligations of the policyholder apply *mutatis mutandis* in the case where the insurance contract is concluded by an agent, including the broker who represents the policyholder. They also apply to the insured (if the contract is concluded for the benefit of a third party), unless the insured is unaware of the insurance.

317. In this respect, the provisions of marine insurance are more internationally oriented. The provisions of Articles 304 et seq. of the Maritime Code concerning 'declarations on conclusion of the insurance contract' follow the British rules on disclosure and non-disclosure as well as representation and misrepresentation.

318. A rationale for the rule is expressed in Article 304 §1 of the Maritime Code. This provision provides that when concluding a contract of marine insurance, the policyholder is obliged to disclose to the insurer all circumstances of which he is or ought to be aware and which may influence the assessment of the risk and the decision of the insurer as to whether to accept the terms of the insurance.

319. The most problematic issue in practice is the question of what the policyholder should know. It is argued that an applicant has a duty to disclose what he constructively knows because this is clearly provided for by law. However, facts which are material need not be disclosed to the insurer if, as stated in Article 268 §2 of the Maritime Code, they are facts which the insurer knows or which are matters of common knowledge.

320. It is very likely that the policyholder will use the services of a broker in arranging the insurance and he may feel that he can avoid his disclosure obligations because he is not personally conducting the negotiations. The Maritime Code prevents the policyholder from avoiding his obligations by imposing the same obligations on an agent in Article 304 §3 of the Maritime Code. Since a broker should be more familiar with marine insurance matters than the policyholder, this provision imposes an additional obligation on a broker. Not only must he disclose everything that his principal must disclose but he must also disclose every material circumstance of which he is aware.

321. When a contract of marine insurance is concluded for the benefit of a third party, the obligation to disclose any material circumstance rests on all the insured parties and their agents or brokers, as well as on the third party, unless the third party was unaware that the contract was being concluded for his benefit.

322. Failure to disclose or provide information shall entitle the insurer to cancel the contract from the outset, and in the event of cancellation, the contract shall be deemed never to have been concluded. In addition, the insurer retains the right to the full insurance premium. However, Article 305 §2 of the Maritime Code states that in the event of non-disclosure or misrepresentation of circumstances required by law, the insurer may not rescind the contract, but is only entitled to a correspondingly increased insurance premium. In this respect, Polish law takes a more enlightened approach to the commercial needs of insureds than UK law, which provides for sanctions in all cases, even in the case of 'innocent' disclosure.

323. It should also be noted that the right to rescind the contract lapses if the insurer does not exercise it within seven days of becoming aware of the circumstance justifying the right to rescind (Article 305 §3 of the Maritime Code).

§2. Payment of Premium

324. A premium represents the policyholder's consideration for insurance cover. It should be noted that there are still premium tariffs, which are a common basis for determining an individual premium. Taking into account various insurance regulations, the premium is calculated on the basis of the risk level and the duration of the insurance cover.

325. Pursuant to the Law on Insurance Activity, the insurer, after assessing the insurance risk, sets the premium at a level that ensures at least the fulfilment of all obligations under the insurance contract and coverage of the costs of conducting the insurance business. However, it is forbidden to use the criteria of sex, pregnancy and maternity in the calculation of insurance premiums, and benefits may not result in the differentiation of insurance premiums and benefits for individuals.

326. The criteria for determining the insurance premium shall be included in the general conditions of insurance coverage, including the criteria for discounts or increases in the basic amounts. The insurer may index the insurance premium and other charges levied on or payable to the policyholder by virtue of the insurance contract concluded, provided that the methods are set out in the standard policy conditions, together with the date from which and the periods within which the indexation is to be carried out.

327. The consequence of the time factor in the premium is that the insurer is obliged to return part of the premium if the insurance contract expires before the scheduled date (Article 813 of the Civil Code). In such a case, the policyholder can claim the return of the corresponding part of the premium. According to the case law developed in recent years on the basis of numerous disputes, insurers may not charge additional fees that reduce the amount of the premium to be refunded. The insurance premium must be refunded pro rata *temporis* without deduction of any handling fees.

328. The premium should be paid at the same time as the policy is taken out unless the parties agree otherwise. Marine insurers often require the premium for a single policy to be paid at the time of acceptance of the contract and, if a policy has been issued, simultaneously with the issue of the policy.

329. Such a rule is derived from the provision of Article 814 of the Civil Code, according to which the period of insurance cover begins on the day following the date of conclusion of the insurance contract, but not earlier than the day following the date of payment of the premium, unless the contract provides otherwise.

330. Of course, it is possible, and in practice it is done, that the premium is paid within a certain period after the conclusion of the insurance contract. If the insurer becomes liable before payment of the premium and the premium has not been paid in time, the insurer may cancel (withdraw) the contract with immediate effect, simultaneously notifying the insured, and demanding payment of the premium for the period during which it was liable. If the contract is not cancelled, it will be cancelled at the end of the period for which the unpaid premium was due. If the premium is to be paid in instalments and one of the instalments is not paid on time, the Insurer's liability can only be cancelled if this has been stipulated in the insurance contract and the Insurer has demanded payment and informed the Insured of the consequences of non-payment within an additional period of seven days.

331. In some cases, a change in the premium amount may result from a change in the risk during the insurance period. In such a case, each of the parties can demand an appropriate change in the premium from the moment when the above-mentioned circumstance occurred, but no earlier than the beginning of the current insurance period. In this case, the other party may cancel the contract with immediate effect within fourteen days of the date on which the request was made. In accordance with the provisions of Article 816 of the Civil Code, the above rule does not apply to life insurance.

332. Notwithstanding the above, the amount of the premium due may change if the amount of the sum insured changes according to the will of the parties.

333. The payment of the insurance premium is always the obligation of the policyholder, even if the insurance contract has been concluded for the benefit of a third party. The insurer can demand payment of the premium only from the policyholder. The Code does not regulate the situation in which the insured may assume the obligation to pay the premium directly if the policyholder fails to do so, or the obligation to inform the insured of the policyholder's non-payment. However, if an outstanding premium is paid by the insured, such payment must be accepted by the insurer.

§3. Obligations in the Case of Insured Event

334. The policyholder has two basic obligations in the event of an insured loss. These are the obligation to notify the insurer and the obligation to take preventive measures.

335. The obligation to notify the insurer of an insured event is not absolute but depends on the wording of the general conditions. The general conditions may stipulate that the policyholder must notify the insurer of the accident within a certain period of time. When an insurance contract is concluded for the account of a third party, this obligation may be imposed on both the policyholder and the insured, unless the insured is unaware that the contract has been concluded for his account. If no obligation is imposed, it cannot be enforced and no negative consequences can be drawn by the insurer.

336. In the event of a wilful or grossly negligent breach of the obligation to notify, the Insurer may reduce the payment accordingly if this breach has increased the damage or made it impossible for the Insurer to determine the circumstances and consequences of the accident. The consequences of failure to notify the insurer of the accident do not apply if the insurer has received information about the circumstances that should have been notified to the insurer within the time limit set for notification. There are many disputes in the doctrine on the interpretation of the right to reduce the payment, in particular, whether the reduction also means the refusal to pay. So far, the doctrine and court decisions have been in favour of the insured. Of course, it should be taken into account that in some cases a late notification may result in the loss, its cause and circumstances not being established at all, regardless of the fault or lack of fault of the insured. In such a case, payment may be refused for lack of proof that the conditions of cover have been met.

337. With regard to the obligation to take preventive measures, it is again the wording of the general conditions of insurance that has the greatest impact. The general rule established by the Civil Code is that, in the event of an insured event, the policyholder is obliged to use the means at his disposal to save the insured property and to prevent or reduce the damage. In addition, the General Conditions of Insurance may provide that, in such a case, the Policyholder is obliged to ensure the possibility of pursuing claims for compensation against the persons responsible for the damage. If the Insured fails to take the above measures intentionally or as a result of gross negligence, the Insurer shall not be liable for the resulting loss and may refuse payment. In the case of insurance for the account of a third party, the above obligations also apply to the Insured.

Chapter 5. Obligations of the Insurer: Payment of Claim

§1. Non-Life Insurance

338. The primary obligation of the insurer is to pay compensation or other benefits in the event of an insured loss. The scope, extent and limitation of the insurer's liability are only generally regulated by law, and the specific issues are to be regulated in the insurance contract and the general conditions of insurance. Specific legal regulations in this respect are only provided for compulsory insurance. The consequence of the vagueness of the legislation is the large number of insurance disputes concerning the method of calculating the loss, the interpretation of exclusions, etc.

339. The insurer is obliged to pay compensation within thirty days of receiving notification of the insured event (Article 817 of the Civil Code). However, if the clarification of the circumstances necessary to establish the insurer's liability or the amount payable is not possible within the thirty-day period, payment must be made within fourteen days of the clarification of all such circumstances. However, the Insurer must pay any undisputed part of the claim within the basic period of thirty days. It is expressly stated that the insurer must exercise due diligence in assessing the insured's claim. As emphasised by the courts, the insurer should play an active role in the claims settlement process and not just wait for the insured to provide evidence.

340. The insurer is obliged to pay compensation to an injured third party without delay in respect of liability insurance. If the injured party, prior to the notification, demands compensation from the insured party responsible for the damage and the insured party refuses, the insurer is in default from the date of the aforementioned demand. SN of 9 June 1995, III CZP 69/95 OSINC 6/95.

341. The provision of Article 817 §2 of the Civil Code does not entitle the insurer to abandon (postpone) the claim settlement procedure until the moment of the final conclusion of the court proceedings in relation to a motor vehicle accident insured against civil liability. SN of 10 January 2000; III CKN 1105/99.

342. The compensation paid by the insurer is in the form of a term claim. However, the insurer shall not be in default with regard to the amount stated in a statement of payment sent to the insured, if the insured does not specify his claim in terms of an amount after receiving the statement of payment. (SN of 6 July 1999, Act III CKN 315/98).

343. Articles 28 and 29 of the Act on Insurance Activity also impose some important obligations on the insurer regarding the settlement of claims. First, it is stated that the insurer shall pay compensation or other benefits on the basis of acceptance of a claim or on the basis of its own findings obtained in the procedure described below (Article 29) or on the basis of a settlement concluded with the claimant or a valid court decision.

344. Article 29 sets out the insurer's obligations after a claim has been reported to the insurer. Upon receipt of a notice of an insured event, the insurer shall, within seven days from the day of receipt of the notice, notify the policyholder or the insured, if they are not the persons who made the notice, of the insured event and initiate proceedings to establish the facts of the insured event, the legitimacy of the submitted claims and the amount of the indemnification, as well as notify the claimant, in writing or in any other manner to which the claimant has consented, of the documents necessary to establish the liability of the insurer or the amount of the indemnification.

345. If the insurer does not pay a benefit within the legal or contractual time limits (generally thirty days), it must inform the claimant in writing of the reasons why it is impossible to meet all or part of the claim and also pay an undisputed part of the benefit. If a benefit is not due or if the amount due is different from that stated in the claim, the insurer concerned shall notify the claimant in writing, stating the circumstances and the legal basis on which the total or partial refusal to pay the benefit is based. The information provided by the insurer should include a reference to the possibility of enforcing claims through the courts.

346. Finally, it should be pointed out that the insurer is obliged to provide the persons claiming a right to a benefit with information and documents collected in order to determine the insurer's liability or the amount of the benefit. These persons may request written confirmation of the information provided by the insurer and that photocopies of documents be made at their own expense and certified as authentic by the insurer. The manner of providing access to information and documents, ensuring the possibility of written confirmation of the information provided, as well as ensuring the possibility of making photocopies of documents and certifying their authenticity, shall not imply that these persons are hindered beyond a justified need, and the cost of photocopies borne by these persons shall not differ from the normal market cost of such services.

347. As a rule, the insurer is liable only for damage classified as *damnum emergens*, although this principle does not apply to business interruption insurance. The Civil Code, in its section on insurance contracts, does not define what type of damage can be compensated under insurance contracts (partial and total loss), thus leaving the issue to an agreement between the parties. However, general terms and conditions of insurance usually leave this issue open, which is then interpreted by a court in the event of a dispute.

348. Partial loss occurs when a damaged vehicle can be repaired and the cost of the repair does not exceed the value of the vehicle on the date the insurer determines the compensation. Total loss occurs when the insured vehicle is damaged in such a way that it cannot be repaired or the cost of repair would exceed the value of the vehicle. S.A. I Acr 30/92.

349. The law does not provide a standard rule for calculating the loss, i.e., whether it should be based on the market value or the replacement value, whether it should be gross or net. One of the few issues regulated (as a consequence of the concerns) is the issue of Value Added Tax (VAT). According to the Law on Insurance Activity, if a person entitled to compensation who is not a VAT payer submits an invoice (invoices) to an insurance company for the settlement of transport damage, the insurance company is obliged to include VAT in the compensation.

350. One of the most important issues in relation to coverage is the question of causation. Taking into account the general provisions of the Civil Code (Article 361), a loss must be a normal consequence of the risk insured against, so that if an adequate cause of the loss is not a risk insured against, the insurer is not obliged to indemnify. In addition to the above, the idea of sine qua non-rules has been adopted, according to which it is necessary to prove the existence of both causal links between a risk insured against and a loss itself. However, these rules are binding only in liability insurance, where the insurer stands in the shoes of the policyholder who is liable for the damage caused to third parties. In insurance other than liability insurance, an insurance contract usually provides coverage only for direct losses, excluding the same liability of the insurer for consequential losses.

351. In order to determine the amount that the insured may recover in respect of a loss arising out of an insured event, it is necessary to consider the extent of coverage, the measure of loss and indemnity, and a deductible, if any.

352. One of the most important issues is the regulation of Article 824^1 of the Civil Code, according to which the amount paid by the insurer cannot exceed the value of the damage unless the contract provides otherwise. A limitation of liability is a matter of agreement between the parties only if the sum insured is fixed by contract. In such a case, liability is determined by the sum insured, the insured value and the extent of the damage.[15]

353. If the same insured object is simultaneously insured against the same risk by two or more insurers for sums which together exceed its insured value, the policyholder may not claim any benefit in respect of the loss. As between the insurers, each of them is liable to the extent that the sum insured assumed by them remains in the sum total resulting from the double or multiple insurance. If, in such a case, it has been agreed in one of the insurance contracts that the sum paid by the insurer on account of the insurance may be higher than the loss suffered, the insurer may claim indemnity only from that insurer in respect of the part bearing the loss.

354. The issue of multiple insurance raises many doctrinal doubts in Polish doctrine, which focuses on the question of whether double insurance and multiple insurance are two different concepts or whether they should be recognised as one and interpreted only in the context of over-insurance and relations between insurers covering the same risk under two or more insurance contracts. According to some authors, there are currently no categorical reasons for maintaining the doctrinal distinction between double and multiple insurance, and the latter fully deserves the

15. D. Fuchs, K. Malinowska & D. Maśniak, Kontrakty na rynku Ubezpieczeń, Wolters Kluwer 2020.

conventional name of double insurance. However, the normative specificity of Articles 824 of the Civil Code and 8241 of the Civil Code is necessary and, at the same time, sufficient reason to establish a difference in insurance terminology between the notion of double insurance and multiple insurance, the distinction of which is useful in the case where the insurance protection is provided simultaneously, according to the principles mentioned above, by two or more insurance companies. Of course, the Polish legislator's lack of consistency in this area is ultimately undesirable. It is also worth mentioning that there is no double insurance if the scope of protection is complementary on the basis of agreements concluded with different insurers.

355. Double or multiple insurance cannot be equated with the invalidity of the contract(s). At most, the insurer who learns of the occurrence of such a circumstance after the indemnity has been paid may demand a reasonable reimbursement of part of the sum paid, in accordance with the parity provided for in Article 814 §2 Civil Code. However, a proposal should be considered to unify the construction of double insurance both in land and marine insurance, which, in the author's opinion, should primarily mean the introduction of a solution in Article 8241 of the Civil Code corresponding to the content of Article 303 §3 of the Civil Code. At the same time, in view of the different interpretations of the scope of the article in question, it seems to be the right proposal to modify the double (multiple) insurance so that it also covers civil liability insurance, as is the case in maritime insurance.

356. This provision does not seem to apply to civil liability insurance, which does not have the concept of insured value. This is the prevailing opinion of the Polish doctrine, which states that: 'The basic meaning here is the argument that the concept of insurance value, which is a necessary element of the hypothesis resulting from Article 8241 § 2 of the Civil Code, does not exist in civil liability insurance'; Article 8241 §2 of the Civil Code can be directly applied only to property insurance other than civil liability insurance. In the case of civil liability insurance, the category of 'insured value' does not exist, so it cannot be said that the total sum insured exceeds the insured value. However, it is not excluded that the parties may agree to apply this rule to TPL insurance, but the wording must be modified accordingly.

357. Multiple insurance is precisely regulated in the Maritime Code with regard to marine insurance. Article 303 provides a comprehensive definition of multiple insurance. In essence, multiple insurance is defined as two situations: (1) when an object of insurance has been insured against the same peril for the same period by two or more insurers for sums which together exceed the value of the insurance; or (2) when, for other reasons, the sum of indemnity which would be payable separately by each of these insurers exceeds the loss to be indemnified.

358. The separable alternative used by the legislator suggests that multiple insurance may occur in maritime practice separately in the first or second situation. While in the first case, the legislator is undoubtedly referring to a criterion already established in national practice and literature for the identification of insurance cover, in the second case the legislator is clearly focusing on the situation in which the excess of the value of the damage over the additional amounts of compensation as benefits payable by the insurer is due to titles which do not necessarily originate in the multiplication of insurance cover in property insurance, but may relate to maritime civil liability insurance.

359. In both cases, the consequence is that the policyholder has the right to claim from each of the insurers the payment of compensation in accordance with the contract concluded with them, but the policyholder cannot obtain from them jointly any compensation in excess of the loss. In the event that the Insured has deliberately taken out multiple insurance, the Insured must immediately notify the Insurers concerned and inform them of the content of the insurance contracts concluded. A deliberate breach of this obligation by the policyholder will deprive him of the right to compensation (*see* Article 303 §3 of the Code).

360. In maritime relations, there are also agreements between insurers whereby each insurer's share of the indemnity is determined in proportion to the indemnity it would have to pay if it were the sole insurer and the amount of the indemnity that would be due to each of these insurers under the agreement concluded (Article 303, paragraph 2 of the Code).

§2. Marine Insurance

361. There are two main types of loss regulated by the Maritime Code: partial (which simply means 'average', whether 'general' or 'particular') and total (either 'actual' or 'constructive'). General average is a matter of great interest to a shipping community and to marine insurers and is therefore the subject of a separate chapter in Book V of the Maritime Code entitled 'General Average' (Articles 250 et seq.). This institution covers extraordinary sacrifices or expenses deliberately and reasonably incurred for the purpose of preserving a vessel, its cargo and freight from a common peril.

362. The Maritime Code defines 'general average' and provides only general rules establishing the basic principles of this institution in accordance with the York Antwerp Rules (YAR). It was considered inappropriate to include detailed rules on general average in the Maritime Code since the YAR are almost invariably referred to in the standard forms of transport and insurance documents in use. Nevertheless, in view of the fact that such an exceptional case may arise, Article 255 §2 of the Code provides that, in the absence of agreement between the parties, the adjuster should, when adjusting a general average loss, apply 'rules generally accepted in international maritime trade', by which is meant the YAR.

363. The Maritime Code does not say much about particular average, which is a partial loss of the insured property caused by an insured peril. However, in standard clauses, a particular average is defined as a partial loss of the insured property, with the exception of general average, which does not include particular charges.

Apart from technical definitions, in Polish practice particular average simply means a partial loss of the insured object caused by a fortuitous event which is a peril covered by the policy.

364. The Maritime Code uses the term 'total loss' in connection with the expenses specified in Article 325 (incurred for the purpose of preserving the subject matter of the insurance, averting the loss or reducing its extent, determining the nature and extent of the loss, drawing up general average statements or selling the subject matter of the insurance, as well as other expenses incurred in accordance with the insurer's instructions), which are reimbursed in the ratio of the sum insured to the insurable value. The Insurer is obliged to reimburse such expenses even if the sum of the expenses together with the indemnity exceeds the sum insured. This is an example of an actual total loss.

365. It sometimes happens that the insured object, be it a vessel or goods, is placed in a situation where it has not actually suffered a total loss, but where the cost of preventing such a loss would be greater than the value of the object when salvaged. In such a situation, the insured would simply accept the loss and abandon the property rather than incur a greater loss to salvage the property. Article 329 of the Maritime Code specifies the circumstances under which the insured may claim constructive total loss. The insured may set a reasonable time limit for the insurer to declare whether it will exercise its right to claim. However, the insurer who has paid the full sum insured in accordance with the Code cannot demand that the rights to the insured object be transferred to him. For this reason, in literature and in practice, this institution is called 'abandonment of the insurer'.

366. From a legal point of view, abandonment is defined in Articles 330 et seq. of the Maritime Code, which concerns the abandonment of the subject of insurance by the insured. It provides that the Insured may demand payment of the full sum insured against surrender of the rights to the subject of the insurance/abandonment to the Insurer if there are grounds for believing that total loss of the subject of the insurance is inevitable or that everything in it would entail expenses disproportionate to the value of the subject of the insurance. Such abandonment is unconditional and, once accepted by the Insurer, is irrevocable. The Insured must notify the Insurer of the abandonment in writing, stating the circumstances justifying the abandonment (Article 331 §1 of the Maritime Code). In this article, the legislator has described in detail the period within which a notice of abandonment may be given. In principle, it is no later than six months from the date on which the insured became aware of the circumstances justifying the abandonment. When notifying the abandonment, the Insured is obliged to inform the Insurer of any real rights encumbering the subject of the insurance and of any other insurances relating to it, as well as of any restrictions on the power to dispose of the subject of the insurance known to him.

367. It should also be noted that the rights to the subject of the insurance are transferred to the Insurer when he declares that he accepts the waiver.

§3. Life Insurance

368. The primary obligation of the insurer, even in life insurance, is to pay compensation or other benefits in the event of an insured loss. The scope, extent and limitation of the insurer's liability are regulated only in general terms in the legislation, and the specific issues are regulated in the insurance contract and the general insurance conditions.

369. The legal provisions of the Civil Code do not distinguish between life and non-life insurance with regard to the payment of claims. However, the nature of the claim is different, since the claim in life insurance is not compensatory in nature. Therefore, as stated in §1, the insurer is obliged to pay compensation within thirty days from the date of receipt of the notification of the insured event (Article 817 of the Civil Code). However, if the clarification of the circumstances necessary to determine the Insurer's liability or the amount payable is not possible within the thirty-day period, payment must be made within fourteen days of the clarification of all such circumstances. However, the Insurer must pay any undisputed part of the claim within the basic period of thirty days. It is expressly stated that the insurer must exercise due diligence in assessing the insured's claim.

370. Some important obligations concerning the settlement of claims are also laid down in Articles 28 and 29 of the AIRA (*see* §1 of this chapter).

371. If the insurer does not pay a benefit within the statutory time limit (generally thirty days), it must inform the claimant in writing of the reasons which make it impossible to satisfy all or part of the claim and also pay an undisputed part of the benefit. If a benefit is not due or if the amount due is different from that stated in the claim, the insurer concerned must inform the claimant in writing, stating the circumstances and the legal basis on which the total or partial refusal to pay the benefit is based. The information provided by the insurer should include a reference to the possibility of pursuing claims through the courts.

372. Finally, it should be pointed out that the insurer is obliged to provide the persons claiming a right to a benefit with the information and documents collected in order to determine the insurer's liability or the amount of the benefit. These persons may request written confirmation of the information provided by the insurer and that photocopies of documents be made at their own expense and certified as authentic by the insurer. The manner in which access to information and documents is provided, the possibility of obtaining written confirmation of the information provided, and the possibility of making photocopies of documents and certifying their authenticity, shall not result in more burdensome requirements for such persons than are justified, and the cost of photocopies borne by such persons shall not differ from the normal market cost of such services.

373. As a general rule, the insurer is only liable for damage classified as *damnum emergens*, although this principle does not apply to business interruption insurance. The Civil Code, in its section on insurance contracts, does not define what type of damage can be compensated under insurance contracts (partial and total loss), leaving the issue to an agreement between the parties. However, general terms and conditions of insurance usually leave this issue open, which is then interpreted by a court in the event of a dispute.

374. Partial loss occurs when a damaged vehicle can be repaired and the cost of the repair does not exceed the value of the vehicle on the date the insurer determines the compensation. Total loss occurs when the insured vehicle is damaged in such a way that it cannot be repaired or the cost of repair would exceed the value of the vehicle. S.A. I Acr 30/92.

375. The law does not provide a standard rule for calculating the loss, i.e., whether it should be based on the market value or the replacement value, whether it should be gross or net. One of the few issues regulated (as a consequence of the concerns) is the issue of VAT. According to the Law on Insurance Activity, if a person entitled to compensation who is not a VAT payer submits an invoice (invoices) to an insurance company for the settlement of transport damage, the insurance company is obliged to include VAT in the compensation.

376. One of the most important issues in relation to coverage is the question of causation. Taking into account the general provisions of the Civil Code (Article 361), a loss must be a normal consequence of the risk insured against, so that if an adequate cause of the loss is not a risk insured against, the insurer is not obliged to indemnify. In addition to the above, the idea of sine qua non-rules has been adopted, according to which it is necessary to prove the existence of both causal links between a risk insured against and a loss itself.[16] These rules however are binding only in third-party liability insurance, where the insurer steps in the shoes of the policyholder liable for the damage caused to third party. In insurance other than liability insurance, an insurance contract usually provides for coverage only for direct losses, excluding the same liability of the insurer for consequential losses.

377. In order to establish the sum which the insured can recover with respect to a loss resulting from an event insured, it is necessary to examine the extent of coverage, the measure of loss and compensation and a franchise/deductible if it is provided.

378. One of the most important issues is the regulation of Article 824^1 of the Civil Code, according to which a sum paid by the insurer cannot exceed the value of the loss unless a contract provides otherwise. A limit of liability is a matter of arrangement between parties only in case when the sum insured is fixed by a contract. In such a case, liability is designed by the sum insured, insurance value and extent of loss.[17]

---

16. Z. Brodecki, *Insurance Contract Law in Poland.* Gdańsk: Info trade, 1993.
17. B. Kucharski, Świadczenie ubezpieczyciela w umowie ubezpieczenia, Wolters Kluwer 2019.

Chapter 6. Insurance and Third Parties

§1. Insurance in Favour of Third Party

379. An insurance contract is always bilateral in the sense that its parties are always the insurer and the policyholder (who is usually also the insured). However, an insurance contract may also be concluded in favour of a third party (who is not a direct party to the contract, but a party to the insurance relationship in the sense that he has a direct claim against the insurer).

380. There are two types of third-party insurance. The first is insurance for the account of a third party, and the second is insurance for the account of the policyholder, where the third party is the beneficiary. However, the latter is only characteristic of life insurance (Article 831 of the Civil Code). The issue of third-party insurance does not cover the issue of liability insurance, since the subject of this type of insurance is the liability of the policyholder (however, this type of insurance can also be concluded in favour of the third party, where the policyholder insures the liability of other persons (insured)). This issue will be discussed later.

381. The possibility of concluding a contract in favour of a third party is directly expressed in Article 808 of the Civil Code. The same concept is provided for in Article 296 of the Maritime Code. The third party is granted the right to receive compensation directly under the insurance contract. However, he is also obliged to fulfil certain obligations, except for the payment of the premium, which should always be paid by the policyholder. Pursuant to Article 808 §2 of the Civil Code, the insurer may raise objections under the insurance contract against the third party that affect the insurer's liability.

382. The Civil Code imposes various obligations not only on the policyholder but also on the insured third party. These are the obligation to properly declare the risk, the obligation to mitigate the loss in the event of the occurrence of the insured event, the obligation to notify the insurer of the occurrence of the insured event, and the obligation not to voluntarily cause the insured event.

383. As mentioned above, a third party for whose benefit the insurance contract was concluded may demand direct payment of the indemnity from the insurer. The indemnity can only be paid to the policyholder with the consent of the third party.

384. In accordance with the provisions of the Maritime Code, a third party in whose favour the contract was concluded may demand the enforcement of the insurance contract if the policy is in his possession. Payment to the policyholder may be made as long as the policy remains in his possession.[18]

---

18. Z. Brodecki, '*Insurance Contract Law in Poland*', 26 et al.

§2. Assignment of the Contract to Third Party

385. *Ex lege* transfer of rights and obligations arising from the insurance contract to a third party is provided for in the Civil Code only in one situation – in case of change of ownership of the insured property. In this case, the old and the new owner of the insured property are jointly and severally liable for payment of the premium due for the period up to the date of transfer of ownership. (Article 823 of the Civil Code).

386. The assignment of rights under the insurance contract is also possible under the general rules. This construction is commonly used in credit relationships, where a credit institution is assigned the right to compensation from the insurer in the event of destruction of the insured property, or the right to a benefit from the debtor's life insurance policy.

§3. Status of the Third Party Injured in the Third Party Liability Insurance

387. The status of the third party – the injured party – is relevant to liability insurance. There is only one provision in the PCC dealing with this issue, which is contained in Article 822. According to its provisions, the injured third party has a strong position vis-à-vis the insurer once the insured event has occurred and the liability of the policyholder has been established.

388. First, in accordance with the provisions of Article 822, paragraph 4, of the Civil Code, the third party may bring an action directly against the insurer (*actio directa*) in respect of any type of liability insurance, not only compulsory. There are no additional requirements (such as bankruptcy of the insured, etc.). The direct action is based on the general rules of law applicable to the liability of the policyholder, i.e., rules on tort or contractual liability. Of course, in the case of voluntary TPL insurance, the insurance cover may be limited in the insurance contract and the insurer is liable only within the limits of the cover agreed in the insurance contract. In addition, the insurer can raise any objection to the extent of the policyholder's liability.

389. Second, the position of the injured third party cannot be affected by the actions of the policyholder after the occurrence of the insured event. The insurer may not plead against the person entitled to compensation that the policyholder or the insured has breached his obligations under the contract or the general terms and conditions of insurance, if this occurred after the occurrence of the accident. Thus, the right of the injured party is not affected by a grossly negligent or intentional breach of the duty of prevention after the occurrence of the insured event.

Chapter 7. Termination of the Insurance Contract and Limitation of Actions

390. There are several legal concepts that can lead to the termination of insurance cover. We should distinguish between the possibility of withdrawing (cancelling) the insurance contract and termination by notice. In addition to the above, there are legal circumstances in which the insurance contract terminates by operation of law.

§1. Withdrawal from the Contract

391. Legislation provides for the possibility of either party withdrawing from the insurance contract for various reasons. The relevant provisions are contained in the Civil Code and in the legislation on compulsory insurance.

392. According to the current legislation, only the policyholder can terminate the insurance contract. The relevant provisions have been transposed into Polish law on the basis of the second-generation insurance directives (currently included in the Solvency II Directive). Pursuant to Article 812 of the Civil Code, the policyholder may withdraw from the contract within thirty days of its conclusion (in the case of natural persons) and within seven days of its conclusion (in the case of legal entities) if the insurance contract was concluded for a period exceeding six months. No reasons need to be given for such withdrawal. However, in the event of cancellation, the Insurer is entitled to the premium for the period during which cover was provided.

393. In the case of marine insurance, the policyholder may cancel the contract at any time prior to the commencement of the risk covered by the insurance (Article 298 of the Maritime Code).

394. The possibility for the insurer to withdraw from the insurance contract is provided for in the Maritime Code. According to Article 305, the insurer may withdraw from the contract in the event of a breach of good faith on the part of the policyholder, i.e., in the event of misrepresentation when concluding the insurance contract. The insurer may also cancel the contract in the event of an aggravation of the risk caused by or with the consent of the policyholder unless the aggravation of the risk is in the mutual interest of the insurer and the policyholder or for the purpose of saving human life (Article 315 of the Maritime Code).

§2. Termination upon Notice

395. The termination of the insurance contract by notice should be considered separately for life and non-life insurance, although there are common reasons for both types of insurance. Termination of the insurance contract by notice by the insurer is possible only in special circumstances, i.e., either in cases provided for by law or for important reasons specified in the insurance conditions. Termination of the life insurance contract with notice by the insurer is possible only in the cases provided for by law.

396. Based on the legal provisions, the Insurer has the right to terminate the contract with immediate effect only if the insurance cover comes into force before the payment of the premium or its first instalment and this premium or instalment is not paid in time. In such case, the Insurer may also demand payment for the period of insurance (until the termination). If the next instalment is not paid on time, the insurance cover can only be cancelled if this effect is provided for in the insurance conditions and the Insurer has demanded payment with an additional period for payment (at least seven days).

397. Both parties may terminate the non-life insurance contract in the event of a significant change in the risk. First of all, either party may demand an appropriate change in the premium (from the moment the risk change has occurred), and the other party may terminate the insurance contract with immediate effect by giving notice to the other party no later than fourteen days from the demand for a change in the premium (Article 816 Civil Code).

398. As mentioned above, the insurance contract may also be terminated by notice for important reasons, provided that this possibility and the reasons for termination are included in the insurance conditions. In this respect, the doctrine raises some objections regarding the nature of important reasons. It seems that important reasons must be circumstances of an extraordinary and unexpected nature, such as the cessation of the business activity of the policyholder, misrepresentation discovered by the insurer, and the like. It should also be noted that there are some doubts as to whether the important reasons for cancelling the insurance contract can only give the right to cancel to the insurer or whether it should be guaranteed to both parties on an equal basis.[19]

399. In the case of life insurance, Article 830 of the Civil Code expressly provides for the right of the insured to terminate the contract at any time by giving notice in accordance with the policy conditions. If the policy conditions do not provide for termination, the policyholder may terminate the contract with immediate effect. In practice, the above provision applies to long-term life insurance contracts, as personal insurance other than life insurance is usually written on an annual basis. The Code also provides for a presumption of termination by the insured. Unless the contract provides otherwise, the insurance contract is deemed to have been cancelled by the insured if the premium has not been paid by the date specified in the insurance conditions, despite the fact that the insurer has previously sent a reminder to pay within an additional period. Pursuant to Article 830 §2 of the Civil Code, the consequences of non-payment of the premium should be brought to the attention of the insured in a notice.

19. D. Fuchs, K. Malinowska & D. Maśniak, Kontrakty na rynku ubezpieczeń, Wolters Kluwer 2020.

§3. Expiration by Law

400. In addition to cancellation or termination by notice, the insurance contract may expire as a result of a specific circumstance provided for by law. In this respect, the general legal provisions that provide for the termination of contracts in the event of the death of one of the parties or the deregistration of the legal entity that is a party to the contract, as well as the inability of one of the parties to pay, are applicable. In addition, a non-life insurance contract may expire if the subject matter of the insurance is transferred to a third party so that the policyholder loses the insurable interest. Termination does not occur if the parties, with the consent of the insurer, agree that the purchaser shall assume the insurance rights and obligations (Article 823 of the Civil Code).

§4. Limitation of Actions

401. The Civil Code provides for specific limitation periods in relation to the insurance contract, after the expiry of which neither party may validly bring an action before a court. According to Article 819 of the Code, the limitation period is three years. This period should be calculated from the date on which the insurance payment is due to the insured or third party. This rule corresponds to the time limits imposed on the insurer for the settlement of the claim.

402. The limitation period is suspended from the moment when the insurer is notified of the claim or the occurrence of the insured event. It starts running again from the moment the insurer issues a statement.

403. In liability insurance, this period is determined by the provisions of contractual liability for a particular type of obligation or tortious liability.

404. In marine insurance, the limitation period is five years from the date on which the claim becomes due (Article 299 of the Maritime Code).

Part III. Property and Liability Insurance

Chapter 1. Fire Insurance

405. Polish companies have assets worth PLN 2.8 trillion. Entrepreneurs own machinery and buildings worth PLN 1.8 trillion. To this should be added over PLN 1 trillion of current assets in the form of inventories, receivables and short-term investments, which can also be covered by insurance. The value of business assets insured against fire and other natural disasters in Poland is around PLN 1.7 trillion. Almost all large companies, 92% of medium-sized companies and 87% of small companies in our country have this type of policy.

406. One of the biggest losses in recent years was estimated at PLN 110 million. The factory of the German company Coko-Werk burned down in 2015, but thanks to the support of the insurer, the company managed to restart after sixteen months.[20] The indemnity covered 100% of the material damage (plus business interruption costs). The largest industrial loss in the history of the Third Republic of Poland was a fire at the Turów power station on Christmas Day 1998.[21] A consortium of three insurers paid out PLN 220 million in compensation for damage to one unit of the power station, which, taking inflation into account, could be equivalent to a loss of around PLN 1 billion today (report by the Polish Chamber of Insurance).

407. Fire insurance can be both compulsory and voluntary.

§1. Compulsory Fire Insurance

408. There is one type of compulsory fire insurance in Polish law.[22] It is regulated by the Act on Compulsory Insurance and has historically been considered one of the most important types of compulsory insurance due to the low insurance awareness among farmers. However, this approach is now being questioned and there are numerous calls for this type of first-party insurance to be made voluntary.

20. https://media.ergohestia.pl/attachment/1085541.
21. https://www.reuters.com/article/world/explosion-rocks-pge-power-plant-in-southern-poland-idUSBRE86N1NK/.
22. M. Orlicki, Ubezpieczenia obowiązkowe, 2011.

Fire insurance covers farm buildings against fire and other accidental events. Farm buildings must be insured not only against fire but also against hurricane, flood, drowning, torrential rain, hail, snowfall, lightning, explosion, landslide, mining subsidence, avalanche or aircraft crash. All these events are defined in the legislation on compulsory insurance. As far as fire losses are concerned, these have been defined as losses resulting from fire activity that has moved beyond a fireplace or started without a fireplace and spread by its own power. There are some exclusions from coverage, namely: (1) damage caused intentionally by the policyholder or a person for whom the policyholder is responsible or a person who shares a common household with the policyholder; (2) damage caused as a result of gross negligence by the above-mentioned persons; (3) mining damage as defined by the Mining and Geological Law; or (4) damage caused during an earthquake.

409. A farm building covered by compulsory insurance is defined by law as a building that is an integral part of the farm, has an area of more than 20 m^2, as defined in the building regulations, and is owned by a farmer.

410. Certain farm buildings are excluded from compulsory insurance. This exclusion applies to buildings which, according to their technical condition, have been worn down to 100% of the relevant standard, buildings which are to be demolished following a final decision by the competent authorities, as well as tents and foil tunnels.

411. The obligation to insure a building against fire and other specified perils arises as soon as a building has a roof. Coverage commences upon conclusion of the contract and payment of the premium or its first instalment unless the Insurer has agreed a later date for payment of the premium or its first instalment, in which case coverage commences upon conclusion of the contract.

412. The insurance coverage ends when the contract is terminated, i.e., usually at the end of the twelve-month period in which it was concluded, or at the end of the three-month period following the declaration of the insurer's bankruptcy. The insurance also terminates in the event of the transfer of the holding to another person. The rights and obligations resulting from such an insurance are transferred to the new owner and the insurance expires in due course (at the end of the twelve-month period for which it was concluded) unless the new owner cancels it in writing (with thirty days of notice).

413. A person who takes over a farm where the agricultural buildings are not insured is obliged to conclude the insurance contract at the latest on the day of taking over the farm. In the case of termination of the insurance contract, the owner of the farm buildings who terminates the contract should conclude the new insurance contract by the last day of the insurance coverage under the terminated contract.

414. It is also important to note that if a farmer does not give written notice of termination to the insurer at least one day before the end of the twelve-month period, the insurance is automatically extended for the following period. However, such renewal shall not take place if the premium for the previous twelve-month period has not been paid or in the event of the liquidation or bankruptcy of the insurer. In the case of automatic renewal, the insurer is obliged to confirm the conclusion of the contract with the insurance document within fourteen days from the day of its conclusion.

415. In addition, not later than fourteen days before the expiration of the twelve-month period for which the insurance was concluded, the insurance company is obliged to provide the policyholder with information on the insurance for the next insurance period, including, *inter alia*: (1) the determination of the amount of the insurance premium; (2) an instruction that the amount of the stated premium may be changed; (3) information on the right to terminate the existing insurance, as well as the form, possible method and date of such termination; (4) information on the effects of such termination and the effects of failing to give such notice of termination.

416. If the owner of the agricultural buildings is simultaneously insured by two or more insurance companies, at least one of the contracts for the insurance of agricultural buildings having been concluded on the basis of automatic renewal, such insurance may be terminated by the policyholder, but the insurer may demand payment of the insurance premium for the period during which it was liable. If several insurance contracts for the same agricultural building with the same insurance period have been concluded with the same insurer, only one premium is due.

417. The Act on Compulsory Insurance also establishes a minimum sum insured for this insurance, which is equal to: (1) the real value of the building in its new state less wear and tear; or (2) the new value in the case of new buildings and other buildings whose wear and tear does not exceed 10% on the day the insurance contract is concluded (the wear and tear standards for agricultural buildings are determined by the insurer in accordance with the provisions of the Building Code). The sum insured will be determined on the basis of: (1) the price list used by the Insurer to assess the value of the buildings; (2) the enclosed price calculation for the construction works, which will be prepared by an authorised person for this scope of activity after the execution of the works, in accordance with the principles of the calculation of contract works and the methods of price determination that are currently binding in the construction industry, or on the basis of expert estimates. The Insurer is obliged to update the value of the building accepted for insurance, but not more often than once a year, if a change in the prices of building materials, labour and other material costs has caused an increase or decrease in the value of the building of at least 20%. The updated value of the building is the basis for determining the new sum insured.

418. The insurance contract should provide for the obligation to refund the premium in certain circumstances, including where agricultural land loses its character as an agricultural holding, or where the insurance contract is terminated prematurely. The return of the premium for the unused insurance period is possible for each full month of the unused insurance period. The amount of the monthly premium to be refunded is set at one-twelfth of the premium due for twelve months of insurance.

419. The extent of damage to a building will be determined on the basis of (2) the cost estimate prepared by the company carrying out the reconstruction or repair work, which shall be determined in accordance with the rules on calculation principles and pricing methods for construction works currently in force in the construction industry, taking into account the previously used materials, dimensions, constructions and equipment; if the sum insured has been fixed at the actual value, the actual wear and tear of the building shall be taken into account from the date on which the insurer's liability commenced until the date on which the loss occurred.

420. Furthermore, the sum insured for the loss of the farm building will be reduced by the residual value of the objects that can be used, rebuilt or reconstructed, or increased, within the limit of the sum insured, by the documented costs of cleaning the site of the loss up to 5% of the value of the loss.

421. The degree of wear and tear of the building shall not be taken into account in the case of minor damage, which shall be valued at the equivalent of EUR 100, calculated at the average exchange rate published by the Central Bank and in force on the day the indemnity is determined.

§2. Voluntary Fire Insurance

422. The Polish insurance market currently offers very comprehensive fire insurance on a voluntary basis. Since there are only minor differences in the terms and conditions of voluntary fire insurance offered on the Polish market, it would not be risky to present the above insurance terms and conditions in a complex form.

423. Subject of insurance. Insurance products are basically offered in two forms, either as universal insurance dedicated to various types of property, including movables and real estate or as insurance dedicated to specific types of property (usually movables) due to the specifics of the risk in the given branch of industry (such as cargo, hull or machinery breakdown). Universal insurance products are described below.

424. The subject of the insurance can be any property owned by the policyholder for both commercial and private use. Some types of property, such as documents, files, currency, securities, works of art, jewellery and other articles made of silver, gold and platinum, can be insured only by means of a separate insurance contract, which defines the conditions and the insurance sum of such coverage. Insured property is usually tied to a specific location (and the associated protection against loss), although it is also possible to insure property in different locations or during certain processes, such as moving, transportation, exhibitions, trade fairs, etc. Fire insurance for property is subject to the existence of basic protections. These do not entitle you to a discount, but they are a prerequisite for coverage. Additional types of protection over and above those required by law may give the insured a discount if they are used.

425. Extent of Insurance Coverage.

426. Typically, fire insurance provides coverage against the basic scope of risks (FLEXA), including: (1) fire and direct lightning; (2) aircraft damage; (3) explosion; (4) hurricanes and storms, floods, torrential rain and hail; (5) leaks from water supply and sewerage systems and technological equipment; (6) avalanches, earthquakes and subsidence. However, a popular type of insurance is also the all-risk property insurance, where an insured accident is a broadly defined sudden event, independent of the will of the insured, where fire is only one of the risks covered.

427. As a rule, the insurance also covers damage to the insured property caused by rescue operations in connection with one of the insured events (listed above) and as a result of the disappearance of the insured property during such events. However, the Insurer's liability does not cover the disappearance of cash, securities, documents, stamps and numismatic collections, works of art, silver, gold and platinum objects, as well as jewellery, unless the aforementioned objects have been insured under a separate contract.

428. As a general rule, only direct losses are covered in the form of a reduction in assets (within the limits of the insured property), while indirect losses are covered on the basis of additional clauses (subject to an additional premium) and may concern such losses as coverage of the costs of renting replacement equipment or premises, or through other insurance products such as business interruption insurance.

429. In addition to the direct loss, the Insurer is also obliged (by default) to cover the expenses incurred by the Insured, such as: (1) costs related to rescue operations undertaken by the Insured in order to prevent, mitigate or limit the loss and which were justified by all the circumstances surrounding the insured event (preventive measures are also an obligation of the Insured, *see* below); (2) the cost of removing the debris resulting from the loss, as well as the cost of dismantling and removing the parts that cannot be reused; (3) the cost of safeguarding and protecting the insured property in the event that it is directly threatened by the occurrence of the loss.

430. The 'loss' is defined as physical loss or decrease of the value of the insured property as a result of destruction, damage or loss thereof. Furthermore, 'fire' is usually defined in a similar way as in compulsory fire insurance and includes '*a fire which has penetrated outside of the hearth or which arose without a hearth and is in position to expand uncontrolled*'.

431. Insurance cover is usually subject to a number of exclusions which can be categorised as: (1) the exclusion of certain types of property from cover (e.g., cash, jewellery) or which are not specific to the insurance product (e.g., personal property in commercial insurance and vice versa); or (2) property located in a particular place or under particular circumstances (property not in use, property undergoing renovation or repair, etc.) (e.g., cash, jewellery) or which are not specific to the insurance product (e.g., personal property in commercial insurance and vice versa); or (3) property located in certain places or under certain circumstances (property not in use, property under renovation or repair, property located outdoors, etc.); (4) certain types of damage (e.g., wear and tear, etc.); (5) damage resulting from certain types of events (e.g., war, riot, etc.). These exclusions may be absolute or relative, i.e., there is the possibility of extending the subject matter or scope of cover under additional clauses for an additional fee.

432. The most common exclusions include:

- losses caused by an act of war, state of emergency, strike, etc.;
- damage caused by water to water buildings and installations (including those under construction), with the exception of damage caused by tidal waves of any size and force that were not foreseen at the time the water building or installation in question was designated and that occur as a result of very exceptional circumstances;
- damage caused by the Insured as a result of explosions carried out for production and exploitation purposes;
- losses in fuel or explosive engines caused by explosions related to their inherent function or by explosions due to the normal pressure of gases concentrated inside them;
- losses caused by flooding where this is due to the poor condition of the roof or the failure to secure openings in the roof or other parts of the building;
- losses caused by prolonged exposure to moisture as a result of leaks in the water supply and sewerage system;
- losses caused in the Insured Property as a result of interruptions in the supply of electricity to machinery, equipment and production and refrigeration equipment;
- damage caused to kinescope lamps as a result of their explosion at the manufacturer's premises;
- in the case of subsidence, damage within the meaning of the Mining Act or caused by earthworks carried out;
- damage caused intentionally by the Insured or by a person for whom the Insured is responsible, as well as damage caused by gross negligence on the part of the Insured.

433. The asset may be insured at its actual value, i.e., after deduction of the surrender value, or at a new value. Actual value insurance is usually used to insure fixed assets (e.g., buildings, structures, machinery, equipment, etc.), current assets (e.g., raw materials, semi-finished products, finished products, spare parts, etc.), crops, livestock, etc. Only fixed assets at replacement value can be insured.

434. There are three standard sums insured systems: fixed sums, joint and several fixed sums and 'for risk' sums. The joint and several sum insured system is used to insure property located at many sites, but for which the insured keeps a collective account. For the first risk, only the personal property of the insured's employees can be insured.

435. In the case of fixed-sum property insurance, the insurer determines in detail how the sum insured is to be calculated for each type of property. For example, in the case of fixed assets insured for their new value, the sum insured should be equal to the initial value documented in the accounting books. However, in the case of fixed assets insured for their actual value, the sum insured should not exceed the actual value shown in the accounts. In addition, buildings and buildings under construction, reconstruction and repair insured for fixed sums should be calculated at the level of the total cost of construction, reconstruction or repair. In the system of joint and several insurance for fixed insurance sums of fixed and current assets, the insurance sum should correspond to the total value of the property located in many places and locations but at the same time in the possession of the insured. Finally, in the case of insurance of the personal property of the insured's employees for the first risk, the sum insured should be an amount obtained by multiplying the number of employees and the amount by the average value of such property.

436. The insured is obliged to observe all generally applicable rules concerning prevention, and in particular fire protection, construction and operation of technical equipment and technical supervision thereof, the insurer may refuse in whole or in part to participate financially in the loss, if this occurred as a result of the insured's failure to observe the safety rules or as a result of the insured's consent to their infringement.

437. There are several obligations of the insured in this regard. Some of them result from the legal regulations (namely those contained in the Civil Code), while others should be included in the insurance conditions and should be provided to the Insured prior to the conclusion of the insurance contract. With regard to preventive measures, the law stipulates that in the event of a loss, the Insured is obliged to take all available measures to mitigate or prevent further aggravation of damage to property in imminent danger.

438. The other obligations depend on whether they have been included in the insurance conditions. These include the obligation to notify the insurer of the insured event (within a certain period of time, which should not be too short, otherwise it may be considered an abusive clause). This obligation is fulfilled even if the insurer receives relevant information from another source.

439. Other examples of such standard obligations are the prohibition to change the factual situation of the property before the insurer's verification; to allow the insurer to take all necessary steps to determine the circumstances of the subject loss and the amount of indemnity, as well as to provide the insurer with the necessary explanations and evidence. In the latter case, however, the Insurer is obliged to inform the Insured of the documents required and to provide a list of them.

440. The indemnity will be assessed with the participation of the Insured. Compensation will be paid within thirty days from the date of notification of the insured event. There may be an extension of the deadline or a partial payment in the event that it is not possible to settle the claim within the standard deadline (although the insurer is obliged to act with professional diligence in order to comply with this deadline). Furthermore, the insurer is obliged to pay the undisputed part of the compensation within the standard period of thirty days. It is also standard practice for the insurer to pay a portion of the estimated loss in advance, especially if the claim is expected to take a long time to settle.

441. Once the Insurer has paid compensation to the Insured, it shall be subrogated to all its rights against the third party responsible for the damage, up to the amount of the compensation paid. At the request of the Insurer, the Insured is obliged to assist in the pursuit of recourse claims against third parties and to provide the Insurer with the necessary documents and information.

Chapter 2. Loss of Profits Insurance

442. Loss of profits insurance was introduced to the Polish insurance market at the end of the 1990s, following the example of insurers operating abroad (USA and Western Europe). Thus, this type of insurance operates in Poland under its original English name – 'Business Interruption' or 'Loss of Profits' insurance (called also 'BI'). It is currently offered by almost all insurers operating in Poland.

443. BI insurance protects against the loss of profits and other costs of continued operations (e.g., fixed costs) in the event of an insured loss. This type of insurance is concluded in addition to ordinary property insurance, which covers physical damage to insured property as a result of an insured event. The most common risks covered by this type of insurance in Poland are fire and other natural catastrophes or all-risks insurance related to the breakdown of property or machinery.

444. Another peculiarity of loss of profit insurance is that it does not cover the actual damage to the insured property – which is the role of ordinary property insurance – but the loss of profit suffered as a result of the above-mentioned event, which is excluded in principle in the latter. The sum insured is equal to the profit calculated as turnover minus variable costs or net profit plus fixed costs.

445. The usual exclusions in this type of insurance, in addition to the standard exclusions in property insurance, include the lack of financial means to restore the property, the prohibition of reconstruction by the competent authority, the cost of fines and contractual penalties, etc.

446. The specific feature of the business interruption insurance is the indemnity period, which begins on the day of the occurrence of the damage and lasts as long as the damage has a negative impact on the insured activity (within the maximum indemnity period established in the policy, which usually does not exceed twelve months, depending on the type of business insurance).

447. Regarding the form and manner of concluding an insurance contract for loss of earnings, it should be noted that, despite the fact that general insurance conditions are prepared by insurers, the contract is usually concluded on the basis of individual negotiations, especially when brokers are involved. It reflects the individual and specific needs of the insured companies.

448. The purpose of the insurance is to protect the client's loss of profit – in insurance terms, not accounting terms – resulting from downtime caused by physical damage to the insured property. It is therefore a kind of 'overlay' on the property insurance, e.g., all-risk property insurance, all-risk machinery insurance, and all-risk electronic equipment insurance, which will not work if there is no material damage caused by the event specified in the insurance contract. This means no more and no less than a lack of cover for incurred costs and losses that are not the result of, for example, fire or flood. You should also bear in mind that insurers do not cover standard events such as the effects of biological agents or viruses.

449. Therefore, the vast majority of claims relating to the COVID-19 virus, which relate to loss of profits resulting only from the downtime itself and not from damage to property – even indirectly caused by the pandemic – were not covered. Of course, many insurance programmes have extended coverage with additional clauses, e.g., relating to lack of access to a site, and decisions by public authorities, but the individual circumstances of a case will determine whether specific costs are recoverable. This applies to both local and international schemes. Nevertheless, as cases in the UK or the US have shown, ambiguous provisions in policies, their clauses and extensions or GICs have put considerable pressure on the insurance market to cover at least some of the costs incurred. Currently, the situation in the UK is causing the most emotion, as the Supreme Court ruled that, depending on the terms of the policy, insurance clauses relating to restricted access or the outbreak of disease may be applied to protect against the consequences of the COVID-19 pandemic, irrespective of property damage, thus obliging insurers to cover losses in the event of partial or total closure of premises and in the event of mandatory closure orders.

450. It is worth noting that Polish law is not based on precedent, as is the case in the UK or America, which means that we should not expect a similar ruling in Poland, which could be a binding interpretation for the entire market or a ruling that would directly determine the procedure in similar cases. Rather, there will be individual attempts to obtain compensation through the courts, using ambiguous provisions in the insurance terms and conditions or the insurance contract itself, in order to obtain at least partial compensation for losses incurred by businesses, particularly in the hotel industry, as a result of the closure of operations. The Polish regulator has not commented on this issue.

451. It is important to note that the current situation has contributed to the development of insured parties' awareness of the existence of special insurance products such as BI. Although this solution is not new, there is still a lot to be done in Poland to make this insurance a standard. However, the pandemic has strongly challenged the approach of insurers and their reinsurers to offering business interruption insurance. Insurers are taking a closer look at BI accounts and are cautious about potential interest in extending this cover. As might be expected from the approach to terrorism insurance following the 9/11 attacks in the US, property insurers are seeking to limit any COVID-19-related claims by offering appropriate clauses in both new business and renewals.

Chapter 3. Transport Insurance

452. Transport insurance is one of the more complex branches of insurance. First of all, there are different categories of entities with insurable interest and their subject matter varies depending on the type of transport and the type of insurance interest. This is because they concern the means of transport (hull), the cargo transported, the carrier's liability and the liability of the owner of the vehicle. Insurance can be subdivided according to the type of transport, i.e., land transport, sea transport, inland waterways and air transport.

453. Historically, marine insurance has been the most developed branch of insurance, with a very strong influence of the international market. According to the Polish Maritime Code (which is based on the Maritime Insurance Act of 1906), the subject of marine insurance may be any financial interest related to maritime navigation and assessable in terms of money. In particular, the subject matter of marine insurance can be: vessel, cargo, freight, passage money, charter hire, expected profit from cargo, commission on general average expenditure, obligations arising from civil liability or a claim secured on the vessel, cargo or freight.

454. The current practice of transport insurance seems to be in line with international practice, with the exception of the provisions that impose compulsory insurance in this respect.

455. Cargo and hull insurance are offered on a voluntary basis, while liability insurance is often compulsory.

§1. Cargo Insurance

I. General

456. Goods in transit are subject to partial or even total destruction. For this reason, it is connected with issues of transport insurance, which is one of the most prominent methods of risk management. It is the insurance of goods in transit, which belongs to the basic group of transport insurance. The scope of cargo insurance coverage is determined by the insurance terms and conditions adapted to the specifics of the possible risk. Cargo may be insured along the entire transport route specified in the transport documents, using one or more means of transport, including necessary transshipment activities or temporary storage along the transport route. Cargo insurance is one of the most complex types of insurance used in foreign trade transactions, especially in maritime transport.

457. Two factors influence the complexity of cargo insurance. One of them is the need to determine precisely, on the basis of the contracts applicable in international trade, which of the parties to these contracts bears the risk of damage to the cargo during transport, and from what point in time. The second factor is the participation of many entities in the process of international transport, which affects the civil liability of each of them.

458. The subject of insurance may be goods transported at the risk of the insured. Therefore, the insurable interests in cargo insurance can be attributed, in principle, to the owner of the cargo or other entity bearing the risk of loss. Neither the carrier nor the forwarder has an insurable interest in cargo insurance when acting on their own behalf. However, if they are acting in agreement with an authorised entity, i.e., the owner of the cargo or the forwarder to whom the right to dispose of the cargo has been granted, these entities are entitled to take out cargo insurance. In this case, they may also become beneficiaries of the payment of compensation in the event of damage to the cargo. In conclusion, the insurance interest is on the side of the party bearing the risk of loss, i.e., the shipper.

459. Typically, the risk of damage in transit is borne by the owner of the cargo. He also has the so-called insurance gesture. Who should be considered the owner of the cargo during transport? This depends on the specific circumstances and, above all, on the economic operators themselves and the risks they bear. This question is regulated by specific legal provisions, for example, on the legal effects of the contract of sale. For example, Article 548 §1 of the PCC stipulates that the benefits and burdens associated with the sale of goods, as well as the risk of their accidental loss or damage, are transferred to the buyer at the moment of delivery. However, the provision of Article 544 §1 of the Civil Code states that if the seller has to send the goods to a place that is not the place of performance of the service, in case of doubt, the delivery is deemed to have taken place at the moment when the seller has entrusted the goods to a carrier engaged in the transport of goods of this type for delivery to the place of destination. It should be noted that the provisions in question refer to the moment when the risk of damage to the goods is transferred to the other party.

460. The insurance covers the transportation of the cargo from the moment of its departure from the place of dispatch to the moment of its delivery to the place of destination, as well as necessary transshipment operations and temporary storage of the cargo on the route of transportation (the protection may also cover loading or unloading operations).

461. The subject of the cargo insurance contract is the integrity of the cargo. The subject of cargo insurance may be, *inter alia*, goods of a commercial nature commonly found in commercial transactions, defined in the contract of carriage as cargo, exhibition and fair goods, works of art, property of displaced persons and other non-commercial goods. In practice, there are various conditions of damage coverage, which are constructed according to the needs and possibilities of the insuring entity.

462. The scope of coverage is practically based on the Institute Clauses developed by the Institute of London Insurers, which are applied in both marine and inland cargo insurance. They have full practical application on the Polish market as well. The most important ones are Institute Cargo Clauses (A, B, C), Institute War Clauses, Institute Strike Clauses and Institute Exclusion of Radioactive Contamination Clauses. Institute Cargo Clauses (Clause A, 2009; Clause B, 2009; Clause C, 2009) are commonly used in international cargo insurance. They are universal in nature, being applicable to most types of cargo transported by various modes of transport. Three sets of clauses are most commonly used: A, B and C. They differ mainly in the scope of the insurance cover, the so-called risk clause.

463. In clauses B and C, the scope of insurance cover is limited to closed lists of risks, and the burden of proof for damage resulting from them lies with the insured. This is not the case with Clause A, which is based on the all-risks principle and requires the insured to prove that the loss was fortuitous and unavoidable. Again, the insurance covers the risk of loss of or damage to the insured property, with the exceptions set out in clause A, paragraphs 4.1–4.7, which are identical to the exclusions in the Convention.

464. Accordingly, Clause A does not cover:

– loss, damage or expense caused by the Insured himself;
– ordinary leakage, ordinary loss of weight or volume, or ordinary wear and tear of the insured goods. It applies only to such cases which have the appearance of ordinariness and are to be expected in the ordinary course of carriage;
– loss, damage or expense caused by insufficient or inadequate packing or preparation of the insured goods for the voyage. It is often disputed whether the packing of goods is considered sufficient and appropriate for the type of cargo being transported. Packing or preparation of the insured goods in accordance with generally accepted trade customs and practices will be deemed to meet the above criteria. If the packaging forms an integral part of the insured cargo and is found to be inadequate, the loss or damage may be considered to have been caused by a latent defect in the insured goods;
– loss, damage or expense caused by a latent defect or natural characteristic of the insured object;
– loss, damage or expense directly caused by delay, even if caused by the peril against which the insurance was taken out. Such a provision indicates that the passage of time cannot be treated as a risk against which cargo in transit can be insured;
– loss, damage or expense resulting from the insolvency or financial failure of the owners and operators of the vessel;
– loss, damage or expense resulting from the use of any weapon of war involving nuclear energy or radioactive material.

465. The term ‘all risks’ covers any loss or damage to the insured cargo which is accidental and unforeseeable. It therefore does not apply to certain or highly probable situations such as latent defects, natural characteristics or loss or damage attributable to the insured’s own actions. The burden of proof lies with the Insured, who must prove that the loss was caused by a risk that was not excluded and that occurred during the period of cover. It should be noted that the concept of loss or damage is understood as physical damage to the insured cargo and not as intrinsic or consequential financial loss, even if caused by the occurrence of the insured risk. Consequently, the insurance does not cover costs or expenses other than those customarily incurred in the process of determining the extent and amount of damage, such as sorting and segregation of damaged cargo, or the cost of cargo surveys. Latent defect is defined as the inability of the cargo to survive in good condition during a normal voyage, assuming that the shipowner has exercised all due care and attention to the cargo as required by the contract. Natural perils are those caused by the natural behaviour of the insured cargo in the circumstances in which it is transported.

466. Clauses B and C contain an exclusion in addition to those contained in Clause A. This is the exclusion of wilful damage, destruction of the insured goods or any part thereof as a result of an unlawful act by any person. This includes acts such as throwing cargo overboard without reasonable cause, arson or sabotage resulting in the sinking of the vessel. Cargo insurance written under Institute Type C clauses, which provide so-called limited coverage, covers loss or damage arising from the same causes as under B clauses, with one exception. C clauses do not cover loss or damage caused by earthquake, volcanic eruption or lightning.

467. A cargo insurance contract does not have to be periodic; it can be a one-off contract. The goods to be transported may be insured under a general insurance contract – called a general policy – in which case all or only some of the goods transported at the policyholder's risk during a given period are covered.

468. In the practice of transport business, special rules of interpretation have emerged, the so-called INCOTERMS. These clauses are often referred to as the seller's conditions of carriage to the consignee and relate to the determination of the amount of financial obligations of certain parties to the contract of carriage. Their content has been specified by the International Chamber of Commerce in Paris. Only two INCOTERMS formulas contain a clearly defined obligation of basic insurance of goods – CIF (used in maritime transport) and CIP. All other formulas define precisely the moment when the risk passes from the seller to the buyer, with the seller deciding whether or not to insure the cargo. When defining the terms of delivery, it is important to remember that the assumption of transport and insurance by one party to the contract means that the other party does not receive any benefits from the possession of the goods. Typically, insurance coverage is also limited by deductibles for small damages (franchise), damages caused by the inherent vice of the transported goods and as a result of the sender's fault.

469. Typical insurance conditions on the Polish market provide for specific obligations of the insured. In the event of a loss, the Insured is obliged to: take all reasonable measures to mitigate the loss or prevent its aggravation; notify the police if the loss occurred as a result of theft, robbery or a traffic accident; obtain a proper report from the carrier in the event of a loss; allow the Insurer to determine the circumstances of the loss and its extent.

470. The extent of the damage to the insured property is determined on the basis of the value of the damaged or lost property at the prices prevailing at the time of the damage. Within this general principle, there is a specific provision that in the case of the property of private individuals and companies, the value is determined on the basis of a proper invoice showing the purchase price of the goods or, in the absence of such an invoice, on the basis of the actual cost of purchase or production of the goods, reduced by wear and tear at the time of the loss. Non-fulfilment can only lead to the refusal of cover if the insurer can prove gross negligence or wilful misconduct, which can lead to disputes between the insurer and the insured.

471. After the indemnity has been paid, the insurer is subrogated to all rights against the third party actually responsible for the damage, up to the amount of the indemnity paid. After the indemnity has been paid, the insurer is subrogated to all rights against the third party actually responsible for the damage, up to the amount of the indemnity paid.

II. Marine Cargo Insurance

472. Marine cargo insurance covers goods imported and exported or re-exported by import/export companies by sea or sea/land transport. Cargo insurance is usually based on general contracts between insurers and various import/export companies.

473. The basic features of marine cargo insurance are set out in the Polish Maritime Code. According to it, a policyholder who has concluded a general contract of insurance is obliged to notify the insurer of every shipment or arrival of cargo covered by the contract immediately upon learning of its shipment or arrival, specifying in each case the vessel, the route, the cargo and the sum insured. If the Insured has wilfully or grossly negligently failed to comply with this obligation, the Insurer may cancel the contract, retaining the right to the insurance premiums that would have been due if the contract had been duly performed by the Insured. The right to withdraw from the contract expires if the Insurer does not exercise it within three days from the day on which the Insurer becomes aware of the policyholder's breach of duty.

474. In Polish marine cargo insurance practice, the London Institute clauses are used, i.e., Free from Particular Average (FPA); With Average (WA); and All Risks (AR) or combinations of these clauses. Branch clauses are also used for special cargoes such as cotton, timber, etc. The FPA and WA clauses may include theft, pilferage and non-delivery risk, while the AR clauses may cover heating and sweating in appropriate cases. The importer/exporter also covers the expected profit in accordance with Incoterms or as agreed with the insurer.

475. The insured value of goods transported by sea is usually the invoice value, increased by the expected profit and the costs of transport, insurance and customs duties paid abroad. The sums insured are determined by the insured. Premiums are calculated according to tariffs that take into account the type of vessel, the type of cargo, the voyage, the season and the range of risks covered. Goods are divided into four categories according to their nature and susceptibility to maritime transport.

476. It is worth mentioning that there is also a clause applied by the insurer – the so-called transit clause – which ensures the continuity of the insurance cover for the entire duration of the transport of the goods, regardless of the mode of transport. In other words, the insurer's liability begins when the goods leave the warehouses specified in the policy and ends when they arrive at the final consignee's warehouse.

III. Air Cargo Insurance

477. In air transport, as in other types of transport, cargo insurance is based on International Cargo Clauses (ICC), which are commonly used in the Polish insurance market. Air cargo insurance is often combined with cargo insurance for other modes of transport under one policy. At the same time, insurers offer Institute Cargo Clauses specific to air transport, such as Institute Cargo Clauses AIR (excluding sending by post) 1/1/2009 CL.387, or the extension of basic cover to include war risks in accordance with Institute Clauses: 3.6.1. for sea transport: Institute War Clauses Cargo 1/1/2009 CL.385 (Institute War Clauses Cargo 1/1/2009) 3.6.2. for air transport: Institute War Clauses Air Cargo 1/1/2009 CL388 (Institute War Clauses Air Cargo 1/1/2009). Cargo insurance in international transport is particularly popular because of the carrier's ability to exempt itself from liability in situations related to the nature of the goods and force majeure.

§2. Liability Insurance in Transport

I. General

478. Transport liability insurance is subject to more specific rules and conditions than cargo insurance. This is due to the need to adapt the insurance cover to the binding liability regime. In the case of domestic transport, this will be the regime of the PCC, Transport Law or Aviation Law. In the case of international transport, however, the carrier's liability is often based on international or European legal acts, which also impose an obligation to insure the carrier against liability. Examples are the liability insurance of air carriers and aircraft operators in respect of passengers, baggage and cargo, the liability insurance of air carriers and aircraft operators in respect of third parties or the insurance of air carriers in the event of accidents with mail, standardised by Regulation No. 785/2004 (Regulation, 2004). In the case of air carrier liability, there is now a largely unified air carrier liability regime within the EU.

479. An example of unification is the air carrier liability and insurance regime (in particular for the carriage of passengers), which was implemented by Regulations 2027/97 (Regulation, 1997) and 889/2002 (Regulation, 2002). This regime refers to the principles of the Montreal Convention and extends its scope to domestic carriage. Previously, Community legislation had mainly referred to the Warsaw Convention (1929), without depriving it of its binding force (although the Montreal Convention takes precedence, which is important in the field of carrier liability, particularly with regard to the limits of carrier liability). In essence, therefore, we have a double unification of the regime of carrier liability, since on the one hand analogous rules of liability are adopted for national and international carriage, and on the other hand it is unified throughout the EU. Given this high degree of standardisation of the rules on air carrier liability throughout the EU, the introduction of uniform rules on air carrier civil liability insurance did not require the application of the Directive. The Regulation regulates only some of the most basic issues, such as the scope of the insurance, the amount of the guarantee and the obligations of the air carrier. The Regulation therefore focuses on the elements of the insurance contract that are most important for the standardisation of social relations, leaving other issues to be clarified at the level of national legislation.[23]

480. An example of another type of insurance regulated by the Regulation is the liability insurance of a maritime carrier in respect of the carriage of passengers. In this case, the rules governing the liability of a passenger carrier have been unified on the basis of the Athens Convention, which regulates this very category of liability of a maritime carrier (Convention, 1974). In this case, moreover, we are dealing with the aforementioned category of liability insurance, in which the obligation to take out insurance has a variant character. In this case, this means that the carrier is obliged to guarantee the financial interests of potential victims, but the conclusion of an insurance contract is one of the alternative forms of guarantee that the carrier can choose from. However, in view of the need to protect the interests of the injured party in the case of another form of security, the Regulation provides that the injured party may bring an *actio directa* not only against the insurer but also against the provider of the other form of financial security. In turn, the defendant – whether an insurer or another entity – may use the same defences that would be available to the carrier. However, the Regulation itself does not regulate in detail the basic rules of such security in the same way as the Regulation on air carrier liability insurance but refers directly to the rules of the Athens Convention.

II. Third-Party Liability Insurance of Land Carrier

481. National and international carrier liability insurance is one of the most popular types of transport insurance. The subject of the insurance is the carrier's liability for non-performance or improper performance of the contract of carriage. The general terms and conditions of liability insurance provide for insurance coverage of the carrier's liability in road transport for damage caused during the performance of the concluded contract of carriage – for non-performance or improper performance of the contract of carriage (theft, damage or destruction of goods, delay

23. Konert 2010.

in delivery). The scope of insurance coverage depends strictly on the carrier's liability regime. It can cover all types of risks to which the insured may be exposed in the course of his professional activity as a carrier, from the moment the goods are accepted for carriage to the moment they are handed over to the consignee, as well as delay in the delivery of the goods or failure to deliver the consignment.

482. According to the Transport Law and the CMR Convention, the carrier is liable for the goods entrusted to him from the moment of loading at the consignor's premises until the moment of unloading at the consignee's premises (to the extent that he is responsible for the loading and unloading operations). The scope of protection can be freely defined according to the specific nature of the transport performed. This is usually done by including appropriate provisions in the scope of cover, e.g., gross negligence of the company's own employees, damage caused by persons under the influence of alcohol or drugs, theft during stops in unguarded car parks or petrol stations, delivery of the goods to an unauthorised person or inclusion of additional costs after the damage.

483. As there is no obligation to insure in domestic transport, the optional carrier's liability insurance may include certain types of damage, such as parking outside guarded car parks; cover for transport carried out with all vehicles without the obligation to notify the insurer; extension of cover to transport carried out by subcontractors; extension of cover to gross negligence on the part of the carrier, drivers and subcontractors; Extension of cover to wilful misconduct; cover when the carrier is not named on the waybill; cover for transport of ADR goods; cover when goods are handed over to an unauthorised person; cover for damage caused by immigrants entering the load compartment; cover for damage caused by theft of goods; cover for damage caused by failure to comply with road traffic regulations; cover when the ATP certificate is not up to date.

484. Common standard limitations of loss or damage (unless specifically covered as above) include: wilful misconduct or gross negligence on the part of the insured; improper packaging of the goods or during the loading process if both loading and unloading are carried out by the consignor, consignee or person acting on their behalf; natural characteristics of the goods; the use of a vehicle which is not suitable for the transport of certain goods or which does not meet the technical requirements for this type of vehicle; the transport of animals; the transport of dangerous goods such as self-igniting explosives, poisonous, radioactive, corrosive and infectious materials; the performance of transport services by a person without the necessary qualifications and licences; the use of a vehicle which is not authorised by the authorities for public transport.

485. There are also some other exclusions as far as the insurer's liability is concerned, such as all types of fines, claims by persons transported by the insured person, damage to works of art, numismatic and stamp collections, as well as other types of valuables, claims related to damage caused as a result of war, riot, etc.

486. The Insurer's liability shall not exceed the limits established for the carrier's liability by the CMR Convention or as agreed with the Customer. According to Article 23 paragraphs 1 and 3 of the CMR Convention, the carrier is liable for transport damage up to the amount of 8.33 SDR (Special Settlement Unit) per 1 kg of missing gross weight (it refers to both lost and damaged consignment). Furthermore, the compensation shall not exceed the value of the cargo from the place and time of acceptance of the goods for carriage and shall not include the loss of profit which the person entitled to the compensation expected to make on account of the importance of the transported cargo for the person entitled to the compensation, e.g., its importance for the production of the consignee. In addition, the carrier is obliged to refund or not to claim the freight, as well as to reimburse customs duties and other expenses related to the carriage, in full or in proportion to the lost cargo.

487. These obligations are also of an indemnity nature, but their inclusion in the scope of cover depends on the individual terms and conditions of the insurance. The limit of liability may be increased by the sender's declaration in the consignment note of the value of the goods exceeding the limit provided for in Article 23 paragraph 3 of the CMR Convention (but it cannot include loss of profit). In this case, the amount of this declaration replaces this limit and the carrier is liable up to this amount. The standard insurance conditions usually do not cover the extended liability based on Article 24 of the CMR Convention. For this purpose, the carrier usually needs to obtain coverage based on an additional insurance clause (subject to an additional premium).

488. Furthermore, the limitation of the carrier's liability does not apply if the damage was caused by wilful misconduct or negligence. In this case, not only does the limitation of amount (i.e., 8.33 SDRs per kg of cargo lost) not apply, but the carrier's liability also extends to the loss of profit suffered by the injured party.

489. With regard to the obligations of the insured under the carrier's liability insurance, it is worth mentioning those relating to the proper care of the cargo transported. From the very beginning, i.e., From the moment of accepting the cargo for transport, the insured must fulfil several obligations: to check the contents of the bill of lading with regard to the weight, quantity, marks, numbers, visible condition of the cargo and its packaging; to enter in the bill of lading any reservations regarding the above; to notify the insurer as soon as possible; to notify as soon as possible the Insurer's representatives or any other independent surveyor in order to have a report drawn up describing the circumstances of the loss and, in particular, its causes and extent; if the damage is discovered at the time of delivery of the goods to the final consignee, the Insured should draw up, together with the consignee, a loss report or arrange for a surveyor who will be able to draw up such a document.

III. Third-Party Liability Insurance of Freight Forwarder

490. Forwarder's liability insurance covers damage caused by the insured's failure to perform, or improper performance of, forwarding services. This includes, among other things, dispatching and collecting consignments, drawing up forwarding instructions, advising on transport, concluding transport contracts and arranging transport, drawing up documents relating to transport, loading, unloading and storage of consignments. Despite the fact that OCS insurance has been present in the Polish market for many years, defining the difference between forwarding and transport activities is difficult and often leads to misunderstandings.

491. The basic criterion distinguishing the contract of forwarding from the contract of transport is the content of the order. If the order is only for transport from point A to point B, without any additional logistical operations, it should be assumed that the given entity is acting as a carrier and not as a forwarder. The nature of the contract does not depend on whether the entity has its own fleet of vehicles and performs the transport itself or through subcontractors – other carriers. This insurance is voluntary in the Polish insurance market.

492. In Poland, the scope of a forwarder's liability is regulated by the Civil Code (chapter on the contract of forwarding). According to its content, the Freight Forwarder is responsible for the carriers and sub-carriers he uses for the execution of the order unless he is not at fault in their selection. The Freight Forwarder is also liable for the loss, shortage or damage of the goods during the period from their receipt to their delivery to the Carrier, the Sub-carrier, the Customer or the person designated by him.

493. The subject of the insurance is the third-party liability of the Freight Forwarder for damages resulting from the non-performance or improper performance of the Forwarding Contract, which the Policyholder (the Freight Forwarder) bears in accordance with the provisions of the Civil Code (Chapter: Forwarding Contract). The basic scope of the insurance covers activities that are part of the everyday work of a forwarder, such as: the conclusion of transport contracts, preparation and completion of transport documents, preparation of forwarding instructions, registration of consignments for insurance and customs clearance, inspection of consignments for quantity and weight, marking, packing and repacking, supervision of loading, possible reloading and unloading of goods, temporary storage of consignments. The basic scope of the insurance does not normally include liability assumed by the insured, civil liability as a road carrier (contractual) under the provisions of the CMR Convention or the Transport Act, incorrect completion of customs documents, gross negligence on the part of the policyholder or a person acting on its behalf, under its authority or on its instructions, storage of goods for more than thirty days.

494. Popular clauses on the Polish market that extend the insurance cover include damage to containers, pallets, platforms, packages and receptacles, damage caused by gross negligence, caused by defrosting and failure to maintain the transport temperature, which may give rise to claims against employees, persons connected with the company, members of the family of the owner of the company or entities connected with the Insurer by capital, damage caused by loss of cargo as a result of burglary, damage caused by theft of the means of transport together with the goods, loss of or damage to the goods entrusted to the carrier during the performance of forwarding activities, the contractual third-party liability of the road carrier (in domestic and/or international transport) or third-party liability for the transport of dangerous goods, live animals, money and other documents, works of art, philatelic and numismatic collections.

IV. Third-Party Liability Insurance of Shipowners (P and I)

495. The operation of a shipping business involving the carriage of goods by sea and the use of the ship as a very special and complicated means of transport exposes shipowners to a high risk of causing various types of damage to third parties, both *ex delicto* (in tort) and *ex contracto*. With regard to the principle of liability, an increasing number of court judgments provide that shipowners may be held liable under the principle of strict liability.

496. The scope of the shipowner's liability is determined by both national and international law. In the past, the Polish Maritime Code incorporated the system of the two Brussels Conventions on the Liability of Shipowners and Others of 1924 and 1957 and, more recently, the system of the IMCO Convention on the Limitation of Maritime Claims of 1976. Accordingly, the shipowner is in principle liable without limit for his acts, but in respect of certain obligations his liability is limited to the sums provided for by the said Convention. The obligations to which the principle of limited liability applies include:

a. damage caused to third parties by the negligent act of the master, a member of the crew, a pilot or any other person involved in the operation of the ship;
b. damage to goods accepted for carriage or other property on board the vessel;
c. the bill of lading;
d. damage arising from a navigational error made in the course of the performance of the contract;
e. salvage and removal of wreck;
f. salvage compensation;
g. the owner[3]s share in general average; and
h. contracts or other legal transactions entered into by the master during the absence of the ship from the port of registry for the purpose of preventing the ship from proceeding or continuing the voyage, unless necessitated by the inadequacy or defect of the ship's equipment or supplies at the commencement of the voyage.

497. Some of these obligations, i.e., (a), (d), (f) and (g), are at least partially covered by the hull policy, but all the remaining and further obligations are covered by the TPL policy. In particular, this policy covers the shipowner's liability in connection with:

- the loading, carriage, unloading and delivery of the cargo;
- damage to property not covered by the hull policy;

- death or bodily injury to persons on board (stevedores, pilots, etc.) and losses sustained by the vessel during rescue operations at sea;
- losses incurred as a result of accidents or sickness of persons involved in the navigation and management of the vessel;
- fines imposed on the vessel; customs duties and certain costs, e.g., quarantine; oil pollution damage;
- oil pollution damage;
- wreck removal;
- towage costs;
- losses arising from the participation of the cargo in general average and not otherwise covered by insurance.

498. In the Polish legal system, there are four types of compulsory insurance in maritime transport. The first one is the compulsory insurance of the shipowner's liability for maritime claims based on Article 102a of the Maritime Code, based on the 1976 Convention on Limitation of Liability for Maritime Claims. The second type of compulsory insurance is the insurance of the carrier's liability for damage to the passenger's person or property, introduced on the basis of Article 182 §1 of the Maritime Code, based on the Convention on the Carriage of Passengers and their Luggage, signed in Athens on 13 December 1974. Another type of insurance is the mandatory insurance of the carrier's liability for damage to the person or property of a passenger in international carriage, pursuant to Regulation No. 392/2009 of the European Parliament and of the Council on the liability of carriers of passengers by sea in the event of accidents.

499. The fourth type of insurance is the compulsory insurance of the shipowner's liability for pollution caused by oil carried in bulk as cargo, provided for in Articles 272 and 273 of the Maritime Code. This is a variant insurance, i.e., the shipowner has the right to choose the financial security in the form of insurance resulting from the provisions of the CLC Convention. The insurance is based on the International Convention on Civil Liability for Oil Pollution Damage, adopted in Brussels on 29 November 1969. The last type of compulsory civil liability insurance is the shipowner's bunker oil pollution insurance, provided for in Article 271b of the Maritime Code, similar to the previous one, which gives the shipowner the right to choose the form of security. The insurance obligation is based on the International Convention on Civil Liability for Bunker Oil Pollution Damage, adopted by the International Maritime Organisation in London on 23 March 2001.

500. In addition, the provisions of Article 110.3 of the Maritime Safety Act of 18 August 2011 require the owner or captain of a commercial marine yacht, with the exception of a yacht provided without crew, to have civil liability insurance covering the person in charge of the yacht and personal accident insurance covering all persons on the yacht. The owner's liability insurance in connection with the operation of the yacht provides protection in case of damage caused to third parties in connection with the operation of the yacht (e.g., in case of collision, damage to the quay), but does not cover damage caused to the captain, crew and passengers. The law does not specify the minimum amount of cover.

§3. Casco Insurance

I. General

501. Casco insurance is voluntary and can cover various types of damage caused by accident or theft. Due to their voluntary nature, they are relatively less regulated and there is some freedom in setting their exact terms by insurance companies and their clients. In the Polish insurance market, the ratio of vehicles with AC insurance to vehicles with third-party insurance has been very stable in Poland in recent years (data 2012–2016), oscillating around 26%. The ratio of casco gross written premium to MTPL gross written premium was between 55% and 70%; however, following price increases in MTPL, it fell below 50% in early 2016. Excluding this price shock, the value relationship between the two motor insurance markets in Poland appears to be relatively stable.

502. Depending on the type of Casco, this type of insurance protects the vehicle against various events. In most cases, comprehensive insurance covers damage caused by:

– accident and collision with other vehicles, persons, animals or objects outside the vehicle;
– damage to the vehicle by third parties or animals;
– theft or attempted theft of the vehicle, its parts or accessories;
– fire or explosion;
– weather phenomena such as floods, submersion, hurricanes, hail, lightning, landslides, avalanches, etc.

503. Depending on the scope of the contract, the insured may receive compensation in cash or in the form of a cashless repair of the vehicle in any garage or in a garage belonging to the insurer's network of partners, using original or replacement parts. As a rule, collision insurance also covers damage that has not occurred in road traffic. As a rule, Casco is valid not only in Poland but also abroad. Although this type of insurance is voluntary, it is usually sold on the consumer market (usually among mass risks) and as such is subject to control from the point of view of abusive provisions.

II. Marine Hull Insurance (Casco)

504. Seagoing merchant vessels owned by Polish shipowners are insured under Lloyd's policy conditions and the so-called Institute Clauses. Although two types of policies are traditionally used, the time policy (The Institute Time Clauses-Hull) and the voyage policy (The Institute Voyage Clauses-Hull), Polish practice prefers the former. However, ships are not insured for a period exceeding one year.

505. The primary obligation of the shipowner to claim compensation from the marine insurer in connection with a loss of the vessel is to keep the vessel in a seaworthy condition, i.e., to properly man, equip, supply, load and provide the vessel with all necessary documents for a sea voyage. If the shipowner has complied with all of the above, the insurer may be held liable for the following losses to the vessel resulting from:

- sinking;
- collision with another vessel;
- an accident during loading or unloading;
- fire or explosion;
- any latent defect in machinery or hull;
- negligence of the master, officers, crew and pilots;
- a collision with an aircraft;
- general average and salvage expenses.

506. However, the hull insurance does not cover damage to the insured vessel caused by:

- age or wear and tear;
- starting a voyage in an unseaworthy condition, inadequately equipped or manned, or without essential documents, unless such defects are latent in the vessel or are caused by circumstances that could not have been prevented despite the Insured's due diligence;
- structural defects or mechanical damage to the vessel's machinery (unless an endorsement has been included which provides for the Insurer's liability for latent defects in machinery), provided that they have not been caused by perils covered by the insurance;
- negligent conduct of the Insured;
- demurrage or other delay.

507. There is a general rule in the Polish Maritime Code that in the event of a collision between vessels, the insurer is obliged to pay adequate compensation for the damage to the insured vessel and to settle the claims of third parties who have suffered damage as a result of the collision, even if the total amount paid in both cases would exceed the sum insured. In this respect, hull insurance is a combination of traditional property insurance and liability insurance.

508. The insurable value of the vessel may be determined by an agreement between the two parties to the insurance contract, the so-called taxed value. In the event of a constructive total loss, the taxable value, and not the actual value of the vessel, will be the basis for calculating and paying the insurance indemnity. As a result, the insured may in some cases receive a higher indemnity than the actual extent of the loss.

509. It is common practice for hull insurers to apply a deductible that usually does not exceed 3% of the insurable value of the vessel. This is not only the case for general average claims.

Chapter 4. Liability Insurance

§1. General

510. The liability insurance sector in Poland is currently experiencing rapid growth, both in terms of the types of liability insurance and the number of policies concluded. This is a reflection of the development of the Polish economy and the need of entrepreneurs for more and more protection in view of the high risk of their activities. In light of the above, all non-life insurers operating in the Polish insurance market offer various types of liability insurance adapted to the different needs of Polish companies.

511. The demand for liability insurance is determined by many factors. One of them is the insurance obligation, i.e., the obligation of certain entities to use the insurance protection in the specified scope and time. This compulsion is based on the conviction that potential damaging parties are not sufficiently aware of the need for insurance and the need to protect the interests of injured parties. Liability insurance is a special type of non-life insurance. It differs from property insurance in many ways, not only in the subject of insurance and the type of risk covered but also, for example, in the entities entering into the insurance relationship, the nature of the damage and the amount of compensation, or the relationship between the value of the insured person's property and the amount of damage.

512. The subject of such insurance is the civil liability of the policyholder or the insured as a result of damage caused to third parties by the policyholder or persons for whom the policyholder is liable. By concluding an insurance contract, the insurer undertakes, in return for the payment of a certain insurance premium, to compensate for damage caused to third parties as a result of an event provided for in the contract and for which the policyholder or insured is liable [Civil Code, 1964, Article 822]. The insurer's liability is not limited by the value of the insured object. The insurance covers the risk of claims by third parties injured as a result of an act or omission of the policyholder or insured who is liable for the damage.

513. Third-party liability insurance not only covers the property of the person responsible for the damage but also protects the injured party against the risk of that person's insolvency. The injured party has the right to pursue his claims directly against the insurer of the person who caused the damage. This rule (*actio directa*) is mandatory for all types of civil liability insurance, both compulsory and voluntary, and does not depend on the bankruptcy of the insured.

514. The maximum liability of the insurance company, and therefore the maximum amount of compensation that the injured party can obtain from the insurer, is determined by the guaranteed amount. This amount does not limit the liability of the polluter. It can therefore happen that the amount of the claim, determined on the basis of the extent of the damage, exceeds the amount of the guarantee. In such a situation, the injured party can claim compensation for the part of the damage not covered by the guarantee directly from the person who caused the damage. If it turns out that the amount of this claim exceeds the value of the existing property of the perpetrator of the damage, the liability will also be charged to his future property.

515. The Insurer will pay the indemnity proportionate to the liability of the policyholder, but not more than the amount of the guarantee. The indemnity may also cover the expert's fees and expenses incurred by the policyholder in mitigating the loss and court costs. However, the possibility of offsetting these additional expenses usually requires prior agreement and acceptance by the insurance company.

516. Apart from product liability insurance, professional indemnity and D&O insurance are undergoing the most significant development. At present, a large proportion of the liberal professions are required by law to take out professional indemnity insurance to cover potential losses arising from the exercise of their professional activities. As far as insurers offering liability insurance in Poland are concerned, the growing competition in the market means that almost all insurers operating in the field of property insurance offer various types of liability insurance, ranging from general (public) liability insurance, to product liability insurance, to professional liability insurance, including D&O liability insurance.

517. Most of the standard policy wordings for liability insurance are based on those previously used in Western Europe, some of them on the 'claims made' principle (PI, D&O), some (GTPL and PI) on the 'occurrence' or 'act committed' principle.

518. General policy conditions for this type of insurance are closely linked to the legal basis of the liability covered. In order to achieve sufficient coverage, the General Policy Conditions must reflect the legal provisions governing the particular type of liability with regard to the scope of insurance, otherwise, it may appear that, despite the conclusion of an insurance contract, the insured liable to cover a damage caused to a third party cannot obtain any compensation. The other characteristic of liability insurance is that the cover applies only to third parties, i.e., in the case of tortious liability, which excludes the contractual liability of the insured, the injured third party must be a person who has no contractual relationship with the insured in relation to the insured activity.

519. In general, liability insurance provides coverage for certain risks in the event that an insured person, in connection with the performance of certain activities or as a result of owning certain property, is held liable under mandatory law for damages caused to third parties as a result of death, bodily injury or impairment of health, damage to or destruction of property. General liability insurance covers only the insured's tortious liability. Contractual liability may be covered by a separate agreement.

§2. Public (General) Liability Insurance

520. With regard to general liability insurance, the insurer's liability is very broadly defined as a result of the wide scope of liability that can be imposed on the insured. According to Article 415 of the PCC, the insured is liable for any damage caused to a third party as a result of a wrongful act or omission. In addition, in some cases, the liability arises even if the insured is not at fault. The scope of general liability includes the obligation to compensate for actual damage caused to a third party and for loss of profit (*damnum emergens* and *lucrum cessans*).

521. Beyond and in addition to these rules, the insurer undertakes to pay the costs of the expert, to establish the circumstances of the event, to reimburse the insured person for all the costs incurred in order to prevent aggravation of the damage and, finally, to bear the financial burden of all the necessary costs and expenses related to the defence of the insured person in court.

522. At the same time, the Insurers exclude from the general liability cover:

- damages caused intentionally by the Insured;
- damage caused as a result of work or services carried out by the Insured in a defective manner, if such damage was caused to the Insured's contractual partner;
- damage caused to property as a result of prolonged exposure to: temperature, gases, water, steam or moisture, smoke, soot, etc.;
- damage caused to property that was actually used by the Insured through renting, hiring, leasing, storage or as part of the Insured's industrial or professional activities. The same applies to property used for similar purposes;
- losses caused directly or indirectly by radioactive substances;
- losses suffered by the family members of the Insured;
- losses resulting from the contraction of an infectious disease of which the Insured knew or should have known;
- losses resulting from acts of war;
- losses caused by the disappearance or theft of cash, jewellery, securities or other valuables;
- fines of any kind imposed on the insured person.

523. The standard cover can be extended by:

- Subcontractors' Liability Clause – liability of the Contractor for damages caused by its subcontractors in connection with the execution of works, services or other activities entrusted to them.
- Liability for damage to movable property under the entrepreneur's care or control – liability of the entrepreneur for damage caused to property (other than his own) which he has taken possession of in connection with the running of a business.
- Employer's liability – liability of an entrepreneur for damage suffered by employees as a result of accidents at work.

- Product liability (although sometimes included in the standard cover) – liability of the entrepreneur for damage caused to third parties as a result of placing a defective product on the market.

524. The insurer's liability is limited to a guaranteed sum established for each or all of the events giving rise to the insured's liability to third parties. In accordance with the terms of the insurance contract, the insured person is obliged to follow certain procedures in the event of an incident that may give rise to a claim by an injured third party. In addition to some obligations of a routine nature, such as the obligation to take all possible measures to avoid aggravation of the damage, to preserve all evidence of the event that has occurred, to notify the insurer immediately, but not later than fourteen days after such an event, the insured person is also obliged, in the event that the injured party has initiated legal proceedings, to provide the persons designated by the insurer with the appropriate power of attorney to protect the interests of the insurer and the insured person in court. Furthermore, the Insured should not settle the claim without the prior consent of the Insurer. Although some of the above provisions (conditions) may differ slightly from one insurer to another, in most cases, they are quite similar.

§3. Product Liability Insurance

525. Product liability insurance is now usually an extension of the corporate client's liability insurance – public liability. It is usually sold as a package and cannot be bought separately. It is aimed at companies that manufacture and market products, as well as importers. The insurance covers the manufacturer's liability in the event that a product is placed on the market that poses a risk to the life and health of users, the environment and other property.[24]

526. There are two main product liability insurance products on the market. These relate to the marketing of a dangerous product:

- (defective) product liability insurance;
- Product recall insurance – which takes into account the specificity of the risk and the needs of the insured by requiring, among other things, a product recall plan or, in a simplified formula, as clauses in product liability insurance, but then with a low limit of liability; the coverage may cover only recalls ordered by authorised authorities or extend to other incidents, such as the insured's own decisions, under agreed conditions.

527. An important element of a product liability policy is the territory (coverage is either domestic or both domestic and international, although it is difficult or expensive to obtain coverage for the territory of the USA, Australia and Canada).

---

24. M. Krajewski, Ubezpieczenie odpowiedzialności cywilnej według kodeksu cywilnego. and K. Malinowska-Kamińska, Product Liability Insurance 1 *Prawo Asekuracyjne* (2000).

528. Typical policies cover bodily injury and property damage, including consequential damages; pure financial loss usually requires an extension of coverage at an additional premium; most non-US insurers exclude punitive damages from coverage; the scope of product liability insurance covers losses suffered by third parties as a result of the use or consumption of goods specified in the policy and which have caused death, bodily injury or impairment of health, damage to or destruction of property. Irrespective of the amount of damage caused by an event, the Insurer's liability is determined by the civil liability of the Insured in connection with the damage caused, up to the Guaranteed Amount, which is the upper limit of the Insurer's liability.

529. In addition to the damage caused to third parties, the insurer is obliged to reimburse the insured for the costs of experts and surveyors, as well as for the costs of legal defence.

530. However, the insurance does not normally cover damage which the manufacturer is obliged to cover under a guarantee or warranty; damage caused as a result of the withdrawal from the market of a certain range of goods and products; damage caused by acts of war or the use of nuclear energy.

531. Similar to general liability insurance, in product liability insurance, the insurer imposes on the insured a duty to cooperate in the settlement of the claim as a result of the third party's claim, especially if the third party has initiated legal proceedings against the insured.

§4. Environmental Insurance

532. As in other EU countries, the Environmental Liability Directive introduces the 'polluter pays' principle. Its main objective is to make companies that have caused environmental damage financially responsible. As a result, the rules on environmental liability are very restrictive, which in turn should encourage Polish companies to seek insurance coverage for their potential liability for environmental damage. The Act of 13 April 2007 on the Prevention and Remedying of Environmental Damage (Journal of Laws 2007, No. 75, item 493) introduced liability for environmental damage in a scope that goes far beyond the protection provided by the application of the relevant extension clause in the company's liability insurance. The greatest importance should be attached to liability under the Act on Prevention of Environmental Damage and Remediation of Environmental Damage, where liability is of an administrative-legal nature and its scope also covers elements of the environment that are in the possession of the entity that uses the environment. The entity using the environment is responsible not only for the damage caused to third parties but also for the damage caused to the elements of the environment. The aforementioned law defines a detailed scope of activities that the responsible entity is obliged to undertake in order to ensure that the environment is restored to its pre-damage state. In essence, these regulations apply to virtually all business entities and impose a new, broader scope of liability for environmental damage.[25]

533. However, this insurance is not compulsory, which has a negative impact on the level of insurance among Polish companies. The issue of environmental insurance has recently become the subject of public discussion, and many insurers currently see an opportunity for the future in the development of this type of coverage, especially in light of the new environmental protection laws. There is a growing demand in the market for this type of protection against events that often have serious financial consequences (especially for small businesses).

534. The main purchasers of environmental liability insurance in Poland are local authorities and entrepreneurs. This type of insurance is purchased mainly by medium and large companies. This is especially the case if their activities include, even as a secondary activity, the collection and production of waste or the operation of waste disposal sites, for which they must obtain the necessary permits. The environmental policy can be a form of cover for claims relating to such activity, which is required by the authority issuing the permit. This fact was reflected in a temporary surge in interest in such insurance when the amendments to the Waste Act came into force. However, most local authorities and entrepreneurs limit themselves to adding environmental clauses to their liability policies.

535. In the context of liability for environmental damage, it is important to define environmental damage, which is a change in the state or natural elements (ecosystem) assessed in relation to the initial state, caused directly or indirectly by the activity of the entity using the environment. The damage may affect: water, land, protected species and natural and legal persons. According to the principles of liability, any entity that has caused environmental damage may be required by public authorities to take preventive and corrective measures: (1) clean-up of the site, restoration of the habitat, recovery of the site's population, remediation of contaminated soil, relocation of protected species from contaminated waters, creation of new breeding sites, creation of alternative habitats; (2) compensation to natural and legal persons; (3) reconstruction and restoration of the contaminated ecosystem; (4) possible litigation costs, including legal defence costs. The legislation has introduced the 'polluter pays' principle. This means that in many cases liability will be imposed regardless of actual fault. In addition, in certain legal situations, the owner (landowner) will also be liable. This will be the case if the damage was caused with the owner's knowledge or consent.

536. Liability for environmental damage under recent changes in the law goes beyond the scope of standard general liability insurance. First, general liability insurance does not cover management liability. It covers damage caused to third

25. D. Maśniak, Ubezpieczenia ekologiczne, 2011.

parties (personal injury, property damage or pure financial loss) and protects the civil liability of the insured, but not directly the environmental damage covered by the administrative liability regime.

537. Standard public liability insurance excludes environmental damage, although it usually offers the option of purchasing what is commonly referred to as an environmental clause. The majority of third-party liability insurance products on offer do not provide full coverage for environmental damage and only offer coverage for damage that is more incidental to pollution – bodily injury, property damage resulting from the emission of polluting substances – insurers usually limit coverage to sudden damage and often introduce a specific time period, e.g., seventy-two hours, for reporting damage – this is a very serious limitation because in the case of environmental damage, reporting damage usually takes much longer. As a result, a typical insurance policy will cover only a marginal portion of the potential damage and, because of the shortened time period of occurrence, the potential cost will also be limited. The underlying risks that can cause extensive damage and very high costs will still be outside the protection provided. In addition, some clauses provide protection to ensure that the costs of removing pollutants are covered. However, long-term damage, the cost of restoring the environment to its pre-damage state, compensation for ecosystem damage – damage to biodiversity (damage to protected species, natural habitats) and other elements of the environment, and administrative liability remain outside the scope of protection. As this extension is part of the general liability policy, the insurer only covers bodily injury and property damage caused by emissions to third parties. Alternatively, it may also cover the costs of removal or clean-up and disposal, but only those incurred by third parties. The insured's own costs are not covered. Such additional clauses cover bodily injury and property damage to third parties occurring during the period of insurance as a result of an event specified in the GCU (i.e., discharge, spread, release, emission of smoke, fumes, soot, acids, alkalis, toxic chemicals (liquid or gaseous), surplus materials or other substances polluting the soil, atmosphere or water) and cover such damage only if several criteria are met. The first requirement is that the event must have occurred within the scope of the insured activity and be confirmed by the relevant service. The market standard always provides coverage only for damage that is more incidental to environmental pollution – personal injury or property damage resulting from the emission of pollutants. In addition, some clauses provide cover for the cost of removing polluting substances. However, the scope of protection does not cover long-term damage, the cost of restoring the environment to its pre-damage state, compensation for ecosystem damage – damage to biodiversity (damage to protected species, natural habitats) and other elements of the environment.

538. The most comprehensive solution is dedicated environmental insurance, known as 'stand alone' policies. This insurance only covers environmental damage and various costs associated with cleaning up the damage. What is special about environmental liability insurance is that it covers not only the cost of cleaning up and removing pollution from someone else's land but also the cost of cleaning up your own land. Importantly, such insurance can also cover damage caused by gradual events (e.g., slow release of pollutants into the ground). The insurance will cover costs related to damage to protected species or restoration of natural habitats. Optionally, environmental insurance can also cover the costs of the insured's business interruption, transport damage, risks associated with contract work and historical damage – this is very important because the law states that liability can be transferred if no more than thirty years have passed since the emission or other event that caused the immediate threat of environmental damage or the damage itself. The following costs are covered by environmental insurance Clean-up costs – full cover for the costs of cleaning up and repairing property damage. This applies to both your own and third-party property; Remedial and Preventive Measures – coverage for costs associated with measures taken to prevent or minimise the effects of environmental damage; Biodiversity Damage – coverage for environmental damage in the full range of remedial, supplemental and compensatory measures relating to water, land surface, protected species and natural habitats; Business interruption – coverage of financial losses resulting from business interruption; Third-party claims for bodily injury or property damage – coverage of costs related to third party claims for bodily injury or property damage resulting from both sudden and gradual events; Legal defence costs – coverage of costs of defence and legal assistance. This solution is not yet popular in Poland, but recent events, such as the failure of the largest sewage treatment plant in Warsaw, may influence its popularisation.

539. Examples of recent environmental damage in Poland include:

1. Failure of a pumping station in Gdansk – A serious failure occurred at the Olowianka sewage pumping station. In order to avoid the risk of sewage backflow and flooding in the Gdansk districts, the company providing water and sewage services decided to discharge the sewage into the Motlawa River. The Gdańsk Public Prosecutor's Office decided to initiate proceedings under Article 182 of the Penal Code. The case concerns environmental pollution.
2. Leakage of fuel from a tanker lorry – as a result of a traffic accident, the lorry overturned and spilled 4,000 litres of fuel.
3. Brine leak from a pipeline in Inowrocław – the leak was probably caused by a pipeline failure. Research shows that the concentration of chlorides is a thousand times higher than in uncontaminated soil.
4. Oil pipeline rupture near Pruszcz Gdanski – as a result of illegal drilling into a PERN oil pipeline, crude oil leaked into nearby drainage ditches in an undeveloped area.
5. Oil spill in the Oder River – 14.7.2018 Oil leaked into the Oder River in Zakrzowa.

§5. Professional Liability Insurance

540. Currently, most PII is compulsory insurance imposed on professionals by law.

541. The most common types of mandatory PII include:

- insurance for tax advisors;
- auditors' insurance;
- brokers' insurance;
- tourist Agents' Insurance;
- attorneys insurance;
- notaries Public Insurance;
- debt collection insurance.

542. There are many voluntary professional insurance products on the market. Professional liability insurance, at least those that are compulsory, is based on the act committed trigger. The scope of this type of insurance covers damage caused by professionals to third parties as a result of the exercise of their professional activities. The fact that they act on the basis of an order from a third party is taken into account, and their liability is of a contractual nature (as a result of the non-performance or improper performance of their contractual obligations).

543. The terms and conditions of compulsory professional indemnity insurance are issued on the basis of statutory law in the form of executive acts, usually issued by the relevant ministers.

544. Voluntary professional indemnity insurance can be either excess to compulsory insurance or purely voluntary. Both can be designed on the basis of the freedom of contract rule.

Chapter 5. Legal Aid Insurance

545. Legal expenses insurance is usually offered in two forms: either as an add-on to another type of liability insurance or as a separate product. It is a voluntary insurance. Some insurers operating in the Polish market offer legal expenses insurance as a separate product or as a supplement. The insurance covers the costs of legal assistance in civil, criminal and/or administrative proceedings. Legal expenses insurance is available for various lines of business, including: motor, personal, professional or business. Insurance contracts are usually concluded for a period of twelve months.

546. The purpose of this type of insurance is to protect the interests of the insured in legal proceedings. The insurance coverage is usually provided in such a way that the insurer provides the insured with the possibility of legal assistance or that the insurer covers the costs of such legal assistance, including the coverage of court fees.

547. The scope of legal expenses insurance normally excludes the insurer's liability for:

- criminal proceedings against the insured;
- fines and fines imposed on the insured during the proceedings as a result of the insured's intentional conduct;
- wilful omission to conclude a settlement.

Chapter 6. Aviation and Space Insurance

548. The aviation insurance market in Poland is relatively small and not very visible. However, interest in aviation insurance has been growing over the decades, due to the increasing popularity of sports, competitions and air shows, as well as the growing legal awareness of aircraft users. Aviation insurance is mainly aimed at people who use aircraft for tourist, private, rescue or training purposes. The basic principle of traditional insurance markets is that the premiums of the many cover the losses of the few. The aviation insurance market has always differed from most other insurance markets primarily in that both the premium base and the customer base are very limited, with a small number of policyholders.

549. The Polish insurance market follows the global practice of insuring aviation risks on standard reinsurance terms. As far as aviation insurance is concerned, it is in fact a type of transport insurance and therefore, similarly to land and marine transport insurance, it can be divided into four categories: (1) insurance of an aircraft against loss or damage (aero-casco); (2) insurance of the liability of an air carrier and a person using an aircraft (OC); (3) coverage of personal injury and death (NNW); (4) cargo insurance (aero-cargo).[26]

550. There is no space insurance on the Polish market, as the Polish space sector is underdeveloped and there is no local demand for this type of insurance. The Polish space industry consists of designers and manufacturers of space equipment components and there are no integrators of satellite systems. There are also no space operators based in Poland. Satellite insurance is usually offered as co-insurance by several insurers, so it cannot be ruled out that Polish insurers will offer part of the coverage, although no Polish space insurance conditions have been drafted yet.

§1. Aero-Casco

551. This type of insurance is intended for natural or legal persons who own or use civil aircraft for private or professional purposes. As far as the type of aircraft is concerned, Aero-Casco insurance can cover all civil aircraft, such as aeroplanes, gliders, balloons, hang-gliders, parachutes, medical aircraft or seaplanes. The policy is usually taken out for one year, but it is also possible to take out cover for a shorter period.

552. This type of insurance, like hull insurance or autocasco in car insurance, covers the loss of or damage to the aircraft. The main elements of this type of cover include compensation in the event of damage to an aircraft, for example, during a stopover, take-off, flight or overhaul. The cover may be limited to risks on land or extended to risks in the air. Given the variety of aircraft in actual use, there are none of the stereotyped policies or rigid tariffs seen in other lines of insurance. In fact,

26. D. Fuchs, K. Malinowska & D. Maśniak, Kontrakty na rynku ubezpieczeń, 2020.

policies are tailor-made and the premium reflects the risk and the level of cover. For this reason, cover is usually arranged by brokers.

553. In general terms, aero-casco insurance covers losses caused by collision with land and other objects during flight, landing, take-off and modernisation; by fire, lightning, storm, hail, flood or subsidence; by theft or robbery; by any other event caused by third parties other than crew members. Also included are certain incidental losses such as salvage, transportation and claims settlement costs.

554. At the same time, insurers generally exclude from coverage losses caused while the aircraft is being piloted by an unauthorised person; caused by exceeding the agreed flight envelope; during acrobatic flights; caused by leaving the aircraft without proper care; caused while operating an aircraft in connection with its obligatory services for the army; caused intentionally by the insured or by a person for whom the insured is responsible; caused by gross negligence on the part of the aforementioned persons, unless payment of compensation would be justified by the principles of community life, taking into account all the circumstances of the case.

555. Some insurers impose an overriding obligation on the insured to maintain the aircraft in a fit and airworthy condition, to provide it with all necessary documentation and to comply with the relevant aviation regulations.

556. As with marine insurance, the policy may be taken out for an agreed period of time or for a particular voyage. In addition, the policy may be taken out for a specific aircraft or for some or all of the aircraft owned by the insured (so-called fleet insurance).

§2. Third-Party Liability Insurance

557. Liability insurance plays a greater role in aviation insurance. Air carrier liability insurance was mainly introduced by the Montreal Convention and is also widely used by the European legislator. The Convention was approved by Council Decision 2001/539/EC3. As a result, the Montreal Convention for the Unification of Certain Rules for International Carriage by Air has become an integral part of the legal order of the EU. It can therefore be assumed that the basis for Community regulation is Article 50 of the Montreal Convention, which requires the contracting parties to ensure that air carriers are adequately insured to cover their liability under the Convention.

558. The obligation to insure the air carrier and the aircraft operator has also been introduced in the Aviation Act, where Article 209 provides that '1. Air carriers and aircraft operators shall be obliged to take out civil liability insurance for damage caused in connection with their air operations in accordance with Regulation (EC) No 785/2004 of the European Parliament and of the Council of 21 April 2004 on insurance requirements for air carriers and aircraft operators (OJ L 138, p. 1), subject to the provisions issued on the basis of Article 33(2).' Thus, the Polish law does not constitute an independent regulation but is intended to implement the Regulation. What is more important are regulations that define the scope of insurance in the area not regulated by the Regulation.

559. In view of the above, it should be noted that in the Polish legal system, there are five types of compulsory civil liability insurance, the source of which is international law and the law of the EU. These are:

> (3) liability insurance of air carriers for damage caused during carriage of mail by air (Article 209(3) of the Commercial Code); (4) liability insurance of air carriers for damage caused during carriage of mail by air (Article 209(4) of the Commercial Code) (5) liability insurance of ground-handling service providers for damage caused in connection with their aviation activities (Article 209(5) of the said Law).

560. When analysing the nature and content of an air carrier's insurance obligation, it is necessary to start with the structure of the compulsory insurance system in Polish law. This is because it will have an overwhelming influence on the final form of the content of this insurance. First of all, it concerns the legal nature of the obligation to insure, on which the application of the relevant provisions regulating the insurance contract will depend. In the Polish legal system, the obligation to insure arises, in principle, from the Act on Compulsory Insurance, the UFG, the Guarantee Fund and the Polish Motor Insurers Bureau, where Article 3 defines compulsory insurance as any liability insurance, civil liability insurance of an entity or property insurance if the obligation to conclude an insurance contract is imposed by a law or an act ratified by the Republic of Poland or an international agreement ratified by the Republic of Poland. In this respect, Article 4 of the AIA is also relevant, which in the catalogue of obligatory insurances, in addition to the so-called general obligatory insurances, in point 4 lists insurances resulting from separate acts or international agreements ratified by Poland, which impose an obligation on certain entities to conclude an insurance contract. In view of the above provisions, it is clear that only in the case when a given insurance fulfils the conditions set out in Articles 3 and 4 of the Insurance Act, it will be subject to specific rules binding the parties to the insurance relationship specified in the Act. Due to the nature of the insurance imposed on the air carrier, it appears that it fulfils both conditions, i.e., it is third-party liability insurance and it was imposed by an international agreement ratified by Poland.[27]

561. In the field of air transport, Article 7 of Regulation 2407/92 requires air carriers to be insured against liability in the event of accidents, in particular in respect of passengers, baggage, cargo, mail and third parties but does not specify the minimum amounts or conditions of insurance. In addition, the European Civil Aviation Conference adopted on 13 December 2000 Resolution ECAC/25-1 on minimum insurance cover for liability in respect of passengers and third parties. The entities

27. A. Konert, *Ubezpieczenia lotnicze*. Warsaw: Kluwer, 2014.

subject to the insurance obligation are those authorised to carry out aviation activities. The Aviation Law provides for the obligation to insure an 'air carrier', which is defined in Article 2(16) of the Air Law as 'an entity entitled to provide air transport services on the basis of a licence' – in the case of a Polish air carrier, or on the basis of an appropriate act of the competent authority of a foreign state – in the case of a 'foreign air carrier'. In addition, the obligation to insure applies to ground-handling companies and air navigation service providers, which are obliged to conclude an insurance contract against civil liability for damage caused in connection with aviation activities (Article 209.5 of the Law on Aviation).

562. The insurance obligation is defined in relation to the activity carried out, irrespective of the material rights to the aircraft. Thus, air carriers and aircraft operators provide insurance cover for each flight, regardless of whether their interest in the aircraft results from ownership, any form of lease, joint or franchised operation, code-sharing or any other similar arrangement.

563. However, the insurance obligation of air carriers does not apply to State aircraft ('aircraft used in military, customs and police services shall be considered as State aircraft'). The Convention on International Civil Aviation was signed in Chicago on 7 December 1944. excludes the obligation to insure model aircraft with a maximum take-off mass (MTOM) of less than 20 kg, foot-launched flying machines (including powered paragliders and powered hang-gliders), tethered balloons, kites, parachutes (including towed parachutes), aircraft launched by towing aircraft, including gliders, with an MTOM of less than 500 kg, and micro-light aircraft, used for non-commercial purposes or for local instructional flights not involving the crossing of international borders, to the extent that Regulation No. 785/2004 concerns insurance obligations relating to the risks of war and terrorism. However, in the case of 'transit flights over the territory of a Member State by a non-Community air carrier or aircraft registered outside the Community without having landed in or taken off from a Member State, each Member State shall be entitled, in accordance with international law, to require evidence of compliance with the insurance requirements contained in this Regulation, for example by means of random checks'. (Recital 18 of Regulation 785/2004). However, as stated in the preamble of the Regulation, Member States should avoid the obligation of double insurance.

564. In the case of liability insurance of air carriers in respect of damage caused by delay in the carriage of passengers, baggage or cargo, and in respect of damage caused by the carriage of passengers, baggage or cargo, the insurance obligation shall take effect at the latest on the day before the commencement of the air transport operation, in the case of liability insurance of ground handling service providers in respect of damage caused by delay in the carriage of passengers, baggage or cargo, or in respect of damage caused by the carriage of mail by air, the insurance obligation shall take effect at the latest on the day before the commencement of the air transport operation, or, in the case of liability insurance for air navigation service providers for damage caused in connection with their air navigation activity, the obligation to insure arises at the latest on the day before the commencement of the air operation, and in the case of liability insurance for air navigation service providers for damage caused in connection with their air navigation activity, the obligation to insure arises at the latest on the day before the commencement of the air operation. In the case of liability insurance of air navigation service providers for damage caused in connection with their aviation activity – on the day before the commencement of their aviation activity, at the latest on the day before the commencement of their aviation activity.

565. The European regulation contains several important elements for defining the subject and scope of insurance. First, the insurance obligation covers the risk of civil liability of the air carrier, both for personal injury and damage to property. Separate rules apply to civil liability for mail carried, which was excluded from the scope of the Montreal Convention. It is governed by Regulation 2407/92, and Polish law expressly provides for the obligation to take out insurance in this respect.

566. Undoubtedly, an important element of insurance coverage is its temporal scope, commonly referred to as the trigger. In the case of voluntary insurance, the parties are free to define the insured event, which must occur during the insurance period. In the case of compulsory insurance, the determination of the triggering event is one of the elements that create the content of the insurance obligation. This is also the case for an air carrier's civil liability insurance. The Regulation on compulsory insurance of civil liability of air carriers, ground handling companies and air navigation service providers provides that civil liability insurance shall cover damage caused by an act or omission of the insured during the period of insurance in connection with aviation operations. This means that the following triggering act applies.

567. A necessary element of the insurance obligation is the requirement to conclude an insurance contract with a legally defined guarantee amount. In the case of aviation liability insurance, this guarantee amount results from Regulation No. 785/2004, the provisions of the Aviation Act and the Regulation on compulsory civil liability insurance of air carriers, ground handlers and air navigation service providers issued on the basis of this Act. The Montreal Convention does not provide any specific guidance in this regard, other than to state that the insurance should cover the liability of air carriers. This in turn demonstrates the need for national (and European) legislators to calculate liability, which will in principle correspond to the Probable Maximum Loss (PML), a method of risk calculation for large risks.

568. In practice, the above distinctions between conditions and amounts of cover apply, despite the fact that different types of compulsory insurance are marketed in aviation. It is possible to obtain separate cover for liability for damage caused to third parties (so-called public liability insurance), separate cover for passenger liability, or a combination of both types of compulsory insurance in one agreement, then called a Combined Single Limit (CSL), where the sum insured in respect of one event is limited to.[28]

569. The insurers pay compensation in the event that the insured person is obliged by mandatory legal provisions to make good the damage caused as a result of death, bodily injury, impairment of health, destruction of or damage to property. In fact, the insurance cover includes two types of civil liability of the insured person, which derive from different legal regimes: a contractual liability of the air carrier towards the other party to the contract of carriage, and a tort liability as owner and air carrier. In particular, an air carrier is liable for damage caused by death of or bodily injury to passengers as a result of an accident on board an aircraft or while boarding or disembarking from an aircraft; arising in connection with the loss, partial loss or damage of registered goods or luggage during their carriage by air; occurring in the passenger's baggage or personal effects; for damage caused to parties not having a contractual relationship with the Insured as a person using the aircraft, the latter may be held liable on the basis of the general rules of Polish civil law and, in particular, taking into account Articles 434–436 of the PCC.

§3. Consequential Bodily Injury and Death Coverage

570. Usually, this type of insurance covers losses suffered by the crew of the aircraft – pilots, navigators, radio operators, engineers, stewardesses and stewards, training personnel or other individually specified employees of the carrier. The insurance is not compulsory, so the parties are free to agree on the scope of coverage. The scope of the insurance cover is very wide and includes many typical aviation risks, including those related to the actual or intended hijacking of the aircraft, its seizure, arrest or detention, as well as losses incurred during salvage operations. At the same time, however, the insurer is usually exempted from any liability for losses incurred during unauthorised sporting, acrobatic and/or towing flights and during participation in air competitions.

§4. Aero-Cargo

571. For the carriage of goods by air, insurers offer Institute Cargo Clauses (Air), Institute Strike Clauses (Air Cargo) and Institute War Clauses (Air Cargo).

572. Leaving aside both the Institute Strike Clauses and the War Clauses, which provide special cover, it is worth paying more attention to the Institute Cargo Clauses (Air). They include all possible risks for the insurance and at the same time make several reservations with regard to the insurer's liability. With the exception of damage caused by the wilful misconduct of the insured person, they exempt the insurer from all types of liability in connection with any problems that may arise

28. A. Konert, *Ubezpieczenia lotnicze*. Warsaw: Kluwer, 2014.

with the cargo and its packaging that are beyond the insured services as an air carrier (loss of weight, inadequate packaging, inherent vice of the goods, etc.), damage caused by delay, insolvency or financial default of the owners, managers, charterers or operators of the aircraft, and the use of any weapon of war using nuclear energy. In addition, the insurance does not cover losses arising out of acts of war, arrest and dereliction of duty. Finally, the insurance does not cover losses resulting from or caused by strikes, lockouts and similar events, as well as acts of terrorism.

573. The insurance covers not only the air transport but also the entire route from the warehouses or premises or other places of storage to the consignee or other final warehouse, premises or place of storage. The insurance also remains in force during delays for which the Insured is not responsible. In the event of a loss, the Insured is obliged to take all reasonable measures to avoid or minimise such loss. The Insurer undertakes to reimburse the Insured for all expenses duly and reasonably incurred in the performance of such duty.

Chapter 7. Theft and Embezzlement Insurance

§1. General

574. Theft insurance is one of the most common types of non-life insurance concluded on the Polish market and is offered by any insurer operating in the non-life insurance sector. It is concluded both by natural persons wishing to protect their property and by companies. As far as the general conditions are concerned, there are no significant differences in the individual provisions offered by insurers.[29]

575. Misappropriation insurance is a product designed to provide comprehensive protection for direct financial losses incurred by manufacturing and service companies as a result of crimes committed against them. It has only recently entered the Polish insurance market and is usually offered by foreign insurers. Observation of crime and embezzlement trends around the world leads to the conclusion that the number and value of individual losses are increasing. This is due, among other things, to the spread of information technology, which makes it possible to conduct business at a distance, the spread of computer viruses, the modification and destruction of electronic computer viruses and the modification and destruction of electronic information. Many offences are committed in an attempt to cover up previous mistakes. The general practice for this type of damage is to keep it secret for fear of losing the company's credibility.[30]

§2. Subject of Insurance

576. This type of insurance provides protection against the negative consequences of the loss of property as a result of theft. It should be noted that despite advanced technologies used to protect property, the number of thefts does not decrease. That is why theft insurance is very common in Poland. It is also worth mentioning that preventive activity still plays an important role in this type of insurance. It depends to a large extent on the securities used to protect the insured property. The policyholder who provides additional securities can obtain significant discounts – up to 50% of the premium.

577. There is an extensive list of objects that can be treated as the subject of insurance because they are in the possession of the insured. In general, it is movable property that the insured owns or has a legal title to, such as: goods, raw materials, semi-finished goods, packages, stored and out-of-use machinery, apparatus, equipment, spare parts, cash and securities, platinum, gold, silver, pearls, precious stones, property of third parties temporarily taken for the provision of services, equipment and installations of industrial plants, ships, warehouses, shops and

29. D. Gołębiewski in: D. Fuchs, K.Malinowska & D. Maśniak, Kontrakty na rynku ubezpieczeń, 2020.
30. Raport Marsh Financial Lines: Time to Build resilience, https://www.marsh.com/pl/pl/about/media/raport-marsh--financial-lines--time-to-build-resilience.html, accessed 23 Dec. 2024.

offices. As a rule, documents, collections and objects of scientific value are not covered. However, they may be covered by a separate agreement between the parties.

578. Embezzlement insurance (economic crime insurance) covers direct or financial loss resulting from any act of embezzlement or dishonesty committed by an employee. It may also cover damage caused by computer crime, forgery or counterfeiting committed by persons who are not employees of the company, and damage caused by theft.

§3. Scope of Insurance

579. Theft insurance. The insurance covers the risk of loss, destruction or damage to the insured object as a result of theft or robbery. The Insurer is also liable for damage to the security of the premises where the object is located, even if the burglary was unsuccessful, i.e., the perpetrator did not gain access to the insured premises (attempted burglary).

580. Loss is defined as the physical loss or diminution in value of the insured property as a result of the insured event. The standard definition of burglary includes theft or attempted theft of property from the premises or other place secured in accordance with minimum security requirements: (1) after the perpetrator has forcibly removed or opened the security device; (2) after the perpetrator has forcibly removed the security device or opened the entrance using tools; or (3) after the offender has forcibly removed the security device or opened the entrance by using tools or a forged or duplicated key or an original key which has come into the offender's possession as a result of a burglary or robbery of other premises; or (4) by the offender who has concealed himself in the premises before they were locked if he has left traces which may serve as evidence of his concealment.

581. Robbery is usually defined as the taking of property by using or threatening to use physical force against a person, or causing a person to become unconscious or defenceless; it is also considered robbery when a person uses or threatens to use physical force against a person, causing a person to become unconscious or defenceless; robbery also includes the taking of property by force against an object of robbery – the taking of property by force against the object of robbery which was in contact with or connected to a person.

582. The insurance of property against robbery is usually extended to the damage that occurred during its transport. It is common to extend the scope of theft insurance to the risk of destruction as a result of robbery.

583. Crime insurance. The insurance covers direct financial loss suffered by the insured as a result of a criminal act of theft, misappropriation, embezzlement, hacking into a computer system and employee dishonesty. The loss must occur during the policy period and must be reported to the insurer within that period (or within a specified additional claim period after the policy expires). The insurance covers, among other things, the following offences Theft of money, securities or other property of the insured by employees acting alone or in concert with third parties, direct loss of money or securities as a result of their destruction, unexplained disappearance or removal from the insured premises, direct loss of money or securities as a result of their destruction, unexplained disappearance or removal while being transported by the insured, an employee of the insured, a security company or other authorised person, direct financial loss as a result of the forgery or alteration of any cheque, draft, bill of exchange or other promise to pay purporting to have been made by or addressed to the Insured, hacking into the Insured's computer system resulting in loss of money, property or other financial loss as a result of the manipulation, deletion, introduction of fraudulent data or alteration of computer programs.

§4. Limitation in Coverage

584. The standard exclusions for theft insurance include the transport of money within the insured premises; files, documents, manuscripts and data on media of any kind; documents, manuscripts and data on media of any kind; prototypes, models and museum or antique exhibits; antiques, works of art, philatelic collections; antiques, works of art, philatelic and numismatic collections; computer programs unless they are current assets; narcotics, psychotropic substances, payment, credit, charge or debit cards of any kind, property located in an unused building, premises if unused for an extended period of time, property which has passed its sell-by date or has been withdrawn from the market prior to the occurrence of the loss.

585. In the case of *commercial crime insurance*, the standard exclusions on the Polish market relate to fines, penalties or compensation payable by law, errors or omissions by the Insured or its employees, losses caused by persons owning or controlling more than 10% of the share capital or the capital of the Insured, loss of confidential information, loss of confidential information, although the insurance covers loss arising from the use of confidential information in such a way as to assist in the performance of an activity covered by this insurance, indirect and consequential loss, income or profits (including, but not limited to, interest and dividends). In addition, standard exclusions such as war, nuclear risks, government action, etc., are applied.

§5. Types of Insurance and Insurance Sums

586. Depending on the nature of the property, it may be insured under the following insurance system:

- on a fixed sum basis;
- multiple and aggregate fixed sum basis;
- on a first-risk basis;
- on the basis of monthly turnover.

587. The following, among others, can be insured on a fixed sum basis: goods, raw materials in process, semi-finished products, finished products, auxiliary materials and packaging, stored and unused machinery, apparatus, equipment, etc., and property received from third parties for the purpose of providing services. The joint and several fixed sum insurance systems can be applied to all the above types of property, except for property received from third parties for the provision of services. Under the first-risk insurance system, office equipment and furniture, shops, warehouses, factories, ships, etc., can be insured. In addition, cash and other securities, platinum, gold, silver and precious stones can also be insured under this system. The monthly turnover system can only be used to insure cash.

588. For certain types of insurance, the sums insured are determined as follows:

- in fixed sum insurance – the highest daily value of the property provided for the period of insurance according to the cost of its purchase, manufacture or sale;
- in the case of joint and several insurance – the sum insured should correspond to the total value of the property located in many places and locations, but belonging to the same insured;
- in first-risk insurance – the amount of the sum insured is determined by the insured, taking into account a possible total loss resulting from an accident or theft by burglary or robbery;
- in the case of insurance based on monthly turnover – the sum insured may not exceed the above-mentioned amounts, which are provided for certain types of safes and different ways of securing cash during its transportation.

§6. Obligations of the Insured

589. In the event of a loss, the Insured is obliged to immediately take all possible measures to mitigate the loss and secure the endangered property, as well as to make efforts to recover the lost property. In the event of gross negligence on the part of the Insured in the fulfilment of the above obligations, the Insurer will be relieved of any responsibility in relation to the loss that has occurred.

590. The Insured is also obliged to notify the Insurer and the local police of the loss. In addition, the Insured should not change the facts of the case prior to the actual investigation by the Insurer, unless it is necessary to protect the property saved after the accident. The insured is also obliged to allow the insurer to carry out all the work necessary to investigate all the circumstances of the claim and to assess the amount of compensation to be paid. In this regard, the Insured should also provide the Insurer with all necessary explanations and any evidence that may be in the Insurer's possession.

§7. Evaluation of the Loss

591. According to the standard terms and conditions of *theft insurance*, there are some general principles which provide a guideline for determining the extent of loss. In the case of raw materials, semi-finished products, finished products, auxiliary materials, packaging, etc., the extent of the loss will be equal to the cost of their purchase, manufacture or sale at the prices prevailing at the time of the loss. In the case of property taken from third parties for the provision of services, the extent of the loss shall be equal to the value of the property declared by the Customer, increased by the cost of the services already provided. In the case of cash – its nominal value and in the case of securities – their market value at the time of the loss. Similar rules apply to the valuation of losses of platinum, gold, silver, precious stones, etc., taking into account the cost of purchase or production (in the case of products made from such materials). Finally, the losses of equipment in offices, shops, warehouses, ships, factories, etc., are also determined by the cost of their purchase or repair at the time of the loss.

592. Basically, the calculation of the indemnity paid to the insured person is based on the extent of the loss, but there are some additional principles for the assessment of the indemnity when the amount of loss is increased by the expenses incurred by the Insured in connection with a rescue operation carried out, even if it was justified and ultimately proved to be unsuccessful. The Insurer is also obliged to pay indemnity for losses incurred during the period of robbery.

593. The indemnity under the *robbery insurance* will be paid up to the sum insured for the loss suffered as a result of the act or acts described as an insured event. The loss must be a direct financial loss suffered by the Insured anywhere in the world as a result of a single act or a series of related, continuous or repeated acts of employee dishonesty, theft, computer crime, falsification or counterfeiting.

594. Compensation is paid for direct financial loss suffered by a person or organisation where the insured was responsible for the care, custody or control of that person or for the supervision of money, securities or other property. Compensation does not normally include salaries, commissions, fees, bonuses, promotions, awards, profit sharing, pensions or other employee benefits. The direct financial loss must occur before the end of the policy period and be disclosed before the end of the policy period or, where applicable, the disclosure period. The indemnity also includes the auditor's fees paid by the Insured (with the Insurer's approval) for the purpose of determining the nature and amount of the loss covered by this insurance. These fees form part of the sum insured.

595. In calculating the amount of indemnity payable under this policy, the assessment of direct financial loss will be influenced by the following factors: (i) the lower of the monetary value of other property at the time of the loss or the cost of repair or replacement with property or material of like value or quality; (ii) the exchange rates as published by the Central Bank on the day of the loss; (iii) the cost of blank books, cards, storage media and other materials and the cost of labour and computer use to copy or transcribe data for the purpose of reconstructing books, records and electronic data; (iv) the actual cost of restoring the computer, network or electronic commerce services to their working condition prior to the occurrence of the loss.

§8. Regaining Lost Property

596. The Insured is obliged to inform the Insurer immediately of the location of the stolen property, if such information is available, and to take the necessary steps to identify and recover the property. If the property is recovered in the same condition as when it was stolen, the Insurer will not have to pay any compensation, and if it has already been paid, the Insured is obliged to repay it immediately. However, if the insured property is recovered in a damaged or incomplete state, the indemnity will be paid only in the percentage that the value of the lost property remains of its original value at the time the extent of the loss was assessed. In general, the insured is obliged to accept the recovered property. However, more recent practice is that the insured assigns the lost property to the insurer and, if this is the case, the consequences of the recovery of the lost property are dealt with by the insurer as the new owner of the property.

§9. Recourse Claims

597. The insurer is subrogated by the insured with all rights against a person who is actually responsible for the loss up to the amount of the compensation paid to the insured. If the insurer has only compensated the insured for part of the loss, the insured has the right to recover the remaining part of the loss before the insurer's claims. At the same time, however, the Insured is obliged, at the Insurer's request, to provide all possible assistance in the pursuit of recourse claims against third parties responsible for the damage.

Chapter 8. Agricultural Insurance, Hail Insurance, Livestock Insurance

§1. Compulsory Insurance of Third-Party Liability of Farmers

598. Farmers' liability insurance is recognised as one of the most important types of compulsory insurance in Poland, along with motor vehicle liability insurance. This is due to the fact that the Polish economy was strongly agricultural until a few decades ago. Moreover, one of the reasons for the introduction of such a comprehensive system of compulsory liability insurance for farmers was the low level of insurance awareness among this social group. For this reason, this insurance was included among the three main types of compulsory insurance in the 2003 Act on Compulsory Insurance. Thus, the general rules of this insurance are similar to other types of compulsory insurance directly provided for in the Compulsory Insurance Act.

599. The duration of the insurance is twelve months and the automatic renewal of the contract for the next period is provided for according to the same rules as for compulsory motor vehicle liability insurance.

600. The insurance covers the liability of the farmer, as well as the liability of any other person living in the same household as the farmer, or any person working on the farm during the period of insurance, who has caused the damage.

601. The damage covered by the insurance should be related to the ownership of the farm (and, of course, the farming activity) and result in death, bodily injury, impairment of health or loss or destruction of property. The insurance also covers liability for damage caused by slow-moving vehicles (i.e., special category of vehicles defined in the Road Traffic Act), if such vehicle is owned by the farmer in connection with the operation of the farm.

602. There are some exclusions of the Insurer's liability if the claims brought against the insured farmer are subject to Polish law and relate to the following losses: (1) caused by the transmission of infectious diseases other than those of animal origin; (2) damage caused by defective products supplied by the insured person or caused during the provision of services; if such defects cause personal injury, the Insurer is not liable only if the insured person was aware of such defects; (3) Damage, destruction, loss or disappearance of items borrowed or received for use, storage or repair by the person covered by the TPL insurance of farmers; (4) Loss of cash, jewellery, works of art, securities, all types of documents or collections of stamps, coins, etc.; (5) Pollution or contamination of the environment; (6) Resulting from fines, court and administrative fines, as well as fines or penalties related to amounts due to the state budget. Due to the compulsory nature of the insurance, the Insurer may not impose any further exclusions.

603. The insurer who has paid the indemnity has the right of recourse against the person who caused the damage (even if it is the policyholder) if the damage was caused intentionally or subsequently under the influence of alcohol or narcotics or psychotropic substances or substitutes, as defined by the provisions on the fight against drug addiction.

604. The amount of compensation is determined and paid up to the legal limits of civil liability of the insured persons. These limits are as follows: (1) in the case of personal injury – EUR 3,000,000 per occurrence; (2) in the case of damage to property – EUR 1,000,000 per occurrence, the consequences of which are covered by the insurance regardless of the number of injured parties, calculated at the average exchange rate published by the Central Bank on the day the damage occurs.

605. The obligation to take out insurance arises on the day the farmer takes possession of the holding. The definition of an agricultural holding has been included in the law on compulsory insurance, as it is essential for determining whether or not there is an obligation to insure. The farm is defined as the area of arable land, including the area of ponds and the area of land classified as arable land and occupied by farm buildings, which exceeds the total area of 1.0 hectare if it is subject to agricultural tax, as well as the area of such arable land or land, irrespective of its area, if it is used for agricultural production, which constitutes its special branch of production within the meaning of the provisions on personal income tax.

606. The insurance coverage begins on the date of the contract and the payment of the premium or its first instalment. If a later deadline for the payment of the premium or its first instalment has been agreed, the Insurer's liability shall commence from the moment of the conclusion of the insurance, as confirmed in the policy. Such other period for payment of the premium may be agreed if the insurance is concluded: (1) before taking possession of the farm; or (2) for the following twelve months before the beginning of this period.

607. If possession of the farm is transferred to another person after the insurance has been taken out, the farmer's rights and obligations under the insurance contract are automatically transferred to the transferee. In this case, the insurance contract will expire at the end of the period (twelve months) for which it was concluded unless the new owner cancels it within thirty days of taking over the holding. In this case, the insurance cover will be terminated with thirty days of notice and the new owner should take out a new insurance contract to cover his liability.

608. Cover will cease when the contract is cancelled as above. If the insurance contract is terminated earlier than the period for which it was concluded, the policyholder should be refunded part of the premium in proportion to the reduced period of insurance. This refund is not due if the loss covered by the insurance occurred during the period prior to the termination of the contract. The refund is due for each full month of the unused period of insurance. The amount of the monthly premium to be refunded is set at one-twelfth of the premium due for twelve months of the insurance period.

609. The insurance may be cancelled only in the limited cases specified in the law on compulsory insurance, in the following circumstances: (1) a change in the legal or factual status of the farmer which results in the farmer no longer being subject to agricultural tax or personal income tax in respect of agricultural production carried out within the scope of its special branches; or (2) at the moment when the agricultural land loses its character as an agricultural holding; or (3) the lease contract is terminated by the purchaser of the agricultural holding.

§2. Livestock Insurance

610. Under this cover, the insurer undertakes to pay compensation for losses incurred as a result of illness or accident to an animal. Compensation is also paid in the event of necessary slaughter, as confirmed by a veterinarian. The insurance covers cattle, horses, pigs, sheep, goats, fish, etc. The following losses are generally excluded from the insurance: (1) those caused by theft or slaughter; (2) those caused intentionally by the Insured or a person who shares the same household with the Insured or for whom the Insured is responsible, even if the perpetrator did not intend to deceive the Insurer; (3) those caused by gross negligence on the part of the Insured or the aforementioned persons.

611. The sums insured for livestock are equal to the value of the animal provided by its owner, based on the invoice price of the purchase of an animal, or its inventory value, or finally – a value agreed with the Insurer. However, this value should not be higher than the average free market price for a given type of livestock.

612. The amount of the loss incurred is the value of the animal immediately before its death or accident, as estimated by the veterinarian. They take into account the age and musculature of the animal, as well as the average price of livestock in the area concerned. If the meat has been declared fit for human consumption, 100% of the residual value is deducted from the amount of the claim. Irrespective of the indemnity, the Insurer will reimburse the Insured for the costs of medical treatment of livestock that have died or have been slaughtered, as certified by appropriate documents, up to a maximum of 2% of the sum insured.

613. In addition to the standard obligations of the insured person, there are also some special obligations of the insured person. Among other things, the Insured is obliged to observe the basic rules for the care, feeding and use of livestock, to comply with the relevant rules for the prevention of infectious diseases and, in the event of necessary slaughter, to submit the meat to the relevant veterinary examination. The Insurer may refuse to indemnify if one of the first two obligations is not fulfilled as a result of the Insured's wilful misconduct and was the actual cause of the loss. Consequently, for any contributory negligence of the insured person, the insurer is entitled to reduce the indemnity proportionately, if the negligent behaviour had an adverse effect on the extent of the damage that occurred.

§3. Compulsory Insurance of Agricultural Crop

614. The provisions of the law of 7 July 2005 on the insurance of agricultural crops and livestock imply the obligation for a farmer who has received direct payments for agricultural land to take out an insurance contract for at least one of the five risks specified in the law, covering at least 50% of the area under agricultural crops. The insurance obligation is deemed to have been fulfilled if, from 1 July of the year following the year in which the farmer received direct payments, at least 50% of the area under crops is insured against at least one of the risks listed below within a period of twelve months. Co-financing from the national budget is possible.

615. The insurance obligation applies to the following crops: cereals, maize, rape and colza seeds, sugar beet, legumes, potatoes, tobacco and hops, ground vegetables, fruit trees and bushes and strawberries. A farmer is obliged to take out a crop insurance policy with an insurance company that has previously signed a subsidy agreement with the Ministry of Agriculture.

616. The insurance protects crops against, among other things, damage caused by: hurricane, flood, torrential rain, hail, lightning, landslide, avalanche, drought, winterkill or spring frost.

617. The law provides for definitions of the main risks, where, for example, flood – means damage caused by: (a) floods caused by torrential rain (rain with a rainfall coefficient of at least four; if this coefficient cannot be determined, the actual state and extent of the damage at the place of origin, clearly indicating the effect of the torrential rain, shall be taken into account); (b) run-off of water on slopes in mountain and foothill areas. Drought – means damage caused by the occurrence, during any six-day period from 21 March to 30 September, of a reduction in the climatic water balance below the level specified for certain crops. Soil hail – means damage caused by precipitation consisting of lumps of ice. Winter damage – means damage caused by freezing, wetting, evaporation, desiccation or frost during the period from 1 December to 30 April, resulting in total or partial destruction of plants or total or partial loss of crops. Spring frost: damage caused by temperatures below 0ºC during the period from 15 April to 30 June, resulting in the total or partial destruction of plants or the total or partial loss of the crop.

618. Failure to take out compulsory crop insurance results in a penalty of EUR 2 per uninsured hectare. The penalties cannot be applied if the farmer does not take out compulsory insurance because he has received a written refusal from at least two insurance companies that have concluded subsidy agreements with the Ministry of Agriculture.

Chapter 9. Catastrophe Insurance

§1. General

619. One of the threats to business is damage caused by natural catastrophes. The increasing frequency of extreme weather conditions, hurricanes, unexpected winter storms or heavy rainfall has a significant impact on business. Polish insurance companies identify catastrophe risk as one of the main risk concentration factors. The actuarial approach identifies the risk concentration in terms of possible losses caused by catastrophic events, especially floods and hurricanes. The magnitude of catastrophic risks leads to the use of reinsurance to secure insurance activities by limiting the impact of catastrophic phenomena that may adversely affect the financial position of insurers. This is usually done through obligatory reinsurance treaties together with supplementary facultative reinsurance treaties (surplus of losses).[31]

620. There are no general policy conditions for separate catastrophe insurance in the Polish market. However, this does not mean that Polish insurers do not accept catastrophe risks at all. In fact, this type of insurance is becoming more and more popular in Poland, and such risks are quite often the subject of insurance coverage, although they are often spread over several terms and conditions of particular branches of insurance or, however, they are all combined into one product. As far as the diversification into several lines of business is concerned, it mainly concerns agriculture, motor, buildings, marine and aviation insurance. Some of them are briefly presented in other chapters of this part. Catastrophic events are covered by general insurance against fire and other accidents, and cover perils – mainly flood, hurricane, fire, lightning, etc.

621. The contribution of insurance to the financing of catastrophic risks is currently perceived by the population and state authorities as an important problem of modern society, which requires the development of appropriate methods and the establishment of principles for the financing of damage and destruction caused by natural disasters. The effects are sometimes very long-lasting and labour-intensive. The assets at risk are real estate, movable property, equipment, furniture, crops, harvested produce, livestock and others. Therefore, if we look at the results of the insurance market on the basis of a comparative analysis of premiums and claims in Group 8 (Non-life Insurance Division II), i.e., insurance against damage caused by natural forces, which covers damage to property not included in Groups 3–7 of the Insurance Classification, caused by fire, explosion, storm, other natural forces, nuclear energy, landslides or collapses, we can see that the annual premium is increasing by about 7% a year and the number of policies by 11% compared to the period ten years ago. Claims, however, are increasing at a faster rate – around 15% – and the number of payments is up by around 20%.

---

31. For example, *see* the report of PZU of 2020.

622. It should be noted that catastrophic insurance against losses caused by natural disasters is a category of insurance that is developing and becoming increasingly visible in the insurance market. According to recent surveys, more than 60% of households have insured their assets. However, this is usually not comprehensive insurance against all natural catastrophe losses. The purchase of an insurance policy is influenced by the policyholder's sense of security. The majority are willing to insure their property against all possible natural disasters.[32]

§2. Nuclear Risks

623. Nuclear risks are usually considered uninsurable due to their catastrophic nature and almost non-existent demand on the Polish market (there are no nuclear power plants in Poland). Nuclear risks are also perceived as an act of God, which excludes liability in contractual relations, and even if this is not the case, it is the risk that is usually excluded in all types of property insurance products. Even coverage based on the all-risks concept excludes losses arising from nuclear damage caused by nuclear reactors, nuclear damage or damage caused by radioactivity. However, there is one exception in Polish law that directly provides for the need to insure nuclear facilities. It concerns the Law on Nuclear Activity (currently applied to only one entity in Poland).

624. According to the Polish Law on Nuclear Activity of 2000, a person using a nuclear facility is obliged to conclude an insurance contract for civil liability in connection with possible nuclear damage that may result from such activity. The obligation to insure also covers the transport of nuclear material. The obligation to insure arises on the day preceding the first day of operation of the nuclear power plant or on the day preceding the day on which the transport is to begin. The insurance covers the operator's liability for nuclear damage caused during the insurance period (i.e., it is based on the triggering act).

625. The Atomic Energy Act contains specific rules on civil liability for nuclear damage, which change the remedies available to victims of tortious acts in relation to general liability in tort, as well as some principles relating to the insurance contract. It is important to note that the insurer cannot contractually limit the obligation to pay compensation to the victims, so it is the law that defines the scope of liability. The minimum guarantee for an accident is set at the equivalent of 300,000,000 SDRs. However, for transport and scientific nuclear reactors, the guarantee amount is lower and ranges from the equivalent of 400,000 SDR to 5,000,000 SDR.

626. The law does not limit its geographical scope, therefore it takes into account not only domestic but also international legal relations arising from nuclear incidents in case of transboundary radioactive contamination. If the nuclear accident occurs in Poland, the Polish regional courts are competent to resolve disputes

32. A. Kułakowska – Bicz, Catastrophic Events and Their Insurance in Poland in the Light of Empirical Research, Prace i Studia Geograficzne 2014, T. 55 ss. 69–83.

concerning claims for damages. If the nuclear accident occurs abroad, the competence of the court and jurisdiction are governed by the Vienna Convention on Liability for Nuclear Damage of 21 May 1963 (Journal of Laws of 1990 No. 63, items 370 and 371).

627. A claim for compensation for nuclear damage may be made directly against the insurer, in which case the insurer may invoke the limitation of liability and other defences available to the operator.

628. In the event of a lack of insurance coverage, despite the obligation described above, the operator of the power plant is obliged to pay an administrative fine equal to 20% of the minimum guaranteed sum of such insurance. Payment of the fine does not release the operator from the obligation to take out insurance.

629. If the nuclear accident has caused personal damage, 10% of the guarantee sum should be set aside to cover claims relating to such damage. Only if, five years after the accident, the claims for personal damage do not exceed the above amount, the remaining part of the guarantee sum may be used to compensate for damage to property and the environment. The payment of the compensation is guaranteed by the State Treasury to the extent that the damage is not compensated by the insurer or the UFG.

630. Claims for compensation of personal injuries are not subject to any time limitation. Other claims, i.e., claims for compensation of property damage and damage to the environment, are subject to a limitation period of three years from the date on which the injured party receives information about the damage and the person liable for the damage, but the maximum limitation period is ten years from the date of the nuclear accident.

631. The law follows the rule that all liability should be channelled to the operator of the nuclear power plant. The question of who is the operator is left to the definition of this issue in the administrative regulations. The law covers at least two types of organisational units that have undertaken activities specified in the law as public operators (government bodies and the research institute acting on behalf of the state); and/or private operators, including state enterprises acting on their own account and in their own name.

632. The Atomic Energy Act creates almost absolute liability for nuclear damage. The law provides that an operator is not liable only in the case of damage caused by war or intentional fault of a third party or a victim. The law does not exclude liability even if the event is due to an exceptional natural disaster. The insurer must accept this principle.

633. An operator is obliged to pay compensation in the event of a nuclear accident, and such compensation covers losses actually suffered by the injured persons in connection with bodily injury, impairment of health, as well as losses suffered by another person as a result of the death of an injured person; damage to or destruction of property; profits which an injured person could have made if the damage had not occurred; all necessary expenditures which have already been made or will be made after the event causing the damage in order to prevent further damage to people or the environment per se.

634. Such a broad definition of nuclear damage is linked to the principle of full compensation. In reality, the law obliges the state to be involved in the event of catastrophic damage, which means damage exceeding the financial security coverage. The Treasury is only liable for personal damage exceeding the financial security coverage. In the case of non-personal damage, however, it can be assumed that the state budget will be involved in the compensation of catastrophic damage.

635. Beyond and in addition to the normally compensable items of damage to persons and property, the 2000 Act introduces a notable change in Polish civil law. In Article 39 §3, it provides that the right to compensation for damage caused to the environment as common property is also possible. The Minister responsible for the protection of the environment has the exclusive right to claim such compensation and indemnity.

§3. Natural Catastrophes Insurance

636. Catastrophe insurance is offered on the Polish insurance market as part of natural catastrophe insurance (commonly known as flood insurance or natural catastrophe insurance). The need for such insurance is becoming more and more obvious and the statistics of the last few years prove it. The last few years have been an example of how Poland can experience successive periods of drought and episodes of heavy rainfall in a single year, which cause local flooding and river flooding, but do not fundamentally improve the hydrological situation of the country. Floods in recent years have caused significant damage to crops and buildings in rural areas. Insurers are participating in an expert working group to develop a stress testing methodology for drought (and aggregated as a catastrophe risk – blackout risks). Water supply disruptions can have a significant impact on the future profitability of BI. Similarly, a blackout can affect a significant area of the country. These risks are therefore treated as catastrophic, along with floods and windstorms.

637. As mentioned at the beginning, natural catastrophe insurance is generally offered by all insurers engaged in non-life insurance, and it is usually offered as part of a specific branch of insurance (such as agricultural insurance) or as a separate product combining coverage for several specific catastrophes in one insurance contract, usually together with fire insurance.

638. The current disaster insurance system in Poland is essentially based on voluntary insurance. Compulsory insurance exists only for buildings forming part of an agricultural holding: against fire, hurricane, flood, flooding, driving rain, hail, snowfall, lightning, explosion, landslide, fall, avalanche or aircraft crash. These risks are included in the package. Quasi-mandatory insurance is also provided for farmers who have received direct payments under the direct support scheme. This insurance covers the risk of damage to – cereals, maize, rape, colza, hops, tobacco, ground vegetables, fruit trees and bushes, strawberries, potatoes, sugar beet or leguminous crops, from sowing or planting to harvesting – against the risk of damage caused by storm, flood, torrential rain, hail, lightning, cattle, horses, sheep, goats, poultry or pigs – against the risk of damage caused by storm, flood, torrential rain, hail, lightning, landslide, avalanche and as a result of emergency slaughter. In the case of these insurances, the coverage can be AR or selected by the agricultural producer.

639. For example, in the case of compulsory agricultural insurance against fire and other risks, the insurer is liable, in addition to fire, for damage caused by storm, flood, landslide, hail, lightning, avalanche, subsidence and others. According to the descriptions provided by the terms and conditions of the above-mentioned insurance, all the specified perils have been defined. For example, a windstorm is defined as a wind with a speed of not less than 17.5 m/sec that causes massive damage. Flood is defined as the inundation of areas as a result of the rise of water in river beds or standing water or driving rain, as well as the effect of water flows in the mountainside or on slopes. Landslide has been described as a mass of rock or earth sliding down a slope or hillside as a result of the subsidence of voids in the ground or in connection with the movement of ground on slopes. An avalanche, according to the same insurance, is a sudden sliding or rolling down of masses of snow, ice, rocks or stones from the mountain slope. The above definitions are commonly used in other types of insurance covering natural hazards.

640. Catastrophic risks are usually covered by FLEXA insurance, so the scope of insurance usually includes fire, storm, flood, landslide, hail, lightning, avalanche, subsidence, aircraft collision, hurricane, earthquake, automobile collision and others. In certain cases, the insurance can be extended to other perils such as smoke. In addition to the direct losses, the insurer usually covers the costs of security measures, the resulting losses, the costs of debris removal and the costs of preventive measures in the event of the risk occurring. The above extensions are subject to certain limits in relation to the sum insured, as the case law points out: 'The spillage of goods during the extinguishing of the fire is included in the insured risk under the property insurance against fire and other natural disasters' (Supreme Court judgment of 27 July 1999, *sygn. Akt. I* CKN 469/99). The coverage of catastrophic risks is usually voluntary, and only the buildings of agricultural holdings are covered on a compulsory basis.

641. The following items can be insured: fixed assets, turnover assets, property of third parties accepted in connection with the provision of certain services under a contract with the insured, cash, investment assets, and personal property of employees. Under special conditions, some other items may be covered (art collections, etc.).

642. The usual exclusions used by insurers include damage caused by acts of war, states of emergency, strikes and riots, terrorism (which can be covered at an additional premium), and damage caused by radioactive contamination, among others. Natural catastrophe insurance can be taken out as traditional insurance for the risks expressly mentioned in the insurance contracts or on the basis of 'all risks' insurance.

643. The determination of the sum insured also seems to be an important issue and is usually determined as the replacement value, the real market value or the gross/net book value of the insured property. The reinstatement value or real market value seems to be the most favourable for both the insurer and the insured, although the book value is still the most common. For large companies and large industrial risks, insurers also offer the possibility of concluding the insurance contract on the basis of a loss limit – in two forms: MAS – Maximum Amount Sum and PML.

644. As can be seen from the above, direct losses are the only risks covered by compulsory insurance and the majority of risks covered by voluntary insurance. However, indirect losses resulting from business interruption and loss of profit (or increased costs) should also be added to the above. This risk can be covered by a standard business interruption policy or one of its variants: (interruption) or one of its variants: insurance against loss of profit due to a breakdown of machinery and equipment (machinery loss of profit); insurance against loss of profit in connection with the execution of construction and assembly works (advanced loss of profit), insurance against loss of rent due to rental.[33]

---

33. Report of the Polish Chamber of Commerce for 2019.

Chapter 10. Credit and Caution Insurance

§1. General

645. This type of insurance was developed in Poland in the second half of the twentieth century. Initially, Polish insurers began to underwrite credit insurance for Polish companies to cover the export of goods, mainly to developing countries. Today, credit insurance has developed strongly in various directions and is offered for creditors and debtors, domestic and export credits, for commercial and non-commercial risks. The most common types of insurance concluded by Polish entrepreneurs are export and domestic credit insurance, leasing instalment insurance and factoring insurance.

646. Another important aspect of credit insurance in Poland, especially export credit insurance, is state-guaranteed credit insurance. The Act on State-guaranteed Export Credit Insurance of 7 July 1994 provides for such a possibility through the establishment of a special entity, Korporacja Kredytów Eksportowych Spólka Akcyjna, which operates in the form of a joint-stock company in which the State has a majority shareholding.

647. Korporacja Ubezpieczeń Kredytów Eksportowych Spółka Akcyjna (KUKE S.A.) is the only entity that, since 1991, has been providing export insurance to secure trade in high-risk markets guaranteed by the State Treasury. The trade finance instruments offered by KUKE are:

a. insurance guarantees at any stage of the export contract (guarantees of payment of the deposit, proper performance of the contract, return of the advance payment and removal of defects and faults);
b. insurance guarantees of payment of claims under letters of credit are addressed to banks that confirm, discount or post-finance letters of credit issued by foreign banks;
c. Supplier credit insurance is intended for domestic entrepreneurs who participate in tenders organised by institutions or international organisations subject to public procurement (e.g., NATO, Organisation for Economic Co-operation and Development (OECD), UN) or who directly conclude export contracts;
d. buyer credit insurance is intended for banks financing contracts requiring financing for the purchase of capital goods and services;
e. Forfaiting, or buyer credit insurance, is either a direct policy issued to the bank or a policy issued to the exporter with assignment of the claims under the policy to the bank.

648. In addition, KUKE offers credit insurance in the form of: (1) europolisa, designed for start-ups or small businesses; (2) package, designed for entrepreneurs developing export and/or domestic sales on trade credit; (3) policy for the East, designed for entrepreneurs operating in politically unstable markets; (4) Export

Credit Union GAP EX and Export Credit Union GAP EX+, designed for entrepreneurs facing liquidity problems in times of the SARS-CoV-2 coronavirus; (5) individual policy to secure a short-term export contract.

649. In an uncertain market environment, companies are looking for ways to minimise and manage the risks associated with their customers. The insolvency of one or more key customers of medium importance to a company can cause serious liquidity problems and even bankruptcy. In addition to safeguards such as guarantees, letters of credit, factoring or provisions for insolvent debtors, trade credit insurance is considered by many to be the most effective solution, especially for international trade. Of particular importance are insurance products that cover the risk of loss of receivables in times of economic crisis.

650. Export credit insurance is an important part of the process of managing the risk of late payment in international transactions. Its positioning in the market depends largely on the current stage of the economic cycle and the geopolitical situation in individual markets. In times of recession or international political turmoil, their availability tends to decrease, while interest on the part of the buyers themselves, i.e., companies making sales with deferred payment terms, increases. Such a phenomenon is indirectly a key factor influencing the volume of foreign trade and thus the state of individual economies. Therefore, in times when the free market mechanism of self-regulation becomes inefficient, the intervention of the state apparatus is necessary. It can take various forms and sizes, but the overall objective is to help domestic buyers of export insurance obtain products that hedge the risks arising from delayed payment at a level that satisfies them.

651. The most important types of credit insurance, i.e., export credit insurance for commercial risks, non-commercial credit insurance and domestic credit insurance, are described below.

§2. Export Credit Insurance Against Commercial Risks

652. Export credit insurance is one of the forms of securing obligations arising from commercial transactions in foreign trade. The subject of the insurance is the cash receivable due to the insured (or the creditor of the insured) under export contracts for the supply of goods or services. The purpose of this type of insurance is to provide protection against losses that may arise during the performance of export contracts. Losses in connection with such contracts may occur at the production stage or after the goods have been produced but before the price has been paid (credit stage).

653. Commercial risk credit insurance covers losses incurred by the insured as a result of the non-performance or improper performance of an export contract by the foreign contractor if such losses are due to events described as commercial risks.

654. Commercial risks are defined as the debtor's legally confirmed, actual or presumed bankruptcy, or the debtor's persistent failure to comply with the terms of the contract with respect to the payment of claims within the agreed time. A legally confirmed insolvency may occur in the following circumstances:

a. the debtor's bankruptcy has been declared or such a declaration has been refused due to the debtor's lack of sufficient assets (to cover the costs of the bankruptcy proceedings);
b. the debtor has suspended payments and approached all or the majority of his creditors for contracts and has later settled the debts on the basis of the total amount by way of judicial proceedings or amicable settlement;
c. enforcement proceedings initiated at the request of the Insured have failed to recover the full amount of the claim due to insufficient assets on the part of the debtor.

655. There are several exclusions of the insurance cover provided by the insurer. Among other things, the insurance does not normally cover all types of political risks (which are covered by credit insurance for non-commercial risks) and the following:

a. losses incurred as a result of acts of law declared or decisions taken concerning: the introduction of new or the extension of existing export or import restrictions, the withdrawal or restriction of previously issued export and import licences, the seizure, confiscation or nationalisation of the subject of the contract, a company or other property of the debtor, prohibitions or restrictions on the movement of foreign currency or moratoria, devaluation of the currency of payment;
b. losses resulting from acts of war, civil war, revolution, etc.

656. Furthermore, the Insurer is not liable for losses caused by exceptional natural events such as earthquakes, storms, cyclones, floods, volcanic eruptions, etc., as well as the effects of nuclear power and radioactivity.

657. In addition to the above, some insurers exclude from cover losses suffered by the insured person caused in whole or in part by his own conduct or that of persons (including banks) acting on his behalf, in particular when the losses are caused by the non-performance, partial performance or improper performance of the contract by the insured person or by persons who have performed services on his behalf.

658. In addition, the insurance does not normally cover:

a. sums due to the Insured as a result of contractual penalties and default interest;
b. consequential losses;
c. misappropriation of the subject matter of the contract or of the sums due by the debtor, his agents or the Insured.

659. The Insured is also not entitled to indemnification from the Insurer if, as a result of his fault, the foreign private contractor has come into possession of the subject of the transaction.

660. The sum insured is determined as the total of the sums due under the contract, which, at the request of the Insured, will be aggregated with the amount of interest due on the amount of credit granted.

661. The insured person is also obliged to cooperate with the insurer during the execution of the insurance contract and, accordingly, both parties are obliged to exchange information in the event that there is a risk of insolvency on the part of the debtor, or his financial situation has deteriorated, or the debtor has actually become insolvent, the debtor's financing bank refuses to cover its obligations, or the debtor has taken steps to extend the due date for payment of all or part of the amounts due, or has requested a change in the terms of payment.

662. In the cases described above, the Insured is obliged to take all available measures and to comply with the Insurer's instructions in order to avoid or reduce losses.

§3. Export Credit Insurance Against Non-commercial Risks

663. Credit insurance of non-commercial risks includes the following types of risks: political risk, catastrophic risk, risk of protracted default by a foreign public debtor (to which the provisions of the bankruptcy law do not apply) and foreign exchange risk, which is still excluded from insurance in Poland. The non-commercial risk may be insured only as a supplement to the commercial risk insurance, but it is also possible to obtain insurance only for the first type of risk (non-commercial).

664. The political risk is usually defined as the following events:

a. Suspension of payment (moratorium) by the debtor's government;
b. Issuance or amendment of legal acts or government decisions that make performance of the contract impossible;
c. inability to transfer receivables from the debtor's country due to political events or economic difficulties or legal acts/administrative decisions, etc.;
d. issuance of nationalisation acts;
e. war, revolution, riots outside the territory of Poland, etc.

665. The Insurer's liability is excluded in the case of commercial or other risks insured on the basis of other types of credit insurance or even property insurance, which sometimes forces the Insured to take out other types of insurance in addition. In addition, the insurer is not liable for amounts owed by the insured for fines, contractual penalties and default interest, consequential damages resulting from the operation of nuclear or hydro-nuclear power plants and radioactivity.

666. Export insurance is currently experiencing a difficult period due to the war in Ukraine. The scale of payouts is the largest in thirty years. The government has therefore introduced changes to formalise procedures and streamline payouts under insurance and guarantee contracts.

§4. Domestic Credit Insurance

667. Trade credit is the most important form of credit in business transactions. Most entrepreneurs make sales on a deferred payment basis. Since the performance of the parties is not simultaneous, the one who performs first (the creditor) bears the risk of non-performance by the other party. If such a situation arises, the entrepreneur is exposed to losses. From the supplier's point of view, the risk is related both to the delay in payment of receivables and to the subsequent insolvency of the customer. Insurance of trade receivables also serves the purpose of monitoring the risk throughout the insurance period, shortening the time for assessing the solvency of individual counterparties, minimising the costs of gathering information on the financial situation of potential counterparties (transferring all responsibilities to the insurer), long-term investment in the safe development of the company: the policy minimises the occurrence of the risk of non-payment, even if it is not currently high.

668. Insurance of domestic and foreign trade receivables covers the following risks: (a) Legal insolvency of the beneficiary – (e.g., bankruptcy, composition, accelerated reorganisation, etc.); (b) Chronic non-payment – a situation in which the debtor fails to meet his obligations for a strictly defined period of time, counted from the date of the collection order or from the original due date (depending on the wording of the contract); (c) Excess cover ('TOP UP COVER') – allows you to increase the limit granted by the insurer under the basic policy. It allows the applicable limit to be doubled; (d) Non-market risk insurance – insurance of receivables from countries with higher economic and political risks. Loss events include moratoria, transfer restrictions, war, natural disasters or revocation of export licences; (e) Single Risk – insurance covering only a single buyer or a group of selected buyers (selective protection).

669. At present, domestic credit insurance is offered as coverage for undisputed claims against the insured in connection with credit granted to contractors, arising from invoices issued by the insured and not paid within a certain period. As a rule, the insurance cover does not include interest, penalties and additional charges.

670. There are two basic forms of domestic credit insurance. The first is the insurance taken out by the creditor on his own account to cover receivables due from all or part of his debtors (contractors). The second type covers claims arising from a single contract or debtor. The insured party is usually a creditor supplying certain goods under its contracts (debtors). The first type is the most advantageous from the insurer's point of view, as it does not allow negative selection of risk on the part of the insured creditor and all his contracts are covered.[34]

671. The most common feature of this type of insurance is the credit limit set for each contractor and the period of its operation. The financial status of the contractors is monitored by the insurer throughout the period of performance of the contract between the insured and its contractor, and in certain cases (negative factors) the credit limit may be reduced or cancelled, which means that this particular contractor and its debts to the insured are released from the insurance cover.

672. The Insurer's liability in respect of domestic credit insurance arises in the following situations:

a. the debtor has been declared bankrupt or such a declaration has been refused due to the lack of adequate assets of the debtor (to cover the costs of the bankruptcy proceedings);
b. the debtor has suspended payments and approached all or the majority of his creditors for contracts and has later settled the debts on the basis of the total amount by way of judicial proceedings or amicable settlement;
c. enforcement proceedings instituted at the request of an insured person have not resulted in the full recovery of his claim due to insufficient assets on the part of the debtor;
d. there is a prolonged delay in payment of the claim – 30–180 days.

673. As for the exemptions from the insurer's liability, they mostly concern amounts due before the occurrence of an event covered by the insurance. In this type of insurance, the insured is also obliged to inform the insurer of any changes in the contracts covered by the insurance.

§5. Insurance Cautions (Bonds, Suretyships)

674. Despite the fact that insurance bonds are relatively new products on the Polish market, they have developed strongly in the recent period. The essence of an insurance bond is an agreement concluded between the insurer and the policyholder, the subject of which is the issue of a bond (surety). On the basis of such a guarantee, the insurer assumes the role of a guarantor with regard to the timely payment of the specified amount to the beneficiary of the guarantee.

675. The insurance guarantee is not regulated in Polish law, although it is widely used in business. It is subject to a number of different regulations and the parties are free to contract the terms of the guarantee. In view of the above, insurers use international practice when offering guarantee terms. In particular, the rules of the International Chamber of Commerce and the definitions developed by the International

34. T. Sangowski, '*Ubezpieczenia Gospodarcze*', 223 et al.

Credit Insurance and Surety Association are taken into account. The rules of guarantees on the Polish market are also based on court decisions.

676. According to the Supreme Court's jurisprudence, the guarantee has its own legal regime and there is no reason to apply the provisions of the insurance contract by analogy; the insurer's obligation under the guarantee contract does not consist in providing insurance cover for a certain period of time, but in issuing a guarantee document with a specific content required by the beneficiary, for which the remuneration is due in the amount agreed by the parties. The provisions of the mandate contract in Article 734 of the Civil Code apply. The issuance of an insurance guarantee at the request of the principal is an unconditional obligation, payable at the first request of the beneficiary, whereas the liability for indemnification under the insurance of receivables is an obligation that is usually very restrictive and subject to the fulfilment of certain conditions.

677. Despite the similarity of its economic purpose to an insurance contract for the account of a third party, an insurance guarantee order contract (including the contracts concluded by the parties) is not a contract to which the provisions of the Civil Code on the insurance contract apply, even by analogy. An insurance contract is a named contract regulated in detail by the provisions of the Civil Code and laws on the conduct of the insurance business. An insurance contract concluded for the account of a third party (Article 808 of the Civil Code) is always a bilateral contract from which the policyholder derives certain obligations. The policyholder is obliged not only to pay the premium but also to comply with the rules aimed at preventing the occurrence of an accident or limiting the possible extent of the damage (Article 826 of the Civil Code). Some of these obligations also apply to the insured when the insurance is taken out for the account of another person (Article 826, §5 of the Civil Code). However, a guarantee is an institution created by market practice within the framework of the principle of freedom of contract (Article 3531 of the Civil Code), with fragmentary regulations, mainly concerning a bank guarantee. Under the general concept of a guarantee, there are typically three interrelated legal relationships: the legal relationship between the creditor and the debtor, which gives rise to the need to secure the creditor's interests arising from this relationship (the so-called basic relationship); the relationship of ordering the guarantee, under which the debtor on the basis of the basic relationship orders the guarantee from another entity – a bank, insurance company or other – in order to secure the creditor's interests; and the guarantee relationship between the guarantor and the beneficiary of the guarantee. The very structure of the institution of a guarantee makes it difficult to compare it with an insurance contract, since it would be necessary to compare with it both the contract mandating the guarantee and the granting of the guarantee itself, and consequently to compare the position and obligations of the parties to the insurance contract (the insurer, the policyholder and the insured) with the position and obligations of the parties to the contract mandating the guarantee (the mandator and the guarantor) and with the position and obligations of the parties to the guarantee itself (the guarantor and the beneficiary of the guarantee). Thus, the beneficiary of the guarantee is not burdened with any obligation to the person of the guarantor under the guarantee given to him, unlike the insured to the insurer. The beneficiary of the guarantee is only burdened with purely formal obligations in the event of a demand for payment of the guarantee sum if the conditions for its payment are fulfilled.

678. Unlike an insurance contract, the guarantee relationship itself does not consist of an assurance to the beneficiary that he will receive the equivalent of the loss suffered, nor that the guarantor will pay more than the beneficiary's loss in the event of a covered risk. This is because the amount payable by the guarantor to the beneficiary in the event that the guaranteed outcome does not occur is fixed in advance. It is therefore not an indemnity liability, while the mechanism of payment of the guarantee amount and the conditions for claiming it make it easier to satisfy the beneficiary of the guarantee.

679. The amount of the guarantee, which is the upper limit of the insurer's liability for damages, can be given the character of a guarantee in isolation from the amount of the damage (Article 824 of the Civil Code), but even then it does not change the compensatory nature of the liability under the insurance contract. The guarantor's obligation towards the beneficiary is self-executing. Therefore, the guarantor cannot invoke against the beneficiary of the guarantee any allegations arising from the relationship of the guarantee order. An insurance contract, even for the account of a third party, may be concluded as an insurer only by an insurance company that meets the requirements set out in a separate law. However, guarantees may be issued by various entities, including banks and insurance companies. Only in the case of an insurance guarantee is the insurance company the guarantor.

680. The rights of the policyholder in the case of an insurance contract and the rights of the guarantor in the case of a guarantee, including an insurance guarantee, are also different. In the case of an insurance contract, the policyholder is obliged to pay the benefit specified by law and in accordance with the rules laid down therein, i.e., the premium calculated for the duration of the insurer's liability (Article 805 §1 of the Civil Code and Article 813 §1, first sentence of the Civil Code). If the insurance relationship is terminated before the end of the period for which it was concluded, the policyholder is entitled to a refund of the premium for the period of unused insurance cover. These provisions are of a cognitive nature. However, in the case of a contract for the provision of a guarantee, including an insurance guarantee, the benefit of the insurance company in the case of a contract for the provision of a guarantee does not consist in payment but in the provision of the agreed guarantee (a non-monetary benefit), and the guarantor is obliged to pay remuneration to the guarantor. The principles of payment of this remuneration and the determination of its amount are not subject to legal regulations, but, like the institution of the guarantee itself, are determined by the will of the parties, based on the principle of freedom of contract (Article 353^1 of the Civil Code).

681. One of the essential elements of the provision of a guarantee is the payment of the amount guaranteed and not the payment of a commission. The provision of a guarantee without payment is not excluded. The amount of the benefit in the form of the insurance premium and the guarantee commission is also determined differently. In the case of the former, the amount of the premium is determined by the calculation of the risk of the occurrence of an insured event, whereas in the case of the latter, the amount of the premium is determined primarily by the calculation of the risk of refinancing the loan thus granted. This is because, whereas in the case of an insurance contract, it is the risk of the occurrence of a specific insurance event that is important, in the case of a guarantee, where the guarantor assumes the risk associated with the realisation or failure of the project specified in the contract, it is the risk associated with the return of the guarantee amount paid, in the event that the guarantee amount has to be paid.

682. The guarantor acts for the account of another, whereas the insurance company acts for its own account. Thus, the Court of Second Instance rightly held that, in the case of a guarantee, there is no transfer of risk to the insurance company, as is the case with an insurance contract, since the debtor remains responsible at all times for the proper performance of the obligation assumed. Undoubtedly, the insurance contract and the establishment of an insurance guarantee have certain features in common. In both cases, the parties to these contracts are insurance companies, acting either as insurer or guarantor. In both institutions, there is an element of chance. In the case of an insurance contract, the risk of an insured event occurring is usually directly related to the duration of the insurance cover, whereas in the case of a guarantee, the duration of the cover has a lesser effect on the risk of having to pay the guarantee if the result guaranteed by the guarantee does not occur.

683. Both an insurance contract and an insurance guarantee may serve the same economic purpose of protecting the economic interests of third parties, i.e., the insured or the beneficiaries of the guarantee. However, these similarities do not preclude the application of the second sentence of Article 813 §1 of the Civil Code, either directly or by analogy, to the remuneration to be paid to the guarantor by the party issuing the insurance guarantee. It should also be added that the Supreme Court has held that a guarantee is subject to its own legal regime and that there are no grounds for applying the provisions governing an insurance contract to it by analogy (judgment of 17 December 2004, II CK 308/04, unpublished).

684. The definition of a guarantee on the Polish market is based on the definition developed by the International Chamber of Commerce, according to which a guarantee (payable on demand) is any written guarantee, letter of guarantee or payment obligation that provides for the payment of money upon the presentation of a written demand for payment and other documents specified in the guarantee document in accordance with the terms of the obligation. A guarantee is usually an act independent of any contract on which it may be based, and the insurance company as guarantor is in no way bound by the terms of such contract, except that the guarantee may contain references to the terms of the contract. The guarantee usually contains the clauses 'irrevocably and unconditionally' and 'on first demand'. This precludes the guarantor from relying on the underlying relationship between the beneficiary of the guarantee and the policyholder. All the terms of the guarantee should be contained in the guarantee document itself, issued by the guarantor – the insurance company.[35]

685. In order to issue a guarantee, the insurance company signs a guarantee contract with the policyholder, on the basis of which the insurance company undertakes to issue a guarantee. Thus, there are three contracts in the guarantee process: (1) the basic contract between the policyholder (debtor) and the beneficiary of the guarantee (the counterparty of the policyholder); (2) the guarantee contract between the insurance company and the policyholder (debtor under the basic contract); (3) the guarantee contract between the guarantor and the beneficiary (because the prevailing view is that the guarantee must be accepted by the beneficiary, so it is not a unilateral act).

686. The guarantee is classified as an insurance activity in the AIRA and is included in Group 15 of Division II, together with other types of financial insurance. The basic classification in the AIRA divides insurance bonds into two classes:

a. direct bonds;
b. indirect guarantees.

687. In business, insurance guarantees are most commonly used as: (1) contractual bonds guaranteeing the performance of a contract, such as bid bonds, performance bonds, advance payment bonds, or maintenance bonds; (2) customs, tax and similar bonds; (3) fidelity bonds; (4) supply bonds, lease bonds; (5) payment bonds for exporters; (6) environmental bonds.

688. Insurance bonds are commonly used to secure customs and tax claims.

35. R.A. DANKIEWICZ, Ubezpieczenia kredytów eksportowych jako narzędzia wspierające handel międzynarodowy, Insurance of Export Credits as a Tool Supporting International Trade; Annales H – Oeconomia http://oeconomia.annales.umcs.pl.

Chapter 11. Technical Insurance

§1. CAR/EAR Insurance

689. The intensive industrialisation of the Polish economy over the last twenty years has contributed significantly to the rapid development of various branches of engineering insurance in Poland. This chapter will mainly deal with Erection All Risk (EAR) insurance. At present, we can say that the development of these insurances has entered a new phase. More and more often, we are no longer dealing with simple Contractors All Risk (CAR)/EAR contracts, duplicated by the hundreds and thousands, but with real 'tailor-made' projects.

690. Construction and erection insurance (CAR/EAR) is aimed at investors and contractors in construction projects and provides the most comprehensive and consistent protection possible for investments against property damage and, in relation to third parties, also bodily injury. Construction insurance is a standard requirement of banks that lend to construction projects. The most common solution is for the investor or main contractor, who is responsible for the entire contract, to take out insurance for the entire work. In special cases, insurers will also provide cover for selected stages of work carried out by individual subcontractors. We do not recommend such a solution because in this situation there is no one responsible for the consistency and comprehensiveness of the insurance cover. However, there may be significant differences in coverage between the policies taken out by different subcontractors. Due to the large values covered by this type of insurance, insureds typically use a broker to arrange coverage.

691. CAR/EAR insurance provides cover for ongoing construction and installation works against losses caused by risks not excluded from the policy (AR formula). Thus, the policy provides cover for all uninsured events of a sudden and unexpected nature that are not specifically excluded from the cover. Standard cover will include burglary, but you should be aware of the need to adequately secure the site (usually with fencing, cameras and constant surveillance). Insurance covers both force majeure and man-made losses.

692. Typical coverages include: fire, explosion, lightning strike, acts of God (including collapse or landslide, flood, inundation, hurricane, excessive rainfall), structural collapse or failure of installed equipment or facilities due to faulty design, materials, installation or workmanship, burglary, robbery or destruction by third parties, as well as the cost of rescue operations related to the insured events and the cost of removing the remains of the damage.

693. It is also common for insurers to require fire and theft cover The most common exclusions of liability include Acts of war, terrorism, civil commotion, damage caused by confiscation or nationalisation, damage caused by nuclear reaction, radioactive contamination, contamination or pollution by industrial waste, indirect damage such as liquidated damages, interest and losses caused by late or improper performance of construction and installation work, natural wear and tear or long-term deterioration, or defects in the design or materials supplied to the site for which the designer or manufacturer is responsible.

694. In many countries, including Poland, EAR insurance is most commonly offered under the so-called Munich Standard of the reinsurance company Munich Re. According to this standard, the insurer is liable for any sudden and unforeseen physical damage occurring at the site of the insured construction (installation), provided that no circumstance excluding the insurer's liability has occurred. The Munich Standard provides for a basic cover and a large number of endorsements, which are added to the insurance depending on the specifics of the project and the needs of the insured. Supplementary clauses may include both exclusions and extensions of cover.

695. Insurance contracts are concluded for the duration of the works, which is determined by the provisions of the construction contracts. The idea of taking out a CAR/EAR policy is to provide insurance cover for the entire construction or installation process – from the very beginning (e.g., construction of foundations) to the final acceptance of the work or any tests (usually the period of cover also includes the maintenance/warranty period). In this respect, endorsements are often used to ensure that, in the event of a change in the completion dates, the insurer is obliged to extend the previously declared period of cover to the maximum previously agreed. In the absence of such clauses, the extension of the contract requires individual negotiations between the parties.

696. On the Polish market, there are several solutions for the structure of CAR/EAR policies: unitary policies – covering only one specific contract, rotating policies – covering all contracts during the insurance period (usually twelve months) without the need to declare them, rotating policies – so-called open cover – covering all contracts declared during the insurance period under predetermined conditions and insurance rates.

697. Construction insurance is most often priced on the basis of an individual risk assessment and selected cover. Thus, the premium is influenced by factors such as the nature, subject matter and complexity of the construction and installation works, the amount of sums insured for certain categories of property or risks and, in the case of extension of cover to include civil liability, the amount of the guarantee sum, the scope of cover and, of course, the type of investment covered. The underwriting criteria also include the experience of the entities involved in the execution of the insured construction and installation works, the history of previous claims, the location of the construction site and the timing and tension of the work schedule. For this reason, the cost of insurance varies.

698. The sums insured under construction/installation policies are determined on the basis of: (1) the value of the contracted work; (2) the value of the property surrounding the work area; (3) the value of machinery, equipment and materials on the site; (4) the investor's expected profit upon timely completion of the work. The key to the correct estimation of the sum insured is the correct calculation of all components for each participant in the project (addition of the values of individual works, materials, machinery, if any, etc.).

699. Depending on the specifics of a given contract, the insurance contract is most often concluded by one of the parties to the contract (investor or general contractor), while the insured entities are usually all the participants in the process (investor, general contractor, subcontractors, substitute investors, bank, etc.) according to their rights and interests arising from their participation in the construction and assembly process.

700. In Poland, there are various standards of EAR insurance, including:

a. Contractors' All Risks Insurance/Erection All Risks Insurance (CAR/EAR) both in Continental edition (Munich Re/Swiss Re) and according to the standards of the London market and Lloyd's,
b. Advanced Loss of Profits/Delay in Start-up (ALoP/DSU),
c. Civil Engineering Completed Risks (CECR)/Comprehensive Project Insurance (CP),
d. Built Operate Transfer Policy (BOT),
e. Contractors' Plant and Machinery (CPM),
f. Third-Party Liability for Contractors or Erection Risks (TPL),
g. Cargo Insurance/Marine Cargo Insurance,
h. Marine Delay in Start-up (MDSU)/Project Cargo Insurance,
i. Environmental and pollution risks for contractors.

701. As a rule, construction site insurance coverage can consist of up to three parts, called sections:

a. Section 1 – for property insurance
   Covers installations under construction or installation, construction equipment and machinery, construction facilities such as containers, stored materials, and other property of the Insured or under its control.
b. Section 2 – for liability insurance
   This covers the Insured's liability in connection with the performance of construction or installation work. The scope of this cover is normally limited to tortious liability for bodily injury and damage to property caused to persons not connected with the works. This narrow scope of coverage can be extended to include, for example, damage caused to employees (employer's liability) or cross liability between insureds (employer's liability).
c. Section 3 – which deals with financial losses resulting from property damage during the construction period (also known as the investor's loss of profit insurance).
   This section covers losses resulting from delay in the commissioning of the project due to property damage insured under section I. Coverage includes loss

of operating profits and fixed costs incurred between the scheduled commissioning of the facility and the actual commissioning date. The sum insured is determined on the basis of the assumptions of the business plan prepared prior to the investment.

702. The structure of the CAR/EAR insurance enables comprehensive insurance of construction works carried out under a given contract – as both the property (including works, materials, machinery, existing property) and the issue of civil liability of all entities involved in the implementation of a given project are insured, as well as, if section 3 is purchased, the investor's lost expected profit. It is important to note that the insurance contract can only cover section 1 on its own, while sections 2 and 3 can only be covered by the insurance contract if the coverage contained in section 1 is insured.

703. The coverage of CAR/EAR policies can be extended to include, among others, liability for the risk of strikes, riots, liability for cross liabilities, protection during the trial period of machinery/equipment, rectification of defects during the warranty/maintenance period, remuneration of surveyors/experts after a claim, additional costs after a claim, transport risk (CASCO), risk due to designer's errors, risk due to storage of property outside the construction site, risk due to serial damage. It is also possible to extend the coverage with specific clauses for works related to tunnels, bridges, roads, etc.

§2. Machinery Breakdown Insurance (MB)

704. All types of machinery and equipment owned or used by the insured can be covered by MB insurance.

705. Construction machinery and equipment insurance covers sudden destruction, damage or loss of insured property, regardless of the will of the insured. Construction machinery and equipment insurance is an all-risk product, which means that it covers material damage to the insured property caused by all fortuitous events (i.e., events of a sudden and unexpected nature, except those expressly excluded from cover). The most common exclusions are mechanical breakdown, natural wear and tear of consumables, damage caused by the manufacturer or service provider, and damage caused by the policyholder's wilful misconduct or gross negligence. In order to adapt the scope of coverage to the specificities of the insured machinery and equipment, the terms and conditions contain a number of additional clauses that allow for modifications.

706. The scope of coverage may include, *inter alia*, the costs of securing the insured property against damage in the event of an imminent threat of damage, the costs of rescuing the affected insured property to prevent further damage, and the costs of cleaning up the remains of the damage, up to the limit specified in the insurance contract (e.g., up to 10% of the amount of the damage).

707. Machinery is covered after the successful completion of operational tests. Cover applies during operation, assembly and disassembly, repair and overhaul. Cover applies to equipment located at a specific location specified in the insurance document or in a specific territory (country) by virtue of its purpose. A list of equipment with the date of manufacture and stated replacement value is required for the insurance. The cover is therefore not blanket but covers items clearly identified in the policy.

708. Insurance is usually based on a sum insured, which is set at the replacement value of the machinery and equipment declared for insurance or, less frequently and in justified cases, at the actual value.

709. Typical types of machinery covered are: (1) Earthmoving machinery – loaders, bulldozers, excavators, etc.; (2) Construction equipment and supplies – scaffolding, formwork, compressors, generators, barracks, construction containers; (3) Cranes and lifting equipment – overhead cranes, tower cranes, gantry cranes, lifting platforms, forklifts; (4) Road construction machinery and equipment; (5) Pile driving and drilling equipment; (6) Machinery used in gravel and concrete works – crushers, breakers, mills, levellers; (7) Agricultural machinery – combines, seeders, etc.; (8) Public service vehicles and equipment – fire engines, ladders, snow ploughs; (9) Transport systems and rolling stock – at the designated place of insurance; (10) Harbour and working waterfront machinery.

Chapter 12. Cyber Insurance

710. Cyber risk insurance, despite being a relatively new insurance product, is experiencing dynamic changes. This is due to the co-participation in the digital economy, which has not only been one of the forms of human economic activity for a long time but has also become a determinant of civilisational development, and a source of new types of risks. The processes of economic digitalisation have been subjected to the intervention of regulators around the world. In this context, digital insurances can thus even be compared to such socially important ones as climate insurance. Their dimension is no longer just completely private but is becoming part of the functioning of society as a whole. This is a major challenge for a private risk management method such as insurance.

711. Undoubtedly, cyber risk insurance has become a buzzword with significant legislative changes in the area of data protection. However, we must realise that this situation is only one of the elements making cyber risk insurance an indispensable part of social and economic development. Given the contribution of information technology, described as 'a group of technologies that process, collect and transmit information in electronic form' in economic and social life, the management of the risks associated with them places these insurances alongside the most basic types of insurance, i.e., fire insurance, particularly when it comes to the protection of critical infrastructure.[36] The issue of digital risk management has long been on the agenda of both national governments and at the level of the EU (*see*, for example: The European Programme for Critical Infrastructure Protection (EPCIP) formulated in the European Commission Communication EU COM(2006) 786 final; Council Directive 2008/114/EC of 8.12.2008 on the identification and designation of European Critical Infrastructure and the assessment of the need to improve their protection (OJ EU L 345, p. 75)). Dependence on information technologies makes the security of their functioning, including the content of information collected and stored through them, a key issue (The Geneva Association, Ten key questions on cyber risk and cyber risk insurance, November 2016). It is also for this reason that the risks emanating from the use of information technology have become the subject of cyber security regulation at the national level (they were regulated by the NIS Directive and transposed by the Act of 5.7.2018 on the National Cyber Security System (Journal of Laws, item 1560)).

712. The starting point is the notion of cyberspace and cyber security. Central to these concepts is access to information. As a result, cyber risk can be defined as threats to the access and use of information. Thus, in a popular, broad sense, cyber risk is equated with IT risk and defined as the operational risk of using, owning, influencing, and deploying information technology in an organisation managing it. This broad framing is justified by the fact that the consequences of the materialisation of cyber risk can occur regardless of whether the source was a deliberate act or inadvertent human error, and whether it lies in circumstances external to the

36. (C. Banasinski, The Concept of Cyber Security and Cyberspace [in:] Cyber Security. Outline of a Lecture, ed. C. Banasiński, Warsaw 2018, p. 22).

organisation or has its origin within the entity. We have been dealing with cyber risks for as long as we have been dealing with cyberspace itself, i.e., the use, in short, of the Internet and electronic means of communication. One of the first publicised risks associated with the use of cyberspace was the YK2 problem. Although the first types of cyber insurance were already being offered, they did not attract much attention from companies. Besides, insurers themselves took a conservative approach to them. Attitudes began to change in the early 2000s when the first high-profile incidents involving breaches of the electronic payment systems of major US corporations (Heartland Payment Systems and Sony's PlayStation Network) took place. An additional factor became the introduction of the first data breach regulations (e.g., the 2002 regulations in California, or the provisions of the European Parliament and Commission Data Protection Regulation). The development of privacy breach rules and liability has been a milestone in the development of awareness of cyber risk, and the need to manage it comprehensively and thus also consider its insurance as a method to manage part of this risk.[37]

713. Talking about cyber risk insurance, however, requires a more detailed approach to its definitions. These have emerged in recent years by at least a dozen. This diversity is part of the observed problem of the lack of standardisation of cyber insurance (EIOPA 2020). For the purposes of this study, the definitions of cyber risk created for the purposes of insurance coverage are certainly the most useful, and of these, the author, for the purposes of this study, has chosen the definition adopted by the Geneva Association,[38] according to which cyber risk is any risk arising from the use of ICT that presupposes the confidentiality, availability and integrity of data or services.

714. In this regard, it is necessary to refer to the concept of cyberspace, which, for example, the National Institute of Standards and Technology (NIST, 2013) defines as 'a global space in the information environment consisting of an interdependent network of information systems infrastructures, including the Internet, telecommunications networks, computer systems and embedded processors and controllers'. The literature emphasises that although there is no clear definition of cyberspace, it should be viewed through the lens of technical and technological as well as social elements. Thus, the definition has been proposed according to which cyberspace is 'a virtual environment of more or less open communication through interconnected computer systems and information and information links'.

715. Cybersecurity in the above view is caused naturally by features of technology or by human action, such as human error, criminal actions (extortion, forgery), cyber war or cyber terrorism. It is characterised by the interdependence of events and their effects, their potentially catastrophic magnitude, high uncertainty about the optimal modelling method and high potential for fluctuations. Consideration should also be given to the EIOPA definition, adopted from the IAIS, that cyber risk is any

37. (P. Low, Insuring Against Cyber-Attacks, 'Computer Fraud & Security' 2017/4, D. Bradbury, Insuring Against Data Breaches, 'Computer Fraud & Security' 2013/2).
38. Geneva Association, Ten Key Questions on Cyber Risk and Cyber Risk Insurance, November 2016.

risk derived from the use of electronic data and its transmission, including technological tools such as internet and telecommunication networks.

716. Sources of cyber risk, i.e., types of cyber threats, are well described in publicly available reports, both Polish and foreign. Among these, human error, cybercrime and cyber-terrorism are mentioned first and foremost. Added to these are the threats of interdependency, which can lead to internal disruption of an organisation's processes and operations, but also greater vulnerability to the effects of external phenomena, such as fire or flooding. These connotations are exacerbated by the increase in interdependence not only in the area of data exchange between the private and public sectors (e.g., public records available online) but also at the level of the operation of critical infrastructure. For this reason, it can be said that cyber risk connects the public and private spheres and, consequently, prevention must also take place at these two levels.

717. Cyber risk insurance has been known since the late 1990s, when it began to be offered, in collaboration between insurers and software distribution companies, as an added value to high-quality software. While the software itself was intended to provide risk reduction resulting from the use of IT in general, by reducing the likelihood of an incident, the consequences of the materialisation of cyber risk (so-called residual risk) were transferred to the insurer.[39] Today, in the 2020s, the digital economy poses far greater challenges to this type of protection than simply assuming (part of) its financial consequences through the payment of a benefit. These challenges are amplified by phenomena such as a pandemic or an unstable geopolitical situation. This follows from the features of cyber risk outlined above. An analysis of the consequences of its materialisation shows emphatically that they can be comparable in a black scenario to terrorism or catastrophic risk. Even the gaining of experience by the market, including the collection of cyber risk data and the building up of statistics, does not ensure that it will become a risk as easily measurable as typical property insurance. This is also the reason why both the risk itself and its management, including insurance, are becoming the focus of regulators.[40]

718. Cyber risk management consists of a number of activities, of which the company's internal management systems play the most prominent role. They go significantly beyond the designation of responsible IT services, as they alone cannot completely prevent a threat or damage and will not take over management's responsibility in this regard. Among the many measures available to businesses is the provision of ISO compliance, as well as insurance. However, it is important to realise that the latter can in no way replace internal processes, but can only complement them. Internal risk management resources are essential to the proper functioning of any insurance, but in cyber insurance, they play a special role. We are talking about moral hazard, which is of considerable importance in the case of a cyber risk due to

39. (M. Lelarge & J. Bolot, Economic Incentives to Increase Security in the Internet: The Case for Insurance, IEEE INFOCOM 2009, Rio de Janeiro 2009, pp. 1494–1502, G. Strupczewski, Cyber insurance: essence, market and law, PWN 2021, p. 269).
40. EIOPA 2020, Strategy on cyber underwriting.

the dominance in cyber risks of the human factor, which is also the weakest point in the protection against the occurrence of a cyber event.

719. When analysing the role of cyber insurance in cyber risk management, it is important to bear in mind not only the effect on a single organisation but also on a global scale. Thus, it is highlighted that it has undeniable potential in terms of, for example, raising awareness among organisations of the risks and losses that may result from cyber-attacks by sharing knowledge on good cyber security practices and cyber risk management. Insurers' actions on both a micro (in individual insurance relationships) and macro (through public promotion campaigns) scale can effectively encourage investment in risk mitigation, and facilitate response to and recovery from cyber-attacks.

720. Cyber insurance is voluntary insurance regardless of jurisdiction. This means that there are no legislative guidelines as to the object and scope of the protection offered, and there are no standardised terms and conditions of protection. Some standardisation essentially stems from the technical elements and features of cyber risks, which are key to the construction of insurance cover based, for example, on the bow-tie method to identify the sources of the risk and its consequences, which translate into the definition of the insurance accident and the scope of cover. The subject matter and scope of insurance are thus a product of insurance and IT technology to a greater extent than in general insurance. Underwriting cyber risks precisely because of these characteristics is being examined by EIOPA and other regulators worldwide. This is important on two levels, first for building transparent cyber insurance models, devoid of *silent risks*, and also, given the dynamic growth of this risk, for monitoring the security of the insurance market in the context of risk exposure as required by Solvency II.

721. Understanding the specialised nature of cyber risk insurance is key to its proper management and underwriting. This statement would seem self-evident were it not for the fact from a survey of businesses, more than half of whom were confident that cyber risk cover was included in general property, or third-party liability insurance contracts, while only 17% of these contracts included appropriate cover. It is theoretically possible to include appropriate cover in general property insurance contracts, including property, business interruption, public liability or even directors' or employers' liability insurance. However, the insurance market's response to the increasing level of threats is to develop a dedicated subject matter and scope of cyber-risk insurance and offer it as a separate insurance product that can comprehensively provide a threat-compatible level of protection. It combines risks characteristic of different types of insurance, but only when offered under a single insurance contract can it be described as cyber-risk insurance. This is a direct result of the complex nature of cyber risk as defined above.

722. For a long time, protection against cyber risks was provided by more general insurance contracts, i.e., property insurance, business interruption, general liability, and professional indemnity (errors and omissions, professional indemnity).

However, because they were not structured with these risks in mind, they essentially provided, if any, protection against cyber risks by accident. For the most part, however, they are so ill-suited to its specifics that the most critical risks are covered by the insurer's exclusion of liability, or have remained in the realm of 'silent risks'. Thus, in property insurance, there are exclusions for recovery from a cyber-attack, a clear reference to material damage to tangible assets, where damage to software and data is subject to exclusion as intangible damage. Conventional BI insurance does not consequently cover cyber-attacks as not causing material damage. In the basic type of BI insurance, there is usually an exclusion for damage involving a breach of personal data; and in professional indemnity or D&O insurance, cover is sometimes limited to professional indemnity claims against third parties while employee claims for disclosure of their data are excluded, and exclusions apply, for example, for the spread of a virus.

723. Given the above, it is important to come to terms with the fact that cyber risk requires a specific approach and a dedicated product that combines features of different classes of insurance. Thus, the subject matter and scope of dedicated cyber insurance usually cover the three basic types of events that make up cyber risks, i.e., third-party liability, financial risks related to the interruption of the policyholder's business or other costs constituting pure financial loss, and legal expenses insurance. The insured event that determines the subject matter of the insurance (referred to as a cyber incident or event) is usually a malicious (intentional) act of a third party, human error, programming error, breach of privacy, loss of network security, unauthorised use of or access to a computer system, or threats or similar acts against a computer system, as well as such incidental acts as the occurrence of an overvoltage, undervoltage or power outage in an electrical installation.

724. As part of the coverage against the consequences of liability risks, the provisions of the insurance contracts define the events giving rise to the policyholder's liability covered by the insurance and directly related to the incident. The scope of the insurance differs significantly from that of so-called general liability insurance, covering only a part of the insured's potential liability, i.e., resulting from breaches of privacy, data, security and related consequences. The scope of insurance may cover both the indemnity benefit, pursuant to Article 822 of the Civil Code, and the costs of defence against the claim, as well as the so-called incident response costs, which should be qualified as rescue costs, included in a general manner in Article 826 of the Civil Code. However, while the inclusion of claim defence costs is the result of contractual practice due to the voluntary nature of the insurance, the rescue costs, which consist of saving the insured object and preventing or reducing the extent of the damage, are within the limits of the insurer's obligation under Article 826 §4 of the Civil Code.

725. Market practice indicates the application of the above provision, although the remedying of the damage caused by the realisation of a cyber risk often makes it difficult to assess whether we are dealing with damage prevention or just compensation. In both cases, the common denominator should be, as far as possible, the restoration of the previous state from before the insurance accident (e.g., the restoration of computer system functionality, technical restoration, recovery or reinstallation of data or computer programs, including the costs of purchasing software licences necessary to restore such data or computer programmes). The construction of the scope of protection allowing for the coverage of expert costs aimed at preventing the increase of damage brings the nature of the benefit closer to that of a preventive or assistance-type benefit. This refers to those actions that are taken after the disclosure of a data, privacy or security breach and are aimed at preventing or reducing its effects (such as securing data, informing victims, organising a call centre, analysing the causes and effects of the incident, etc.). It appears that the costs of advising the insured regarding the statutory public law obligations relating to the disclosure of the breach and assisting in complying with such obligations will also be of a similar nature.

726. In addition to civil liability, the scope of cover may include the costs of fines and penalties imposed on the insured and the costs of representing the insured in administrative or criminal proceedings pending in or against the insured in connection with the occurrence of an insurance accident (or only certain events qualifying as an insurance accident). This type of risk covered is to be classified as insurance of financial risks, which means that from a civil law point of view, the provisions of the liability insurance contract do not apply, but the general provisions of property insurance do. Of a similar nature will be benefits compensating for business interruption losses due to the unavailability of an IT system, as well as covering business resumption costs incurred in direct connection with the event causing the business interruption. The nature of pure financial losses also includes coverage for damages caused by cyber-intrusion incurred to remedy the data or privacy incident (in this regard, coverage includes both the costs of experts managing the incident and conducting negotiations, for example, as well as amounts paid in ransom), as well as costs arising from amounts paid out in error as a result of a cyber-attack or the use of the policyholder's IT system to execute financial flows. In legal terms, the same construction is adopted by insurance coverage for costs incurred for public relations in connection with the need to protect the insured's reputation (defined as negative publicity resulting from an insurance accident [sometimes included as a crisis communication cost]) by covering the costs of public relations consultants or so-called crisis communication.

727. Another characteristic aspect of insurance coverage is the so-called trigger, i.e., the temporal factor that determines insurance coverage. It constitutes the 'temporal' element of an insurance accident, which – according to Articles 805 and 806 of the Civil Code – must occur during the insurance period. In insurance practice, we are most often dealing with the triggers of claims made, loss occurrence or act committed, and the distinction between these events is of the greatest importance in civil liability insurance, in the manner resulting from the wording of Articles 822 §§2 and 3 of the Civil Code. In view of the fact that cyber risk insurance combines features of various insurances, the definition of an insured accident in terms of time will differ from one coverage to another. Thus, in the section on liability protection, we may be dealing with an insurance accident consisting in the occurrence of a liability event during the insurance period, e.g., a breach of data, privacy or security (act committed), the occurrence of a loss arising therefrom (loss occurrence) or the filing of a claim for damages during the insurance period (claims made). However, the specifics of cyber risk indicate the sometimes considerable difficulty in identifying the timing of the loss event, as well as the complex process of identifying the timing of the damage. For this reason, a fairly common trigger used in third-party liability insurance is the claims-made trigger, providing coverage for damage claims first made during the insurance period or possibly during an additional period, if applicable.

728. This treatment of the insured accident will not apply to the part of the insurance cover that compensates for the consequences of a business interruption or other financial losses resulting from a cyber event. In this respect, the insured accident will be the disclosure of the occurrence of the insured event, i.e., the disclosure of a data, privacy or security breach. This is also a slightly different take from popular forms of insurance for property or financial risks, where the insured accident usually covers the occurrence rather than the disclosure of a specific event during the period of insurance. This difference is clearly due to the nature of cyber risk. Determining the timing of a breach is extremely difficult, if not impossible. The key is its disclosure, which is also consistent with the onset of damage consequences. In addition, in the case of business interruption insurance, we will be confronted with the concept of an indemnity period, which means the period of the occurrence (or disclosure) of the event resulting in the interruption of the policyholder's business, and which must start within the period of insurance – as this is when the insured event must have occurred, depending on its definition. The indemnity period is usually limited in time, e.g., to 180 days, unless the business interruption ends earlier.

729. Undoubtedly important for the assessment of the scope of coverage is the scope of exclusions proposed by insurers. As this insurance is not all-risk, the limitation of coverage should be analysed through the prism of at least two types of provisions. These are not only provisions with strict exclusions but also specific constructions of the definition of insured events, e.g., a limitation of the concept of damage or the scope of indemnity benefits. The risks subject to exclusion from insurance coverage can be grouped into several categories. As it seems, they represent a recurrent market practice. An uninsurable risk under all conditions is the wilful act or gross negligence of the insured, which is also subject to exclusion by law (Article 827 of the Civil Code). This exclusion covers both the policyholder (and thus also persons acting on behalf of the policyholder, who is a legal entity) and the insured pursuant to Article 827 §4 of the Civil Code. Thus, it also applies to such events which, by their nature, can only occur as a result of intentional acts, i.e., infringement of intellectual property of third parties, such as plagiarism, violation of trade secrets, patents, trademarks, trade names, copyrights, licences or any other form of intellectual property rights, as well as intentional collection of data or distribution of information in the nature of spam. Exclusions regarding the sanctioning of specific conduct by the insured are among the most problematic. In the Polish system, the predominant position of the jurisprudence as regards the possibility of limiting the right to benefit only allows for an exclusion of the insurer's liability only in a situation where the breach of duty occurred due to wilful misconduct or gross negligence.[41] Clauses of this type should therefore not be construed to imply a limitation of the insurability of events arising from the ordinary fault of the insured, such as a lack of diligence in monitoring the security system.

730. Another category of exclusions may include the risk of damage to the software itself or other intellectual assets through which the attack occurred, consisting of their loss, destruction or loss of commercial value. This is due to the very difficult estimation of such losses. A risk that is not insurable under cyber risk insurance is also the risk of personal injury, although international experience has shown that it is possible to negotiate the scope of such an exclusion on an individual basis, particularly where liability to an injured third party is involved. The lack of coverage for personal injury liability under cyber risk insurance may necessitate supplemental coverage in this respect under general liability insurance.

731. Another common exclusion is the failure of mechanical or electronic equipment. It consists of excluding from coverage events involving mechanical deactivation of equipment, disconnection of power supply, etc., but should only apply to events that are not in the nature of a cyber-attack (via virus, spam, etc.). Particular attention should be paid to the exclusions relating to war and terrorist risks (such exclusion applies to war, invasion and insurrection) in conjunction with their broad definition. This is because it cannot be denied that incidents will often amount to terrorism or even cyber war.

732. Another type of frequent subject-matter exclusion is the lack of protection for mobile devices such as laptops. In some insurance contracts, the removal of this exclusion is possible on individual terms, e.g., provided that the data on such devices is encrypted. A classic exclusion is the limitation of civil liability protection to that regulated by law, i.e., beyond the basic scope of liability for non-performance or improper performance of obligations in the area not extended under Article 473 of the Civil Code. Furthermore, within civil liability, claims between insureds may be excluded, necessitating separate coverage, e.g., of the D&O type in the event that cyber insurance covers both the company and its directors and officers as insureds.

733. In addition to exclusions specific to cyber risks, insurance contracts also contain a standard range of exclusions for different types of insurance, and this is precisely because of the previously stated combination of different types of risks in a single insurance contract. Such exclusions include war and terrorist risks (albeit subject to the possible possibility of cyber-terrorism coverage), risks of environmental pollution, natural wear and tear on IT systems, use of experimental and unapproved IT infrastructure products, and financial risks associated with securities trading.

41. (D. Fuchs, Komentarz d Art. 827 k.c., Kluwer 2020, p. 403).

734. The specificity of cyber insurance begins at the pre-contractual stage. As in other types of insurance, the basic starting point is risk assessment. The insurer, in seeking to identify it, must analyse factors such as the process of storing data for a large number of entities (persons), the facts regarding the possible handling of payment cards, the circumstances regarding the dependence of the business on the Internet (as to the risk of business interruption), the type of activity in terms of its standard or unique nature, the level of growth of the business through successive acquisitions and, finally, the scale of outsourcing used by the policyholder, including access to the premises, data and system of the policyholder by contractors. The fact is that, as with all new risks, there is still not a sufficient historical database to accurately estimate the risk (including the average loss per event). The lack of a sufficient actuarial base of the consequences of a cyber event makes it difficult to apply a fundamental principle for insurance – the law of large numbers – and therefore to estimate the risk correctly. Therefore, there will be undoubted value in the cooperation of the insurance sector with government administration, including access to data on breaches that are notifiable under the new legislation. Consequently, in order to compensate for the resulting information asymmetry as to the level of risk, insurers are forced to use very precise information acquisition tools. These include pre-audits and advanced questionnaires, as well as specific IT compliance requirements (e.g., requiring confirmation of compliance and security of IT systems by the policyholder), which, despite their value, do not eliminate the risk in the case of strong policyholder relationships with external systems.

735. The above circumstances 'force' a rather close cooperation between the insurer and the policyholder at the risk identification stage, even consisting of the insurer's access to the policyholder's IT systems, auditing the system, internal processes, responsibilities and the way cyber risk is managed. Without it, it is difficult to imagine effective cyber risk management, including prevention and remediation by the insurer. Many times, clauses providing for access to the insurer to the policyholder's systems and the insurer's participation in the management of security systems are present in foreign cyber insurance.

736. The policyholder is burdened with a number of other obligations which, although theoretically not dissimilar in their nature to other types of insurance, take on a special significance in practice in cyber risk insurance. It can be said that there is a far-reaching idea of mutuality and cooperation between the parties. Prior to the occurrence of an insurance accident, the main burden of this cooperation lies with the policyholder, to shift to the side of the insurer at the post-incident stage. For this reason, insurance contracts in Poland often contain provisions imposing an obligation on policyholders to take precautionary measures as a condition of insurance cover. These obligations are in the nature of an insurance duty, as a consequence of failure to observe them the insurer may refuse to fulfil the benefit if they had an impact on the occurrence of an insurance accident. Therefore, it seems necessary to apply Article 827 of the Civil Code, i.e., to prove the insured's willful misconduct or gross negligence in failing to observe such duties. It is undoubtedly helpful for this purpose to formulate the tasks of the insured precisely so that both parties have certainty of the legal situation in the event of an insurance accident for reasons attributable to the policyholder.

737. Market practice indicates the frequent presence of clauses consisting of an obligation on the insured to take all reasonable and possible measures to secure the IT system and prevent the occurrence of cyber-attacks or business interruption events and minimise their negative effects. However, this wording of the insurance contract provision may be considered imprecise. It should be supplemented in the practice of their application by the insured itself, e.g., by introducing security procedures or verifying the existence of such procedures as part of the insurance underwriting process by the insurer. A rather specific type of obligation, not found in any other type of insurance, is the obligation to keep the existence of the insurance cover secret insofar as it relates to cyber extortion subject to an obligation to disclose such information to authorised state authorities. For obvious reasons, however, it is intended to prevent an increase in moral hazard, both on the part of the policyholder and on the part of the perpetrators of extortion.

738. Further types of obligations are actualised in the event of an insurance accident. In addition to the obligation imposed by Article 826 of the Civil Code, insurers standardly introduce provisions clarifying the scope of these obligations and the manner of performance. Above all, the obligation to notify the event, which is repeated in all types of insurance, gains a new dimension in cyber insurance. While judgments of consumer courts have effectively brought out the use of short (even counted in hours) deadlines for notifying the insurers about the occurrence of an insurance accident and this also applies nowadays in the terms and conditions of cyber insurance, it is precisely in this type of insurance that the speed of the insured's action, due to the specificity of information technology, the speed of the spread of the damage and the cascading increase of its size, is justified.

Chapter 13. Miscellaneous Insurances

739. Poles travel a lot, whether for business or pleasure. Insurance protection in connection with travel is provided by many insurers, is extensive and is offered through various channels. There are no significant differences in the scope and conditions of insurance coverage offered by different insurers, although the scope of coverage usually depends on the choice of the policyholder.

740. Usually, the insurance cover for people travelling abroad consists of four separate policies: motor vehicle liability and third-party liability, medical expenses abroad and the consequences of injury or death occurring abroad, and luggage insurance. Motor insurance for international traffic does not differ much from that used in the domestic market (except, of course, for the amount of the premium). In the following, we will discuss the insurance of the costs of medical treatment and the consequences of bodily injury or death occurring abroad.

§1. Insurance of Costs of Medical Treatment and Accidental Death and Dismemberment Abroad

741. The first part of the insurance covers medical expenses incurred by the insured person abroad as a result of a sudden illness or accident. Medical expenses include expenses incurred abroad for medical examinations, treatments, interventions and operations, the purchase of necessary medicines and dressings prescribed by a doctor, as well as hospitalisation. There is also a long list of additional costs and expenses covered by the insurance, such as the cost of transporting the injured person from the place of the accident to the hospital, the cost of the necessary return of the injured person to Poland and the cost of attending to the injured person during the period of his or her return to Poland.

742. There are several exclusions of the insurer's liability. First of all, the insurer is not obliged to reimburse the expenses incurred if there are any medical objections to the insured person going abroad. In particular, the Insurer does not cover expenses related to: special diets, even if recommended by a doctor, stays in sanatoriums and health resorts, medical treatment that was not necessary for the return to Poland, alcohol or drug intoxication, abortion unless it was necessary to save the life of the insured, medical treatment in Poland, etc. The insurance also does not cover the costs of cosmetic surgery, the purchase of spectacles or the repair of dentures, unless they were damaged in an accident, dental treatment, chronic diseases and others.

743. The second part of the cover provides protection in the event of an accident that causes bodily injury, impairment of health and/or death of the insured person. The accident must have occurred outside the insured's control during the period of insurance. If the accident caused the death of the insured person before the expiry of the two-year period prior to the accident, persons such as the spouse, children, parents and other heirs of the deceased will be entitled to the death benefit (in the appropriate order). However, if the insured person suffers a permanent disability as a result of an accident within two years of the date of the accident, he may be entitled to a permanent disability benefit in proportion to the degree of disability. This is a lump-sum payment which does not take into account the occupation or profession of the disabled person.

§2. Insurance of Traveller's Baggage Abroad

744. This policy covers items that are part of the traveller's luggage during his/her stay abroad and that are left in the care of the insured person or entrusted to a professional carrier, left in a luggage office or left in a locked luggage compartment at a railway station, airport, etc., or left in a hotel or locked in a vehicle.

745. The Insurer will pay compensation if, during the period of insurance, the insured luggage is lost, destroyed or damaged as a result of:

a. a duly documented theft or robbery;
b. An accident on land, water or in the air;
c. an accident or sudden illness of a person resulting in loss of control of luggage;
d. fire, lightning, explosion, hurricane, heavy rain, hail, avalanche, etc.

746. However, the following items are excluded from the insurance cover: repatriation effects, means of transport, floating equipment, fuel, valuables, scientific and artistic objects, cash, alcohol, and effects for production or commercial purposes. In addition, the Insurer is not liable for damage caused intentionally or by gross negligence by the Insured or a member of his family, or in connection with the confiscation, detention or destruction of the goods by customs or other authorities, or as a result of wear and tear of the insured object, its spontaneous combustion, perishability, etc. The Insurer is not liable for damage caused by the Insured's own fault, or as a result of the Insured's or a member of his family's gross negligence, or in connection with the confiscation, detention or destruction of the goods by customs or other authorities.

Part IV. Motor Vehicle Insurance

Chapter 1. Motor Vehicle Insurance Against Third-Party Liability

747. The original concept of motor (third party) liability insurance is to protect the policyholder against financial losses that may arise as a result of damage caused to third parties in connection with the ownership of the vehicle. Although this concept is still valid today, it has largely been replaced by a new concept which consists of protecting the victim of a motor accident rather than the person who caused the damage.[42] Such a modern approach has not only been introduced in numerous provisions of civil law, e.g., by supplementing the concept of tort liability or that of strict liability, which must now be assumed by the owner (the owner-like possessor or the dependent possessor) of the vehicle, but has also provided the basis for a compulsory motor vehicle liability insurance system and has led, among other things, to provisions obliging the insurer and the UFG to indemnify the victim. The law provides that the insurer who undertakes the activity within the framework of this type of insurance must accept all the risks raised by the insured, without any right of refusal.

748. Third-party liability insurance extends to the liability defined in Articles 435 and 436 of the Civil Code, which establishes the general principle that a person who, on his own account, operates a business or a machine using natural energy, such as steam, gas, electricity, liquid fuel, etc., is liable for any damage caused to a person or property unless the damage was caused by force majeure or entirely due to the fault of the injured person or a third party for whom he is not vicariously liable. Article 436(1) of the Civil Code extends this type of liability specifically to the 'independent owner' of the mechanically propelled vehicle and to the person to whom he has given possession of the vehicle. The liability defined in these two articles cannot be excluded or limited in advance by an agreement between the parties (Article 437), such an agreement being null and void.

749. According to these provisions, the liability of users of motor vehicles is based on the principle of risk (strict liability), which means that they are obliged to compensate for any damage caused by the use of motor vehicles under their control, irrespective of the fault of the driver. Liability can only be excluded if it is proved that the accident was caused solely by the injured party or solely by a third

42. T. Sangowski '*Ubezpieczenia Gospodarcze*', 163 et al.

party or by force majeure, i.e., an unexpected and unavoidable act of nature. Obviously, any defect of the vehicle itself does not fall under this category and falls under the risk of the owner or possessor of the vehicle.

750. The principle of risk does not exclude the consideration of the contributory negligence of the injured party, since the law rarely encounters clear cases of total responsibility of one party for an accident. Therefore, while the user of a motor vehicle may be exonerated only in the case of a clear case of full responsibility of the injured party, in other cases he/she is entitled to expect a reduction of damages in accordance with the behaviour of the injured party (Article 362 of the Civil Code).

751. Apart from the above, the user may be liable according to the principle of fault expressed in Article 415 of the Civil Code, which provides that 'whoever, through his fault, causes damage to another, shall be liable to make good such damage'. However, in the context of civil liability, this only applies to the claims of 'gratuitous passengers' and to the mutual claims of users in the event of collisions between their vehicles. It follows that a passenger carried free of charge must prove negligence on the part of the user or driver, whereas claims for damages arising from collisions are apportioned according to the respective degrees of negligence of the parties involved. However, the situations in which the principle of fault can be applied are interpreted narrowly, as they are exceptions to the general rules of liability for damage caused by motor vehicles.

752. Compulsory civil liability insurance for owners of motor vehicles is governed by the Act of 22 May 2003 on Compulsory Insurance, UFG and Motor Insurers' Bureau, Chapter 2. This Act provides for a general regulation of all compulsory insurances in Poland, however, TPL insurance is subject to the most extensive regulation, taking into account the relevant legislation of the EU.

753. The obligation to insure applies to every owner of a mechanical vehicle for the entire period of its registration. The insurance taken out by the owner of the vehicle covers any person driving the vehicle. The obligation to take out insurance in accordance with the provisions of the Act does not apply to vehicles for which the place of risk is one of the countries of the EU. The obligation of foreign vehicles concerns the whole period of their stay in Poland.

754. The scope of the insurer's liability and, consequently, the scope of the insurance cover are very broadly defined. Third-party liability insurance covers liability towards third parties who, in connection with the use of the vehicle, have suffered material or non-material damage resulting in death, bodily injury or mental impairment, as well as physical loss, damage or destruction of property. In addition, the law defines damage as related to the use of the motor vehicle damage that occurs when entering or leaving the vehicle, when loading or unloading it, as well as during stopping, parking and parking. In addition, in the case of damage occurring on the territory of Poland, compensation may also be paid if the person who caused damage to another person cannot be identified or if the person who caused both damage to property and damage to another person has not concluded a contract providing for compulsory TPL insurance. In such cases, compensation is paid by the UFG.

755. There are some exclusions of coverage if the claims pursued under third-party liability insurance are subject to Polish law. In this case, the insurer is not liable for the following losses that have occurred: (1) damage, destruction or loss of property caused by the driver to the owner of the motor vehicle; It also includes the situation when the owner of the motor vehicle by which the damage was caused is the owner or co-owner of the motor vehicle to which the damage was caused (however, it should be emphasised that in this case there is full coverage in respect of bodily injury); (2) resulting from the carriage of goods as freight, consignments or luggage, unless the liability of the Insurer is excluded; (3) resulting from the loss of cash, jewellery, securities, documents of any kind or collections of stamps, coins or similar collections; (4) resulting from environmental pollution or contamination.

756. Civil liability insurance protects both the user and the driver since it is clearly designed to cover civil liability arising from the use of the vehicle, regardless of who is in control of the vehicle at the time of the accident. Consequently, neither fault nor wilful misconduct will relieve the insurer of the obligation to indemnify the insured, although the insurer will acquire the right of recovery against a wrongdoer.

757. The Insurer is entitled to recover from the Insured the indemnity paid under the policy if the Insured: (1) caused the damage intentionally or after having consumed alcohol or under the influence of narcotics or psychotropic substances or substitutes; (2) became the user of the vehicle as a result of committing a criminal offence (e.g., theft of the vehicle); (3) did not have the necessary driving licence to drive the motor vehicle, with the exception of the following cases: saving the life or property of a person or during the pursuit of the perpetrator immediately after the commission of the offence by this person; (4) escaped from the place of the event.

758. Compensation will be determined and paid within the limits of the Insured's liability up to the Guaranteed Amount stated in the Insurance Contract. The guarantee sum cannot be lower than the equivalent in PLN: (1) in the case of personal injury – EUR 5,000,000 for each injured person, regardless of the number of injured persons; (2) in the case of property damage – EUR 1,000,000 for one event, the consequences of which are covered by the insurance, regardless of the number of injured persons – calculated at the average exchange rate published by the NBP as valid on the day of the occurrence.

759. For losses occurring in countries where the National Bureaux are signatories to the Uniform Agreement between National Bureaux – Internal Regulations, the Insurer is liable up to the guarantee sum established by the legal acts of the respective country but not less than the above-mentioned sums.

760. As a matter of fact, the heads of damage are defined by the PCC and the amount of damage is a matter of amicable or court settlement. Thus, according to Article 362 of the Civil Code, a wrongdoer is liable for the 'usual consequence of the act or omission which caused the damage' and, within these limits, is obliged to compensate for the actual loss suffered (*damnum emergens*) and the benefit which could have been obtained if the damage had not occurred (*lucrum cessans*). If the injured party has contributed to the cause of the damage, his compensation will be reduced accordingly (Article 362 Civil Code). According to the choice of the injured party, the compensation is either the restoration of the status quo or compensation in lieu of the damage (Article 363 Civil Code). If the damage consists of an injury to health or the body, the injured party is entitled to reimbursement of all costs incurred, including the cost of prostheses and retraining if his disability prevents him from pursuing his previous occupation (Article 444 Civil Code). If his earning capacity has been permanently reduced or his needs have increased, he is entitled to periodic payments to compensate for the loss of further opportunities. He is also entitled to compensation for loss of earnings and for pain and suffering (Article 445 of the Civil Code). The latter allows, in special cases, compensation for moral damage and claims for impairment of the enjoyment of normal life.

761. In the case of a fatal accident (Article 446 Civil Code), the tortfeasor is obliged to reimburse the costs of medical treatment (if any) and the usual funeral expenses. The second category of compensation for death consists of periodic payments to the deceased's dependants. These include the deceased's spouse, children, parents and grandchildren, brothers and sisters, and relatives by marriage if they were entitled to support and were actually supported by the deceased. In the case of widows, for example, eligibility depends on age, earning capacity and responsibility for the upbringing of children. The third heading complements the second, as it consists of compensation to dependants if they suffer a 'substantial deterioration in their standard of living'. As of 2010, the PCC also provides for compensation for moral damage to the deceased's close relatives.

762. In principle, the insurance contract should be concluded for a period of twelve months. The insurance can be concluded for a shorter period only in the listed cases, i.e., if the vehicle is: (1) temporarily registered (for a period not shorter than the period of registration – at least thirty days); (2) registered abroad if the country of the risk location is Poland; (3) a slow-moving vehicle; (4) a historic vehicle. The short-term insurance contract for historical vehicles should be concluded for a period not shorter than thirty days.

763. The short-term insurance contract for a period shorter than thirty days, as far as the permanently registered motor vehicles are concerned, can be concluded by the entity carrying out business activities in buying and selling motor vehicles.

764. The insurer's liability commences upon the conclusion of the insurance contract and the payment of the premium or its first instalment. However, if the contract has been automatically renewed, the liability starts from the date of renewal. If a later deadline for the payment of the premium is specified, the insurer's liability shall commence from the moment of the conclusion of the insurance contract. The parties may freely agree on a different date of commencement of the insurer's liability only in limited cases specified in the Act.

765. The owner of the motor vehicle is obliged to take out insurance: (1) at the latest on the day of registration of the motor vehicle, with the exception of historic vehicles, or – in special cases; (2) before the motor vehicle is allowed to be driven; or (3) before crossing the border, if the owner of the motor vehicle allowed to be driven in Poland has not taken out insurance; or (4) at the latest on the day on which the insurer's liability under the insurance contract ceases; (5) at the latest on the day on which the current insurance contract is terminated in the event of cancellation (as provided for in the Consumer Rights Act).

766. The insurance policy expires: (1) at the end of the period of its conclusion; (2) at the moment of the vehicle's deregistration; (3) at the moment of the contract withdrawal; (4) at the moment of the permanent and complete loss of the vehicle's ownership in circumstances that did not lead to the change of the owner; (5) upon the expiration of three months from the date of the insurer's bankruptcy filing; (6) upon the registration of the vehicle abroad; (7) upon the transfer of ownership of the vehicle to another person and the cancellation of the insurance policy by the new owner; (8) upon the cancellation of the policy as explained below.

767. If the owner of the vehicle has concluded two insurance contracts for the same period with different insurers (which sometimes happens due to the automatic renewal of the insurance of which the owner is not aware), he/she can terminate the insurance contract concluded as a result of the automatic renewal. In this case, the Insurer will be entitled to the premium paid up to the date of cancellation. If there are two or more insurance contracts with the same insurer for the same vehicle, the insurer is only entitled to one premium.

768. The insurance contract may be automatically renewed if the owner does not notify the insurer of its termination at least one day before the end of the insurance period. It will then be considered that a new insurance contract has been concluded for the following twelve months. In order to avoid double insurance in such cases, the Insurer is obliged to notify the policyholder of the extension of the insurance cover for the following period at least fourteen days before the end of the insurance period. The automatic prolongation does not take place only in the case of non-payment of the insurance premium for the previous insurance period or in the case of bankruptcy or insolvency of the insurer.

769. If the ownership of the vehicle is transferred to another person, the rights and obligations under the insurance contract covering the vehicle are automatically transferred to the new owner. However, the new owner has the right to cancel the insurance contract. If the insurance contract is continued, the insurer may recalculate the premium taking into account the risk factors relating to the new owner. The new owner is responsible for paying the premium from the day the vehicle is transferred. The previous owner is also jointly and severally liable for the payment of the premium from the date of transfer of the vehicle until the date on which the insurer is notified of the transfer of ownership.

770. In some cases, it is possible to return the premium for the unused period of insurance if the insurance contract has been terminated in accordance with the provisions of the law. The return should be made within fourteen days of the termination.

771. Conducting insurance activities related to motor third-party liability insurance in Poland is connected with the need to comply with 'soft law' regulations, including the Recommendations on the Settlement of Claims in Motor Insurance issued by the KNF in July 2012. The said Recommendations replaced the Guidelines on Motor Insurance Claims Settlement of 16 December 2014. According to the KNF, the Recommendations contain requirements that derive directly from applicable legislation, Supreme Court rulings indicating best practices to be followed by insurance undertakings, the need to protect the individual interests of policyholders, insureds and beneficiaries under insurance contracts, and supervisory expectations of insurance undertakings regarding the organisation and management of the claims settlement process. The Recommendations cover, *inter alia*, the following issues: timely payment of benefits; payment of benefits in accordance with the principle of full compensation; compliance with disclosure obligations towards beneficiaries; supervision and control by the governing bodies of insurance undertakings over the claims settlement process; internal control in the claims settlement process; supervision and control by insurance undertakings over external entities carrying out claims settlement activities on their behalf.

772. The Recommendations are addressed to domestic insurance undertakings and should also be applied by the main branches of foreign insurance undertakings, taking into account the specificities of their organisation. The Recommendations on the manner of conducting the claims settlement process and determining the amount of compensation under motor third-party liability insurance contracts for damage caused by motor vehicles in motion should also be applied by foreign insurance undertakings with their registered office in the Member States of the EU or the European Free Trade Association (EFTA) – parties to the Agreement on the European Economic Area – conducting insurance business in Poland.

773. In addition to the recommendations, the PFSA issues various opinions on matters relating to motor third-party liability insurance, referring to various issues relating to insurance activity in this area. One of the opinions relates to the issue of the adequacy of premiums. In its standpoint of 6 May 2021, the PFSA discussed the issue of premium adequacy in the insurance referred to in Groups 3 and 10 of Division II of the Annex to the Act of 11 September 2015 on Insurance and Reinsurance Business. In its opinion, the PFSA expressed its expectation that the insurance premium would be correctly determined, i.e., its adequacy in relation to the obligations under the insurance contracts and the costs of the insurance activity performed in accordance with the requirements of the AIRA.

Chapter 2. Personal Accident Coverage

774. The essential issue for the character of personal accident insurance is the definition of an 'accident' as an insured event. The PCC does not define its meaning, therefore the subject of this type of insurance is regulated by the General Insurance Conditions and may differ from insurer to insurer. Despite the above, it is possible to provide a general definition (description) of the meaning of 'accident' as a subject of insurance. According to most general terms and conditions in force on the Polish insurance market, an 'accident' is an event with the following characteristics:

a. it is caused by an external force and has a direct effect on the body of the insured;
b. it occurs suddenly;
c. It occurs against the will of the Insured;
d. it causes permanent injury or death to the Insured.

775. Consequently, any indirect effect of an accident is excluded from the insurance cover, such as death due to mental shock caused by fright. In addition, for the accident to be covered by the insurance, there must be a causal link between the accident and its result in the form of injury or death of the insured.

776. With regard to the above definition of 'accident', certain insurers exclude their liability in certain cases, which results in a limitation of the above definition of 'accident'. The most common exclusions are:

a. The insured causing the accident committed or attempted to commit a crime;
b. the insured intended to commit suicide;
c. the insured was driving without a licence or under the influence of alcohol unless the driving in the above circumstances was in an attempt to save human life or property or in pursuit of a criminal, or the lack of a licence was immaterial to the cause of the accident;
d. the accident occurred in connection with war.

777. As there are no legal regulations concerning NNW (personal accident) insurance, it is usually regulated in the general conditions of insurance:

a. what kind of accidents are covered by the insurance;
b. which consequences of the accidents are covered;
c. the level of benefits (cash and non-cash).

778. Under the NNW insurance, the following benefits can be claimed:

a. a death benefit in the event of death within a certain period of time (usually one year) from the date of the accident;

b. a permanent disability benefit if the claimant is permanently disabled as a result of the accident.

779. The above benefits are usually paid in the form of a lump sum, but some insurers also offer an annuity, which is paid if the insured is permanently unable to carry on his or her occupation as a result of the accident.

780. The amount of the disability benefit is calculated in relation to the degree of disability according to a special procedure established by the insurer. Similarly, the amount of the death benefit and the sums paid for permanent disability may vary from one insurer to another. It should also be noted that both the occupation and the profession of the insured are not taken into account when calculating the disability benefit (as is the case with the social security benefit). The amount of the benefit depends on the sum insured at the time of taking out the policy and the degree of disability. In the event of death, 100% of the sum insured is paid to the beneficiary, taking into account the sums previously paid to the insured as disability benefits.

781. In addition to the two main benefits mentioned above, the insurer is usually required to pay for some other costs, such as the cost of prostheses, medical treatment and retraining for disabled members.

782. Accident insurance in Poland can be offered by insurers operating in the life and non-life insurance sectors. If it is offered by a life insurer, it should be linked to another life insurance contract, in which case it is a supplement to such insurance. If accident insurance is offered by a non-life insurer, the contract may be concluded as a separate insurance, but in practice, it is usually concluded together with autocasco or liability insurance.

Chapter 3. Autocasco Insurance

783. Today insurers offer unified terms and conditions for almost all kinds of motor vehicles irrespective of the type of their ownership. There are actually no substantial differences between the terms and conditions of autocasco insurance written by several insurers developing activities in this field on the Polish market. Below one average terms and conditions of autocasco insurance, which can be treated as very representative of the present insurance industry in Poland, will be presented.

784. The insurance comprises motor vehicles together with their standard equipment. Equipment is considered installations and appliances which are required by Polish traffic law for the maintenance and use of the vehicle according to its assignment, as well as for traffic security and protection against theft.

785. The insurance coverage extends practically to all kinds of traditional motor vehicles such as passenger cars, busses, lorries, trucks, motorcycles, trailers, and caravans, both on the territory of Poland and abroad. An insurance compensation can be paid in case the damage, destruction or physical loss of the vehicle or its standard equipment occurred as a result of:

a. sudden collision with persons, objects or animals;
b. floods, fire, lightning and explosions, hail, hurricanes and other natural forces acting in a sudden manner;
c. sudden impact of thermal and chemical factors of outside origin;
d. the use of the car without the consent of the insured person or theft of the vehicle or parts of it, providing however that they were secured against theft in a way foreseen in the construction of the vehicle unless the vehicle has been left in a closed room or secured space;
e. damage of the vehicle by third parties;
f. damage or destruction of the vehicle in connection with the carriage of persons in need of medical aid.

786. The insurer is not liable for the following losses:

a. those which occurred during driving a motor vehicle by its user or authorised driver under the influence of alcohol or without the qualifications for driving required by Polish law;
b. caused intentionally by the user of the car or the authorised driver and in case when the driver escaped from the site of an accident;
c. caused by unregistered vehicles on public roads;
d. occurred as a result of acts of war;
e. which value does not exceed a certain sum of money;
f. being in consequence of the normal exploitation of the vehicle or which occurred as a result of shocks during driving or of irregularities of the road;

g. concerning damage and destruction of tyres unless they occurred at the same time the damage or destruction of other parts of the vehicle occurred for which the insurer is being held liable.

'Auto casco insurance does not cover damage arisen during the car being driven by the possessor or driver, without the license required by law, even if the lack of the license has not influenced the damage.' SN dated 20 November 1999, sygn. Akt III CKN 475/98 OSN Izba cywilna 4/2000, p. 103.

787. Apart from the above, the insurance does not provide coverage for losses which occurred during car races, competitions, training, testing, etc., as well as caused by additional equipment of the vehicle. However, all losses like those can be, at the request of the insured, included in the coverage by payment of an additional premium.

788. The insurance premium is determined according to the respective tariffs applicable at the time of the conclusion of the contract. Accordingly, the insurance premium depends on the period of insurance, the type, kind and value of the vehicle, the scope of insurance coverage (whether it is only for domestic traffic or for abroad, whether there are additional risks included or not) and the value of additional equipment. In case of disposal of an insured vehicle, all rights and obligations deriving from the insurance contract are transferred to the purchaser, however, the insurer's liability lasts until the end of the insurance period for which the insurance contract has been concluded.

789. Terms and conditions of AC insurance impose some obligations on the insured person or the actual driver of the car when an accident happens such as:

a. to take all proper steps in order to ensure the safety of traffic at the site of the accident;
b. to prevent, if possible, an aggravation of damages;
c. to provide the insurer with all the required information and explanations about the accident;
d. not to conduct any repairs on the damaged car (unless required for continuing safe driving) until a proper survey by the insurer's representatives is arranged;
e. to notify the insurer about the accident as soon as possible, however, no later than seven days from the date of passing the border (if damage occurred abroad).

790. If the insured person has not complied with one of the above-specified obligations and this had some influence on the extent of the damage, the insurer can reject the claim or diminish its scope accordingly.

791. In case of total damage to a vehicle or its total loss as a consequence of the theft or other reason, the insurer will determine the extent of the damage equal to the amount of value of the vehicle at the time of the evaluation of the indemnity, but not higher than the insured sum for which the contract has been concluded. On the contrary, when the insured vehicle has been damaged only in part, the extent of damage is assessed by the insurer according to the actual costs of the repairs of the vehicle carried out in Poland. From the amount of losses that occurred in the vehicle as such and its additional equipment have to be deducted the value of residuals and the share of the insured person which amounts to 10% of the extent of the damage. This can be increased to 20% if during two consequential years damage occurred more than once or even to 30% if during the same period of time damage occurred three or more times. An indemnity has to be paid by the insurer within thirty days from the time when a proper notification about the damage that occurred has been sent to the insurer.

792. Additionally, the insurer undertakes to refund to the possessor or driver of the car some kinds of expenditures which have been suffered in order to: prevent an aggravation of damage, transportation of damaged vehicle from the site of an accident abroad to the nearest repair's services, transportation of the damaged vehicle for repairs to be carried out in Poland, after obtaining prior consent of the insurer (in such a case costs of transportation cannot exceed the value of the vehicle and the sum for which the insurance contract has been concluded) and conduct necessary repairs in order to continue safe driving.

793. Once an indemnity has been paid, the insurer is subrogated to all the rights of the insured person against a third party in relation to the collision that occurred, up to the amount of the indemnity paid. However, this does not apply to persons with whom the Insured lives in the same household or for whom the Insured is responsible.

794. If the Insured does not agree with the Insurer's decisions regarding the amount of compensation paid in respect of the loss or damage, the Insured may take legal action against the Insurer. The Insurer is obliged to inform the Insured of the legal remedies to which he is entitled in such situations. The applicable law and jurisdiction for the settlement of all types of disputes arising from the insurance contract is Polish law.

Part V. Insurance of the Persons

Chapter 1. Accidental Death or Bodily Injuries

795. Accidental death and personal injury insurance (hereinafter referred to as 'accident insurance') may be offered in Poland by insurers operating in the life and non-life insurance business. A life insurer may offer accident insurance only in connection with another life insurance contract. A non-life insurer may offer accident insurance as a stand-alone product.

796. Pursuant to Article 829(2) of the Civil Code, the insurance of the person may cover, in particular, bodily injury, impairment of health or death caused by an accident, as far as the coverage of consequential damage and death is concerned. In the absence of specific provisions in the PCC, the terms and conditions of accident insurance are included in the general terms and conditions of accident products.

797. Essential for accident insurance is a definition of an 'accident' as an insured event. The PCC does not provide a definition of 'accident', so again it is left to the insurers to define it. Although the definition of an 'accident' may vary in detail, a general definition of an 'accident' that is the subject of accident insurance usually refers to an event that has the following characteristics:

– it is caused by an external force and has a direct effect on the body of the insured;
– it is sudden;
– it occurs against the will of the insured;
– causing the injury or death of the Insured.

798. In addition, for the accident to be covered by the insurance, there must be a causal link between the accident and its result in the form of injury or death of the insured.

799. The definitions of 'accident' used by insurers may differ in detail. In particular, it applies to limitations or exclusions of cover, the most common exclusions being that:

– the insured causing the accident was committing or attempting to commit a crime;
– the insured intended to commit suicide;

- the insured was driving without a licence or under the influence of alcohol unless the driving in the above circumstances was in an attempt to save human life or property or in pursuit of a criminal, or the lack of a licence was immaterial to the cause of the accident;
- the accident occurred in connection with war;
- the insured caused the accident as a result of intoxication by alcohol or drugs.

800. Usually, the following benefits can be claimed under accident insurance:

- death benefit if death occurs within a certain period of time (usually one year) from the date of the accident;
- a permanent disability benefit if the claimant is permanently disabled as a result of the accident.

801. The death benefit will be paid to the beneficiary designated by the insured. If the Insurer has not designated a beneficiary, the benefit will be paid to a member of the insured's family in the following order: spouse, children, parents and other heirs.

802. The type and amount of the benefit will be determined once it has been established that there is a causal link between the accident that occurred and the death, permanent disability, medical treatment and incapacity for work of the insured person. This causal link and the degree (percentage) of permanent disability, duration of medical treatment and inability to work are determined on the basis of the documents submitted and the results of the medical examination. The degree of permanent disability should be determined immediately after the end of medical treatment.

Chapter 2. Private Health Insurance

803. Private health insurance is becoming increasingly popular in Poland, mainly due to the inefficiency of the public healthcare system. The scope of private health insurance in Poland usually offers the following services:

- quick access to medical services;
- a personal doctor;
- access to a wide range of medical services, i.e., doctor's consultations, advanced diagnostics, home visits, rehabilitation services and hospital treatment;
- a wide range of options (limits, types of benefits).

804. Private insurance providers, including numerous insurance companies and medical centres, offer a variety of personalised policies tailored to individual needs. However, it is important to note that private health insurance does not guarantee the same universal and equitable access to medical services as is afforded under the public NFZ system.

The scope of services provided under private insurance and the corresponding payments are contingent on the specific policy purchased and the terms of the agreement entered into. Basic policies, typically at lower costs, generally cover limited services such as consultations with general practitioners or specific specialists. Comprehensive services, including complex dental procedures, childbirth, surgical interventions, or hospitalisation, necessitate the acquisition of more extensive and consequently more expensive policies.

805. Private health insurance policies frequently include waiting periods during which access to certain services is restricted. These waiting periods often apply to high-cost services, such as rehabilitation or minor surgical procedures, which may only become available after a defined period, typically ranging from 60 to 120 days following the commencement of premium payments.

806. Additionally, many employers in Poland offer private healthcare packages as a supplementary benefit to public insurance coverage. Individual citizens may also opt to purchase private insurance independently, primarily to secure faster access to medical services beyond those provided under the public healthcare system.

Chapter 3. Life Insurance

807. Life insurance is concerned with the life and health of individuals. Since it is difficult to find specific criteria for determining the monetary value of life and health, there is no compensation payable, but rather a predetermined amount of money (sum insured). This amount bears no relation to the extent of the damage suffered.

808. According to Article 829 of the Civil Code, the insured event in life insurance is the death of an insured person or the attainment of a certain age, whereas the insured event in accident insurance is bodily injury, impairment of health or death as a result of an accident. Under both types of insurance, the insurer is required to pay benefits upon the death of an insured, except that under accident insurance, the death must be the result of an accident.

809. As life insurance is not a contract of indemnity, the insured has the right to receive both the insurance benefit and the compensation to which he is entitled by law if the insured event is caused by the wrongful act of another. Unlike the other branches of insurance, the insurer has no right of recovery from the wrongdoer under Article 828 of the Civil Code. According to Article 833 of the Civil Code, the insured's suicide does not relieve the insurer of its liability under a life insurance policy if the suicide occurred within two years of the commencement of the insurance cover. Suicide implies an intentional act by the insured. Therefore, death resulting from the exercise of dangerous occupations is not considered suicide.

810. Although the contract of life insurance according to Article 815 of the Civil Code is one of the contracts of utmost good faith according to Article 834 of the Civil Code, the insurer cannot cancel the contract on the grounds of misrepresentation within three years from the commencement of the insurance cover.

811. Life insurance policies are usually of a long-term nature. The contract may be terminated by the policyholder subject to the notice period specified in the relevant general policy conditions. There is also the possibility of implied cancellation, which occurs when a policyholder fails to pay the insurance premium as specified in the policy's general terms and conditions, despite being requested to do so by the insurer.

812. In accordance with the principle laid down in the Civil Code, the policyholder is free to dispose of the sum insured in the event of death.

813. The policyholder may designate one or more persons who are entitled to receive the sum insured or make an arrangement for the payment of insurance benefits to the holder of an insurance document. In addition, a policyholder may at any time amend or terminate previous arrangements. It should be noted that the entitlement of the persons designated by a policyholder becomes effective upon termination of the insurance contract. However, the appointment of a beneficiary is invalid if the beneficiary predeceases the policyholder or if the beneficiary intentionally causes the death of the policyholder. In this case, the sum insured will be paid to the policyholder's immediate family in the order specified in the General Policy Conditions, as the sum insured is not part of the policyholder's estate.

814. There are various forms of life insurance available on the Polish market. According to the AIRA's list, an insurance company that has obtained a licence to conduct insurance activities in the field of life insurance may offer insurance products in the following groups:

- life insurance;
- endowment insurance, child endowment insurance;
- unit-linked life insurance and life insurance where the insurance benefit is determined on the basis of certain indices or other underlying values;
- pension insurance;
- accident and health insurance as a supplement to the above types of insurance.

815. Life insurance can be divided into individual and group insurance.

§1. Individual Life Insurance

816. Individual life insurance is becoming increasingly popular in the Polish market. There is a wide range of products available for an individual policyholder in all groups of life insurance, including pure life insurance (covering the death of the insured), investment insurance (where, in addition to insurance cover, there is an investment option where the risk is borne by the insured), pension insurance, child protection insurance and others, including various supplements to the products.

817. Pure life insurance covers the death of the insured during the insurance period. The general purpose of this type of insurance is to provide financial security for the persons who will survive the death of the insured and who have been named by the insured or a policyholder. There are two general types of whole life insurance:

- life insurance, where the insured is covered until the end of his or her life and premiums are paid throughout the period of insurance, usually until the advanced age specified in the contract;
- temporary insurance, where the insurance period is specified in the insurance contract.

818. Annuity contracts may be stand-alone products but are usually associated with pure life insurance products. Their general purpose is to provide a benefit to the insured upon reaching the age specified in the contract.

819. In the case of dowry insurance, the policy is usually taken out to provide financial support for children once they reach a certain age (specified in the general policy conditions). The insurance benefit may be paid as a lump sum or in regular instalments. Dowry insurance usually also covers the risk of death of the parent(s) or the child, depending on the structure of the policy. If the risk of death of the parent(s) is covered, the insurer usually undertakes to pay the insurance premiums until the end of the period for which the policy was taken out. Insurers also offer various riders to the core insurance contract, such as multiplication of the insurance benefit if a parent dies in an accident, additional insurance benefits if a child is injured in an accident, or a pension for a child upon the death of the parent(s).

820. Investment insurance is the most complex type of insurance. It combines the function of a traditional life insurance policy with that of an investment. The insurance premium is divided into two parts – the first part guarantees the insurance cover and the second part is used for an investment. Investment insurance contracts are not classified as pure insurance contracts but as investment contracts.

821. In general, the insurance benefit is paid on the death of the insured (or if the insured lives to a certain age), but the insured is usually also entitled to a redemption of the investment part. In this case, he or she is entitled to a payment known as the surrender value. The complexity of this type of product means that insurers offer a very wide range of this type of insurance. In some cases, they guarantee the amount of the investment part to be paid out, but this is not always the case. Investment insurance with regard to the investment part (unless the payout is guaranteed) is associated with risk. Investment risks in this case are characterised by the complexity of this type of insurance, and investment insurance products in the Polish market have not always been properly offered as savings products.

822. For several years, insurers on the Polish market have also been struggling with the problem of so-called liquidation fees, i.e., amounts charged by insurers due to distribution costs (intermediaries) that reduce the value of the shares/amounts to be invested in the capital fund. Such discounts were applied in the event of early termination of the insurance contract (usually the policy lapses before the tenth anniversary of the contract).

823. Annuity insurance guarantees benefits in the form of regular monthly, quarterly or half-yearly payments from a date specified in the insurance contract until the death of the insured. In practice, these are mainly life annuities, although there is also the concept of temporary annuity. It is paid for the period specified in the insurance contract, provided that the insured is still alive.

§2. Group Life Insurance

824. Group insurance in Poland is vaguely regulated. It is essentially based on a provision of the Civil Code, i.e., Article 808, which sets out very general rules for the conclusion of insurance in the interest of third parties. In addition, the AIRA regulates only a few issues relating to the protection of the insured. Among these rules, the policyholder (the organiser of the group) cannot be remunerated by the insurer.[43] Otherwise, group insurance is largely based on market practice.

825. Group life insurance is offered by many insurers. It usually covers a group of employees or a social group. Group insurance is not a specific type of insurance. It is rather a different method of risk assessment, sales and administration. The period of cover and the sum insured or benefits provided for in the contract are often similar to those offered for individual insurance.

826. Indeed, the main customers of insurance companies offering group insurance are employers who take out group life insurance for their employees. This often makes the employer more attractive in the labour market. From the point of view of the insurance company, the conclusion of a group insurance contract is easier and involves less risk.

827. In order to protect the interests of the insurance company, various obligations are imposed on the employer (the policyholder), e.g., that the persons covered by the group insurance must be employed on the basis of an employment contract and must not take sick leave during a certain period prior to the conclusion of the insurance contract. Very often, a clause in the general terms and conditions of group life insurance that specifies the minimum number of persons that may be covered by a group insurance scheme prevents the insurer from entering into any unfavourable commitments. In addition, in most cases, the insurer requires that all insured persons be covered by one policy and the same benefit scheme.

828. Group life insurance contracts are voluntary, as are all life insurance contracts. The most common groups covered by group life insurance are as follows:

- employees – the most common customers of insurance companies offering group life insurance. The duration of the contract, the sum insured, the type of benefits and the premiums are agreed. A single insurance policy is issued to cover all the insured persons. The premiums are paid by the employer, but the financial cost can often be borne by the employees;
- members of associations – members of various associations, e.g., doctors, lawyers or notaries, may be covered by collective insurance;
- customers of a bank – usually the bank is the policyholder and the customers of the bank are the insured. This type of insurance is designed to protect the interests of the bank or the interests of the bank's customers, usually in connection with a bank loan or credit (payment protection insurance). The insurance premiums are paid by the bank, but the financial costs are borne by the customers. Very often the insurance premium is also credited and paid together with the instalments by the bank's customers.

---

43. *See* more K. Malinowska, Quo vadis collective insurance. Observations on ECJ Rulings Affecting Group Insurance, Gdańskie Studia Prawnicze XXVII – No. 3 (60) /2023.

829. Currently, term life insurance is one of the most common group insurance policies. The length of the insurance period varies. In most cases, insurance contracts are concluded for a period of one year and subsequently extended or renewed.

830. Group life insurance contracts are usually quite complex and are offered with many riders, such as: exemption from the obligation to pay premiums; benefits payable in the event of total or partial disability; insurance of family members and spouses; and others.

831. An appropriate benefit payable on the death of the employee, as in the case of individual insurance, is paid to a beneficiary. Such a person is usually nominated by the insured (but may be nominated by the policyholder in certain circumstances). It is possible to change the beneficiary during the term of the contract. If the beneficiary has not been nominated at the time of the insured's death, the benefit will be paid to the bodies specified in the Schedule.

Part VI. Social Security and Private Insurance

Chapter 1. First and Second Pillar of the Social Security System

832. The social security system in Poland consists of the social insurance and social assistance system, the health insurance system, unemployment benefits and family benefits. The social security system is administered by a number of institutions, including the Social Insurance Institution (Zakład Ubezpieczeń Społecznych, ZUS), the Agricultural Social Insurance Fund (Kasa Rolniczego Ubezpieczenia Społecznego, KRUS) and the NFZ in the area of health insurance benefits in kind. Many legal instruments regulate the legal obligation to insure against certain social risks and the guarantee of benefits in the event of a given risk.

833. The detailed regulations governing individual areas of social security are contained in separate Acts of Parliament, the most important of which are the Act of 13 October 1998 on the Social Insurance System, the Act of 17 December 1998 on Pensions from the Social Insurance Fund, the Act of 20 April 2004 on Individual Old-Age Pension Accounts and Individual Old-Age Pension Protection Accounts (the so-called IKE and IKZE Acts), the Act of 20 April 2004 on Occupational Pension Schemes, and the recently adopted Act of 4 October 2018 on Employee Capital Pension Plans.

834. The types of social insurance and the principles of insurance coverage are regulated by the Act of 13 October 1998 on the Social Insurance System. The Polish social insurance system comprises: (1) old-age pension insurance; (2) disability and survivors' pension insurance; (3) sickness insurance; and (4) occupational injury insurance.

835. The concept of the pension system, which is mainly based on the pay as you go (PAYG) principle, is to be changed in 1999 and replaced by a pillar system. The three-pillar system is a hybrid of the various pension systems currently known (based, among other things, on the Chilean reform concept) and is divided according to the type and institution that collects the funds and then pays them out to the retired person. The first pillar, which is basic and compulsory, is based on contributions paid to the former Social Insurance Institution (Zakład Ubezpieczeń Społecznych – ZUS). The funds are not invested but are mainly used to pay current benefits. The second pillar, which is compulsory depending on age and covers persons born after 1948 (on a voluntary basis) and persons born after 1969 (on a compulsory basis), is based on contributions paid to the open pension funds (OFEs). Those who have not opted for the second pillar, which is voluntary for them, are obliged to pay the entire premium to the first pillar, which is managed by ZUS. The above-mentioned 'instruments' were supplemented by the creation of the legal basis for the third pillar in 1999 and for the so-called fourth pillar in 2004 (*see* below).

836. Until 31 January 2014, participation in the OFE was compulsory for persons born in 1969 or later. Currently, people starting their first job can choose whether or not to join such a fund. From 1 April to 31 July 2016, people who were already members of the OFE could choose whether to continue their membership of the fund. The next opportunity to change their decision will be in 2020. At the end of 2018, there were ten OFEs. They had a total of 15.9 million members (16.1 million in 2017). The value of the investment portfolio of OFEs was PLN 156.6 billion. At the end of 2018, the investment portfolio of OFEs included shares of companies listed on a regulated stock market (85%), bonds (7%), bank deposits (6%) and other deposits (2%).

837. The worsening situation of the first pillar of the pension system, mainly the financial situation of ZUS, due to the demographic and economic situation in the country, led to the introduction of the following changes in this structure: first, by raising the retirement age from 65 and 60 (for women) to 67 for both sexes [however, due to social pressure, this reform was later reversed by the ruling PiS party]; second, by making the second pillar completely voluntary and substantially reducing the amount of the contribution from 7% to 2.92% of the income,31 together with the compulsory transfer of 50% of the funds collected by the pension funds to ZUS in 2014. 92% of income,31 together with the compulsory transfer of over 50% of the funds collected by the pension funds to ZUS in February 2014. In 2020, a total of PLN 155 billion will be transferred to 15.8 million individual retirement accounts opened by private pension funds participating in OFE.

838. If we compare the experience and regulations of other countries, especially EU Member States, we can see that the Polish division of the pension system into pillars is somewhat different. While the common meaning of the first pillar in Europe is usually that the benefits are provided by the state, the second that a pension system is organised by the employer, and the third that individual forms of saving are used, in Poland the first two pillars belong to the state pension system (although they are operated by different bodies and in different ways) and the third is organised voluntarily by employers. Therefore, unofficially, the idea of a fourth pillar has been promoted in order to recognise forms of individual pension saving. After the change in 2019, the second pillar practically lost its importance.

839. Thus, we can say that the Polish pension system is divided into two parts. The first, the basic one, managed by ZUS and pension funds, was created on the basis of the concept of solidarity and the philosophy of sharing and distributing the results of (compulsory) retirement savings among the members of the society. This is the basis for the functioning of the first and second pillars. The second part of the system was based on the individual approach of future pensioners, albeit in forms offered by the state. This is the key to the third (and sometimes fourth) pillar of the pension system.

840. In the compulsory social insurance system, an insured person is a person who is covered by at least one of the social insurance schemes. The Social Insurance Act distinguishes between compulsory and voluntary insurance. Compulsory old-age and invalidity insurance covers employees, members of agricultural production cooperatives, entrepreneurs, persons engaged in non-agricultural business activities, members of the clergy, members of parliament, recipients of unemployment benefits, persons on maternity leave or persons receiving maternity benefit, as well as members of supervisory boards.

841. Persons who do not meet the conditions for compulsory old-age and invalidity insurance have the right to make voluntary contributions to these insurance schemes. The number of insured persons in 2018 was 15,847.6 thousand.

Chapter 2. Third Pillar of the Social Security System

842. When discussing the third pillar of pension provision in Poland, it is important to be aware that the concept is not perceived consistently and in different ways, depending on the approach taken.[44] While formally the third pillar takes the form of one of the government-regulated schemes organised by the employer, the common meaning is much broader and usually includes other forms of retirement savings, both collective and individual. They are also known as fourth pillar schemes.

843. The first idea of the third pillar was introduced in Poland during the period of the general reform of the pension system. A special law was adopted in 1999. The employee pension schemes were intended to supplement the first and second pillars of the pension system. The basic concept of an occupational pension scheme is that it is a voluntary form of the collective system of saving for retirement, organised by employers and financed mainly by the employer and additionally, on a voluntary basis, by the employee. Pension schemes can be organised in one of the forms provided for by the law, i.e., as an employee pension fund, as an agreement with an investment fund, as a group life insurance with a capital fund or in the form of foreign management. From the point of view of tax incentives, it appears to be one of the most favourable forms of pension saving, allowing the systematic accumulation of funds for future retirement benefits, exempt from capital gains tax, although the contribution is still treated as part of the employee's taxable income (but not as income for social security purposes). The benefits are inheritable and exempt from income tax.

844. The following institutions exist within the voluntary funded pension system: (1) Open Pension Funds (*Otwarte Fundusze Emerytalne*, OFEs); (2) Occupational Pension Schemes (*Pracownicze Programy Emerytalne*, PPEs); (3) Individual Pension Accounts (*Indywidualne Konta Emerytalne*, IKEs); (4) Individual Pension Security Accounts (*Indywidualne Konta Zabezpieczenia Emerytalnego*, IKZEs); (5) Employee Capital Plans (*Pracownicze Programy Kapitałowe*, PPKs).

845. The state schemes consisting of individual pension accounts were introduced in 2004 under the name of IKE (*Indywidualne konta emerytalne*), followed in 2011 by individual pension protection accounts (IKZE – *Indywidualne konta zabezpieczenia emerytalnego*). The two forms have many similarities. Both offer the possibility of opening an individual account: IKE or IKZE and choosing the type of investment. They also both include the possibility of concluding an agreement for the management of the IKE or IKZE with the investment or pension fund, the brokerage company, the insurer or the bank (for a savings account). As far as the agreement with the insurer is concerned, the IKE or IKZE account is a form of life insurance (unit-linked products). In both cases, the funds accumulated in the accounts can be inherited. The main differences between IKE and IKZE are the restrictions on transfers, the possibility of payouts and tax obligations. While the

44. *See also* the differences between Poland and other countries as explained above.

funds collected in IKE accounts are exempt from capital gains tax, the contributions are not tax-deductible. IKZE focuses on a tax exemption at the moment of the contribution to the IKZE account, with the benefit paid out being taxable.

846. Occupational Pension Schemes (Pracownicze Programy Emerytalne, PPEs) are a voluntary form of collective saving for old age, organised by the employer in cooperation with employees. The basic contribution is financed by the employer and the employee can declare the payment of an additional contribution, which is deducted from the salary. The funds are transferred by a financial institution chosen by the employer and the employees during the organisation phase of the programme. This institution manages all the funds. The funds accumulated in the employee's account can be paid out, transferred to another PPE or IKE, or returned. Payment of the accumulated savings can be made: (1) at the employee's request at the age of 60; (2) at the employee's request at the age of 55, if he/she has opted for a pension; (3) without the employee's request at the age of 70, if he/she has not previously requested payment; (4) at the request of the survivors in the event of the employee's death.

847. At the end of 2018, there were 1,230 occupational pension schemes and 426,000 people were covered by occupational pension schemes, representing 2.6% of the total number of employees. In 2018, the employers operating the schemes paid PLN 1,310.8 million in basic contributions to the PPEs, while the voluntary contributions of the PPEs' participants amounted to PLN 45.8 million.

848. At the end of 2018, IKE were maintained by a total of fifty-seven financial institutions that included IKE in their offering. The right to pay contributions into an IPE is exercised by a natural person over the age of 16. A minor may make contributions to an IKE in the calendar year in which he/she receives income from work performed under an employment contract, up to the amount of such income. A person may have only one IKE. The contribution to the IKE is taxed and the tax is levied on the income from which the IKE contribution is paid. A person who saves in IKE is exempt from capital gains tax. At the end of 2018, IKE was held by 995.7 thousand people, i.e., 5.8% of the working population. The value of the IKE market in terms of accumulated assets amounted to PLN 8.7 billion (a growth of 9.2% compared to 2017). The majority of IKE assets were accumulated in investment funds (PLN 2.7 billion) and insurance companies (PLN 2.6 billion).

849. Another relatively new form of saving is the Employee Capital Plans (PPK). Employee Capital Plans are a form of voluntary long-term savings programme. The programme is aimed at approximately 11.5 million Polish employees who are subject to mandatory old-age and invalidity pensions. The programme does not apply to the self-employed, members of the uniformed services and farmers. Employees between the ages of 55 and 69 will be able to participate in the PPK on the basis of a declaration of intent. The regulatory framework has been in force since 1 January 2019, following the Act of 4 October 2018 on Employee Capital Plans. Under the Act, employers are obliged to introduce the PPK in their organisation within certain deadlines, with the timetable for joining the PPK depending on the size and type of the company. The introduction date of the PPC depends on the number of employees in the company. From 1 July 2019, the programme will apply to companies with more than 250 employees. From 1 January 2020, the PPK will apply to companies with more than 50 employees and from 1 July 2020 to companies with more than 20 employees. From 1 January 2021, PPKs will cover employees of all other companies. The Employee Capital Plans will constitute a mandatory package of employee benefits. The employer will be obliged to select an institution to operate a PPK and to set up a PPK for its employees. Under the ECP, the employee and the employer pay a basic (compulsory) and an additional (voluntary) contribution to the employee's account.

850. Payments into the PPK account come from three sources: the employer, the employee and the state budget in the form of a subsidy. The funds paid in are to be invested by financial institutions that meet strict criteria. ECPs are supervised by the PFSA in terms of the functioning of the institutions managing the programme. The main purpose of the Employee Capital Plans is to provide additional funds that can be used after the age of 60, or earlier in exceptional circumstances. The funds accumulated in your account are private and are not subject to inheritance. They can be withdrawn at any time. An employer is obliged to enroll its employees in the PPK according to the following rules: (1) employees aged 18–55: compulsory; (2) employees aged 55–70: at the employee's individual request, provided that they have worked for the same employer for at least three months during the previous twelve months; (3) employees aged over 70: cannot be enrolled. The PPK is based on the assumption that it covers not only persons with a permanent full-time job but also part-time workers and workers on a contract basis, as long as they pay contributions to the Social Security Institution. Every employee has the right to join or leave the scheme, including those on parental or maternity leave.

851. In conclusion, even for Poland, the above-mentioned development rate of third/fourth pillar schemes is far from satisfactory and new voluntary forms do not increase the overall penetration index. This is a serious concern for the state, given its inability to provide effective retirement security based on the first or second pillar. There is no doubt that the third pillar (or the third and fourth) should be an important factor in the overall pension system, as it is elsewhere. Most conclusions of various analyses of the issue say that the creation of a legal framework for the existence of the supplementary pension system is not sufficient in the absence of clear and consistent incentives from the state, the most important of which seem to be tax incentives and the promotion of certain schemes in society. The functioning mechanisms of certain forms of individual savings, but also of occupational pension schemes, also lead to their lack of popularity in the general society. This is also the reason why non-state-controlled individual strategies for providing for old age are gaining importance.

852. Among them, life insurance seems to be the most popular and growing. As already mentioned, it is currently one of the forms of employee pension schemes, but it also seems to be the most important form of individual pension provision on the financial market in Poland. This is also in line with the approach of most academics analysing the current pension problems in Poland, who emphasise that any reform of supplementary pension schemes should be of an insurance nature (based on risk assessment), so that the participation of insurers in the reform is inevitable. Such an attitude strengthens the future position of life insurance in the pension system. Irrespective of the academic and government postulates, it is worth presenting the opportunities for the self-development of life insurance as a pension insurance in Poland, taking into account the limited incentives provided by the state.

Part VII. Insurance Intermediaries

Chapter 1. Law of Establishment and Supervision

§1. General

853. As of 1 October 2018, significant changes to the insurance intermediation legislation came into force. They were caused by the transposition of the Insurance Distribution Directive 2016/97 into the Polish legal system. The Insurance Distribution Directive was implemented in Poland by the Act of 15 December 2017 on Insurance Distribution (Insurance Distribution Act, which entered into force on 1 October 2018 after a delay). The implementation is based on minimum harmonisation concepts without 'gold plating', with the exception of the prohibition of links between agents and brokers (although this does not derive directly from the IDD). The national supervisory authority is the PFSA.

854. The new provisions contained in the Insurance Distribution Act generally follow the Insurance Distribution Directive, although many requirements existed under the previous regime and were derived from the Supervisory Authority's guidelines to insurers on the management and appropriateness of products and insurance distribution guidelines. The main changes introduced in the Polish system concern: (1) the obligation to assess needs and requirements; (2) the disclosure of remuneration; (3) the prohibition of personal and capital relationships between agents and brokers, extended by a prohibition to remain in 'other relationships that could jeopardise the performance of brokerage activities honestly, fairly, professionally and in accordance with the best interests of the client'.

855. The Insurance Distribution Act regulates general issues related to insurance distribution, forms of conducting insurance distribution activities, organisational requirements for agents, brokers and employees of insurers involved in insurance distribution, product management and supervision, as well as special requirements for the distribution of unit-linked products.

856. The Insurance Distribution Act defines the concept of insurance (and reinsurance) distributor, i.e., the insurance company, insurance agent, ancillary insurance agent or (re)insurance broker.

857. The activity of insurance distribution may be carried out by an insurance intermediary only or by an insurance company. The conclusion or performance of insurance contracts by a member of the board of directors of the insurer, an agent of the insurer or an employee of the insurer in the name and on behalf of such insurer is not considered insurance mediation. The Insurance Mediation Act imposes certain requirements on the insurer's employees involved in mediation activities. These requirements are the same as those imposed on agents and brokers, although there is no obligation to register employees.

858. With regard to insurance intermediation, insurance distribution may be carried out by two categories of insurance intermediaries, i.e., insurance agents and insurance and reinsurance brokers. In addition, a category of ancillary intermediaries has been introduced (as defined in the IDD). Consequently, insurance intermediation consists of insurance mediation – the performance of insurance or reinsurance mediation by insurance intermediaries. Insurance mediation in the field of reinsurance may only be carried out by insurance brokers. A person may not combine the professions of agent and broker. Agents and brokers may not have any personal or financial relationship with each other or any relationship that would hinder the obligation to act in the best interest of the client. The insurance agent, the insurance broker and the insurance undertaking distributing the IBIPs shall apply organisational arrangements to prevent conflicts of interest so that they do not adversely affect the interests of customers. Distributors shall ensure that the organisational arrangements are proportionate to the activity pursued, the insurance contracts proposed and the type of distributor. They should also take steps to identify conflicts of interest between themselves, including their directors, agents, employees or other persons associated with them, and their customers, or between their customers, arising in the course of carrying on the business of insurance distribution of IBIPS. If the organisational arrangements are not sufficient to ensure that risks of damage to the interests of the customer are avoided, the insurance intermediary must disclose the general nature or sources of the conflict to the customer prior to the conclusion of the insurance contract, in particular informing the customer whether the commission received for an insurance contract depends on the volume of insurance contracts concluded.

859. There is a register of insurance intermediaries, divided into a register of agents and a register of brokers, the register of brokers being further divided into the subcategory of insurance and reinsurance brokers. The register is kept in electronic form by the CSF. Some of the information on agents is also held by the Polish Chamber of Insurance (which discloses it on request). [*See* below for details on the registration of agents and brokers.]

860. According to the Act, the concept of insurance distribution has been introduced, which means 'advising, proposing or performing other work preparatory to the conclusion of insurance contracts, the conclusion of such contracts or assisting in the administration and performance of such contracts'.

861. There are certain exceptions to the regulatory regime that allow insurance distribution to be carried out by entities not licensed under the law. There are two types of situations:

a. First, the provisions of the Insurance Distribution Act shall not apply to entrepreneurs engaged in insurance mediation if all the following conditions are met: (1) the insurance contract or insurance guarantee agreement is concluded in addition to the goods or services provided by the supplier and covers the following risks: (a) destruction, loss or damage of those goods or failure to use the service provided by the supplier; or (b) damage to or loss of luggage and other risks related to travel services provided by that supplier; (2) the amount of the premium payable under the insurance contract or insurance guarantee agreement does not exceed the equivalent in PLN of EUR 600, calculated pro rata on an annual basis; (3) the insurance contract or insurance guarantee agreement is concluded in addition to the goods or services provided by the supplier and covers the following risks: (a) destruction, loss or damage of those goods or failure to use the service provided by the supplier; or (b) damage to or loss of luggage and other risks related to travel services provided by that supplier.
b. Second, the legal regime does not apply to entrepreneurs engaged in the activity of insurance distribution, if an insurance contract or insurance guarantee agreement is concluded in addition to the services provided by the supplier, and the following cumulative conditions are met: (1) the insurance or guarantee agreement covers the risk of non-use of the services provided by the supplier or the risk of loss of luggage or travel-related risks; (2) the duration of the relevant service does not exceed three months; (3) the amount of the premium payable under the insurance or guarantee agreement for one insured person does not exceed the equivalent in PLN of EUR 200; (4) the insurance or guarantee agreement does not cover the risk of loss of luggage or travel-related risks; (5) the insurance or guarantee agreement does not cover the risk of non-use of the services provided by the supplier or the risk of loss of luggage or travel-related risks.

862. In the case where the insurance distributor is excluded from the distribution system, the insurance company takes over some of its obligations towards the customer, such as the obligation to provide information (about the insurer, about the right to make a complaint), as well as the obligation to assess the customer's needs and requirements and to provide the insurance documentation before concluding the insurance contract, and all other obligations related to the customer's best interests.

863. The Polish Parliament has adopted the idea of minimum legal regulation of the circle of entities included in the insurance distribution system. Therefore, the maximum exclusions allowed by the IDD were introduced into the Polish Insurance Distribution Act (IDA). As a result, the following activity is not considered to be insurance or reinsurance distribution: (1) the occasional provision of information to a customer in connection with the entity's business activities other than insurance or reinsurance distribution, where the purpose of those activities is not to assist in the conclusion or performance of reinsurance contracts; (2) the handling of claims against an insurance or reinsurance undertaking, the assessment of claims and the drawing up of expert reports in relation to those claims; (3) the provision of data and information on potential customers to insurance agents, insurance brokers, reinsurance brokers, insurance or reinsurance undertakings, where the undertaking does not take additional steps to assist in the conclusion of the insurance contract, the insurance guarantee contract or the reinsurance contract.

864. Insurance mediation is treated as a business activity within the meaning of the Act of 6 March 2018 on Entrepreneurs (Journal of Laws 2018, item 646 as amended). Therefore, every agent or broker must be registered as an entrepreneur and cannot have the status of an employee.

865. There are several obligations imposed on insurance intermediaries that apply equally to all types of intermediaries. For example, there is a requirement for continuous professional development. The law provides for an obligation to complete at least fifteen hours of training per year. Various forms of training are permitted, provided that they are of an appropriate level and are carried out by persons with sufficient knowledge, training and experience. This must therefore be ensured by the insurer, broker or agent. The training may take different forms, such as a lecture, a seminar or e-learning. In the case of e-learning, the training must be followed by a test.

866. The law also provides for the protection of clients of intermediaries. In terms of consumer protection, Polish law introduces the risk transfer mechanism, which consists of a rule that the payment of the premium made to the intermediary is recognised as being made directly to the insurer. If the insurer pays the claim to the intermediary, the insurer is released from its obligations only when the payment is actually received by the insured.

867. One of the most important issues in relation to the new insurance distribution regime is the obligation to inform and advise the customer. Advising the customer is mandatory for brokers (*see* below), but not for agents. An analysis of the customer's needs and requirements is obligatory for all types of insurance distributors (needs and requirements analysis).

868. Prior to the conclusion of an insurance contract, whether or not it is subject to advice, the distributor must carry out an analysis of the customer's needs and requirements and offer only such insurance that meets the customer's needs and requirements. In addition, the insurance distributor should provide the customer with relevant information about the insurance product in an understandable form to enable him to make an informed decision, taking into account the complexity of the insurance product and the nature of the customer. In the case of non-life insurance, the information takes the form of an IPID (not applicable to insurance of large risks).

869. Polish law introduces minimum requirements for transparency of remuneration received by the insurance distributor. The insurance distributor must inform the customer of the type of remuneration received in connection with the insurance product offered (in particular, whether it is a fee, commission or any other type of remuneration). The distributor must disclose the distribution cost ratio to the customer only in the case of IBIPs. The way in which an insurance distributor is remunerated and the persons by whom insurance agency or brokerage activities are carried out, as well as the persons by whom the distribution activities of the insurance undertaking are carried out, must not conflict with the obligation to act in the best interests of the customer; in particular, the insurance distributor must not make any arrangements for remuneration, sales targets or other arrangements which could provide an incentive to propose to the customer a particular insurance contract or insurance guarantee contract when the insurance distributor could propose another contract which would better meet the customer's needs.

870. Another rule designed to protect customers' rights is the obligation to provide certain information about the agent or broker (e.g., on the scope of liability insurance, etc.). The information should be provided in writing or by any other means available to the entity seeking insurance coverage or the customer; in a clear, precise and intelligible manner; in an official language of the Member State of the EU in which the insurance contract is concluded or in any other language agreed by the parties.

871. The new distribution regime introduces a new set of rules on product supervision and management. The IDA only provides for a general rule in this respect, while the entire system is based on the POG Regulation and the opinion of the Financial Supervision Authority on the application of product stewardship requirements to insurance distributors that are not product manufacturers. Specific recommendations for insurance companies on product stewardship systems were addressed to insurers in 2017.

872. The general rules on product oversight and governance generally apply to all categories of insurance distribution, depending on the role of the agent or broker in the given distribution structure. According to the POG Regulation, both insurers and intermediaries can theoretically be manufacturers of the insurance product and be bound by its obligations.

873. Manufacturers' obligations include, in essence, the obligation to develop, maintain, apply and review a validation process for each insurance product, or significant changes to an existing insurance product, before it is marketed or distributed to customers. The product validation process should identify a defined target market and tailor the distribution strategy to the defined target market, and this information should be made available to distributors. Manufacturers should periodically review insurance products to assess whether the product continues to meet the needs of the defined target market and whether the planned distribution strategy remains appropriate.

874. If an insurance distributor is not a manufacturer, it may still be bound by some requirements imposed by the POG Regulation. Such a distributor must have an appropriate distribution policy and should obtain the product information and understand the characteristics and defined target market for each insurance product.

The distribution policy must be set out in writing and made available to staff. It must be revised and reviewed frequently. This document shall be made available to the Commission of Financial Supervision (CFS). The distributor must provide the manufacturer with relevant sales information on request. In addition, the distributor must inform the product manufacturer and, if necessary, change its distribution strategy if it finds that an insurance product does not meet the interests, objectives and characteristics of the defined target market or has a negative impact on the customer.

§2. Insurance Agent

875. According to the law, an insurance agent is a natural person, a partnership or a legal person (commercial company) who is authorised by an insurance company to conclude insurance contracts on its behalf. Agents are entitled to represent only the insurer (and not the policyholders).

876. The Insurance Distribution Act introduced a new category of agents who may perform agency activities as an ancillary business. An ancillary insurance agent is defined as an entity that, on the basis of an agency agreement concluded with an insurance company entered in the Register of Agents, which is neither a credit institution nor an investment firm, performs an ancillary insurance activity for remuneration, provided that the following cumulative conditions are met: (a) the principal activity of the enterprise is not the distribution of insurance; (b) the entrepreneur distributes insurance only in addition to the goods or services supplied; (c) the distribution of insurance does not relate to a life insurance contract or a liability insurance contract unless such a contract is in addition to the goods or services supplied as part of the enterprise's principal activity.

877. Persons acting as agents must be registered in the register of intermediaries before commencing their activities. The obligation to register also applies to auxiliary agents. While registration is the final prerequisite for the performance of intermediary activities, the agent (before being entered into the register) must be registered as an entrepreneur, pass the examination and conclude the intermediary agreement with the insurance company.

878. Agents are registered at the insurer's request, which should be made within fourteen days of hiring the agent; the insurer should also request deregistration in the event of termination of the agency agreement; the insurer is responsible for the accuracy of the agent's data. In the case of agents acting on behalf of more than one insurer, each subsequent insurer registers the agent separately.

879. In the case of agents, the requirements for registration include: (1) full legal capacity; (2) clean criminal record with respect to certain types of offences; (3) at least secondary education; (4) good moral character; (5) passing an examination organised by the insurer; the agency activity is a business activity, otherwise the natural person should register as an employee of the agent. In the case of insurance agents who are partnerships (without legal personality), the above conditions should be met by all shareholders of these companies if they are natural persons, if the shareholders of these companies are legal persons – at least half of their board members; in the case of insurance agents who are legal persons – at least half of their board members must meet the authorisation requirements.

880. Although the law does not clearly state this, the interpretation of its provisions shows that ancillary intermediaries act in the capacity of insurance agents. Ancillary agents are subject to the same requirements and registration.

881. Persons who fulfil all the requirements laid down in the law may also act as intermediaries, being employed by the other intermediaries. Such persons are not referred to as agents but as intermediaries. It should be noted that such persons must also pass the examination organised by the insurer. They are entitled to perform intermediary activities for the insurers for which their employing agent acts.

882. It should be emphasised that agents who wish to act as agents for more than one insurance company (so-called multi-agents) must pass the examination organised by each insurance company separately and must be registered separately by all the insurance companies they wish to represent.

883. In general, it is the insurance company that is responsible for the agent's acts and omissions. Nothing in the law can limit this liability. The above rule does not apply to the multiagent, who is liable for his own acts or omissions. As a result, the multiagent is subject to compulsory liability insurance. Civil liability insurance covers damage caused by an insurance agent in connection with activities performed on the territory of the Republic of Poland and other EU Member States. Failure to take out compulsory insurance is punishable by a fine. Payment of the fine does not exempt from the obligation to take out TPL insurance.

884. The insurance obligation does not apply if the insurance (multi)agent has its registered office in a Member State of the EU and is covered by liability insurance or an equivalent guarantee in the amount of EUR 1,250,000 for one event and EUR 1,8750,000 for all events for all damages arising in connection with the performance of intermediary activities.

885. The insurance agent may not engage in brokerage activities and may not perform brokerage activities.

886. An insurance agent who has his registered office or place of residence in another EU Member State may perform agency activities in Poland, provided that he is registered in the relevant register in that State. An insurance agent may commence agency activities in Poland no earlier than thirty days after the supervisory authority receives information from the supervisory authority keeping the register of insurance intermediaries in a Member State of the EU about the intention to commence agency activities in Poland. Similar rules apply to Polish insurance agents wishing to pursue insurance intermediation activities in another EU Member State (after notifying the Polish supervisory authority of their intention to do so).

§3. INSURANCE BROKER

887. The role of an insurance broker is to conclude and perform insurance contracts on behalf of the policyholder and to act as an intermediary in concluding an insurance contract for the benefit of the policyholder.

888. Brokerage activities may only be carried out by a legal entity (i.e., in the form of a limited liability company or a joint stock company) or a natural person on the basis of a licence issued by the Financial Supervision Authority. However, in the case of a legal entity performing brokerage activities, such activities may be performed only by natural persons holding the above-mentioned licence.

889. The registration of a broker is carried out automatically by the Financial Supervision Commission after the broker has passed the examination. The registration is connected with the possession of the broker's licence. The registration also concerns the natural persons employed by the brokers, according to the same rules. Brokers are subject to deregistration in case of withdrawal or expiry of the broker's licence.

890. The registration requirements for brokers include: (1) full legal capacity; (2) a clean criminal record for certain types of offences; (3) at least secondary education; (4) good moral character; (5) passing an examination before the Commission; (6) at least two years of experience; (7) PII insurance. In the case of intermediaries established as companies, the above requirements must be met by all partners and half of the members of the board of directors. In Poland, insurance brokerage may be carried out only by natural persons of legal entities, i.e., commercial companies with legal personality (limited liability companies, joint-stock companies).

891. In view of the insurance broker's role as a representative of the policyholder, the insurance broker may not be employed by the insurance company or be a member of its management bodies. In addition, the insurance broker may not engage in agency activities or hold shares in the insurer, except for shares admitted to public trading. The new conflict of interest rules introduced by the Insurance Distribution Act also include the prohibition of any other relationship with agents (as above).

892. The broker must inform the customer, at the time of the first contact with the customer, of the shares held by the insurance company that gives the right to at least 10% of the votes at the general meeting and, if the insurance broker is a legal person, of the shares held by the insurance company that gives the right to at least 10% of the votes at the general meeting or shareholders' meeting.

893. Brokers are obliged to give a personal recommendation to the customer and this does not apply to the insurance of large risks. The advice should be based on a fair analysis of the number of insurance products available on the market in sufficient quantity to make a recommendation on the most appropriate contract and explain the basis on which the recommendation is made, taking into account the complexity of the insurance or insurance guarantee contract and the type of customer, unless the customer declares in writing that he does not wish to receive the advice.

894. With regard to other duties of the insurance broker, he/she should: (1) keep confidential the information obtained in connection with the performance of the insurance brokerage activity, however, this obligation is imposed on the insurance broker even after the termination of the contractual relationship with the customer; (2) present to the insurance company and the customer, upon request, a licence to perform insurance brokerage activities; (3) keep a register of complaints; (4) to keep records on the insurance brokerage activity performed, in particular, powers of attorney to perform insurance brokerage activities on behalf of the client and documents on the broker's remuneration, for a period of ten years from the date of termination of the cooperation with the client. Natural persons performing insurance brokerage activities must present a document authorising them to act on behalf of the insurance broker at the first activity.

895. The insurance broker is obliged to take out compulsory civil liability insurance to cover damages caused to the entity seeking insurance coverage/policyholder, the insurer, the insured and the person entitled under the insurance contract, including damages caused by natural persons through whom the insurance broker performs intermediary activities. The civil liability insurance contract covers damage caused by an insurance broker in connection with activities performed in Poland and other Member States. In the case of a foreign insurance broker, the insurance obligation does not apply if the insurance broker has concluded in a Member State of the EU a civil liability insurance or an equivalent guarantee in the amount of EUR 1,250,000 for a single event and EUR 1,875,000 for all events for damages arising in connection with the performance of intermediary activities and caused to the entity seeking insurance cover, the insurer, the insured or the person entitled under the insurance contract.

896. An insurance broker who has his registered office or place of residence in another EU Member State may perform insurance brokerage activities in Poland, provided that he is registered in the appropriate register in that State. An insurance broker may commence intermediation activities in Poland no earlier than thirty days after the supervisory authority has received information from the supervisory authority keeping the register of insurance intermediaries in a Member State of the EU about the intention to commence intermediation activities in Poland. Similar rules apply to Polish insurance brokers intending to conduct insurance intermediation activities in another Member State of the EU (after notifying the Polish supervisory authority of their intention to do so).

897. Reinsurance brokers are subject to the same obligations as insurance brokers.

§4. Supervision on Insurance Intermediaries Activity

898. The CFS is the sole supervisory authority for the activities of insurance intermediaries.

899. The Commission is responsible for granting and withdrawing insurance intermediary licences and for registering and deregistering insurance intermediaries.

900. The Commission may prohibit the insurer from using the services of an insurance agent and impose the obligation to terminate the agency contract together with the revocation of the power of attorney granted to the agent if it is established that the agent fails to comply with the provisions of the law, due diligence or good practice.

901. The Commission shall revoke a broker's licence if the broker no longer fulfils the conditions for obtaining a broker's licence or at the request of the broker. The licence may also be withdrawn if the broker carries out the activity in violation of the law or in a manner that is seriously detrimental to the interests of the client. If the licence is withdrawn, it may be reapplied for after a period of three years from the date of its withdrawal; during this period, a member of the management or supervisory bodies of the legal person carrying out brokerage activities may not be appointed.

902. Supervision of the activities of an insurance agent shall be exercised by the insurance company on whose behalf the insurance agent acts. The supervisory authority may at any time inspect the activities of the insurer in relation to the use of the services of insurance agents. However, the supervisory authority may apply supervisory measures directly to agents in specific cases of violation of legal provisions.

903. Supervision of the activities of insurance brokers is exercised directly by the Commission. The supervisory authority may, at any time, carry out checks on the activities and financial situation of companies carrying out brokerage activities.

904. The following infringements of the law are subject to criminal liability: (1) agency activities in violation of the requirements for conducting such activities specified in the Act; (2) insurance or reinsurance brokerage activities without the required licence. The above are punishable by a fine, restriction of liberty or imprisonment for up to two years.

905. Any person, other than an insurance or reinsurance intermediary, who uses in a company, in an advertisement or to identify his own business, terms indicating the performance of insurance or reinsurance intermediation shall be punishable by a fine, restriction of liberty or imprisonment for up to one year.

906. If the insurer violates the law on the registration of intermediaries (registration, change of registration or removal from the register) – the supervisory authority may, by way of a decision, impose on the insurer a fine of up to 0.5% of the gross written premium reported by the insurer in the last financial statement submitted to the supervisory authority, or, if the insurer has not been operating or has achieved a gross written premium of less than PLN 20 million, up to PLN 100,000.

907. In the event of a refusal to provide explanations or information in connection with supervisory measures, the supervisory authority may, by decision, impose a fine of up to ten times the average monthly remuneration in the business sector, as most recently published by the President of the Central Statistical Office, on: (1) a member of the management board of an intermediary company or natural person acting as an intermediary; (2) in the case of an insurance intermediary who is a legal person – a fine of up to three times the amount of the commission received in the last three months prior to the imposition of the fine, and in the case of an insurance intermediary or an intermediary offering supplementary insurance who has not received the commission or has not provided information on the amount of the commission received – up to PLN 100,000.

908. In the case of a breach of duties and requirements relating to obligations towards clients, including duties and requirements relating to IBIPs, the Supervisory Authority may, by way of a decision: (1) issue a public statement indicating the person responsible for the breach and the nature of the breach; (2) suspend for a period not exceeding six months a member of the management board of a distributor who is a legal person and who is responsible for the breach; (3) impose on a distributor of insurance or reinsurance who is a legal person a fine not exceeding the amount of: (a) PLN 21,827,500; or (b) 5% of the annual net income from the sale of goods and services and from financial operations or, in the case of an insurance or reinsurance undertaking, 5% of the gross premiums written, as shown in the last annual financial statements for the financial year approved by the licensing authority of the insurance or reinsurance distributor; or (c) twice the amount of the benefits gained or losses avoided as a result of the infringement, if they can be determined; (4) impose on an insurance or reinsurance distributor who is a natural person a fine not exceeding the amount of: (a) PLN 3,055,850; or (b) twice the amount of the benefits obtained or losses avoided as a result of the infringement, if they can be determined.

909. Other sanctions may include: (1) withdrawal of the licence; (2) an order to cease and desist from committing the same act again; (3) issuing recommendations to the insurance or reinsurance distributor.

Chapter 2. Status of Insurance Intermediaries and the Insurance Contract

§1. Status of the Insurance Intermediaries

910. The legal status of the 'agency' and the corresponding 'agent' is governed by the Civil Code (Title XXIII), while the legal status of the ship's agent and the ship broker is governed by the Maritime Code (Chapter 4, sections 2 and 3 on maritime services).

911. Article 758 of the Civil Code provides that the 'agent' acts as a permanent representative in the conclusion of contracts of the specified type for the benefit of the principal and in the latter's name if he is authorised to do so. In case of doubt, the agent is presumed to be entitled to receive payment for the obligations he fulfils and to accept a performance for which he pays, as well as to receive notices of defects and any other declaration concerning the performance of the contract concluded by him on behalf of the principal.

912. The question we need to address is that of determining which party the agent officially represents under Polish law. There is a general rule in the PCC that the agent can represent only the principal. In the case of insurance agents, this rule is reinforced by the provision that the insurance agent can only represent the insurer.

913. In this respect, there is some confusion between the role of the maritime insurance agent and that of the land insurance agent. However, according to the provisions of the Maritime Code, the agent may also act on behalf of the other party to the contract, provided that the shipowner has given his consent. As a general rule, the agent may undertake to act on behalf of both parties to a contract if they have instructed him to do so; he is then obliged to inform each party that he is also acting on behalf of the other party and, in his capacity as an intermediary, he must take account of the interests of both parties.

914. With regard to the remuneration of the intermediary, the intermediary may charge commissions on contracts concluded with his participation. If the amount of the commission is not fixed in an agreement or a tariff, the commission shall be the amount that is customarily accepted in the given circumstances. In the absence of a contract to the contrary, the agent may only claim reimbursement of out-of-pocket expenses incurred in the performance of his duties, provided that the amount does not exceed that which is customary in the circumstances. In order to secure claims for commission and claims for reimbursement of expenses and advances made to the principal, the agent has a statutory right of security over the principal's property received in connection with the agency contract while it is in his possession or in the possession of a person holding it in his name or while he can dispose of it by document.

915. It should be noted that in accordance with the relevant EU regulations, the Civil Code has introduced mandatory provisions protecting the agent's rights to commission, which cannot be changed by the contract. In particular, they concern the right to commission or some form of compensation after termination of the agency agreement, if the principal benefits from the agent's actions during the agency agreement.

916. Brokers do not act on the basis of the agency contract, but usually on the basis of a service agreement between them and the client and the power of attorney granted by the client. It is common practice in Poland that the client (policyholder) does not pay the remuneration to the broker, but the commission (brokerage) is paid by the insurer. To this end, brokers conclude commission agreements with insurers.

917. In marine insurance, the position of the broker is regulated by the Maritime Code. According to the provisions of the Maritime Code, the ship's agent acts as a permanent representative of the ship's operator in a given port or in a given area (Article 191), and the ship's broker acts as an intermediary on the basis of an individual order (each time) (Article 198). It should be noted that the scope of the legal status of 'intermediaries' is much wider and has a different legal status in England than in Poland, which complicates the legal relationship in Polish practice, which is based on the British standard policy.

918. The amount of the broker's remuneration is determined by agreement and, in the absence of an agreement, by custom; in the absence of custom, the broker is entitled to remuneration in an amount that is customary in the given circumstances. However, the broker is entitled to remuneration (commission) if the contract is concluded as a result of his efforts. The amount of the broker's remuneration shall be determined by agreement or, in the absence of an agreement, by a tariff. If the tariff does not contain a relevant provision, the amount of the remuneration is again determined by custom, and if there is no custom, the shipbroker is entitled to remuneration in the amount of what is customary in the given circumstances.

§2. Insurance Intermediaries and the Insurance Contract

919. An insurance contract concluded with the help of an intermediary has direct effects on the policyholder and the insurer. However, Polish law provides for a number of protective measures in relation to insurance contracts concluded with the help of an intermediary or in the case where the contract is concluded for the benefit of a third party (i.e., where the policyholder and the insured are different entities, e.g., in the case of group insurance). The majority of the rules result from the implementation of the EU acquis communautaire, but some of them are a response of the Polish legislator to the shortcomings or malpractices observed in the local market.

920. First of all, it should be mentioned that the rules on customer protection based on the IDD (and previously on the IMD) provide for the mechanism of risk transfer, which consists of a rule that the payment of the premium made to the intermediary is recognised as being made directly to the insurer. If the insurer pays the claim to the intermediary, only the actual receipt of the payment by the insured releases the insurer from its obligations.

921. In the case of an insurance contract concluded on behalf of a third party, in particular group insurance, where the consent of the insured person is required for the provision of insurance cover or where the insured person agrees to finance the cost of the insurance premium, the insurer may not invoke exclusions of cover and the foreseeable consequences of breaches of the insured person's obligations in the event of failure to provide the insured person with the policy conditions before such consent is given.

922. In the case of insurance for the account of another person, especially in the case of group insurance, the policyholder may not receive remuneration or other benefits in connection with the offer of insurance cover or for activities related to the performance of the insurance contract. This does not exclude the possibility of the policyholder financing the cost of the insurance premium. The prohibition on receiving remuneration or other advantages also applies to persons acting for or on behalf of the policyholder, but it does not apply to insurance contracts concluded for the account of employees or persons working for them on the basis of civil law contracts and members of their families, nor to contracts concluded for the account of members of associations, professional bodies or trade unions. The above provisions are intended to counteract the absence of authorisation requirements in the distribution of insurance products (shadow intermediaries).

Part VIII. Reinsurance

923. The reinsurance market in Poland is formed in majority by the insurers writing reinsurance in addition to their substantial business, as none of the biggest global reinsurers has its seat in Poland. There is one original Polish reinsurance company which offers reinsurance for Polish and regional insurance markets. The Polish Reinsurance Company (Polish Re) is claimed to be the leading regional reinsurer active in the market of Central and Eastern Europe. It has operated since 1996 and in 2009 became a member company of Fairfax Financial Holdings Limited, headquartered in Toronto. As for 2021, Polish Re is rated at the level of 'A-' by AM Best.

924. Among the newest developments in the reinsurance market in Poland is the final confirmation by the PFSA of the possibility of cooperating by the Polish reinsurers with third-country reinsurers provided that the latter meet the requirements of Commission Delegated Regulation (EU) 2015/35 of 10 October 2014 supplementing Directive 2009/138/EC of the European Parliament and of the Council on the taking-up and pursuit of the business of Insurance and Reinsurance (Solvency II). This means that reinsurance agreements entered into with such entities may be taken into account in the calculation of the minimum capital requirements provided that the third-country reinsurer has a credit quality of 3 or more.

925. As regards the results of the reinsurance market in Poland, The gross premiums written from active reinsurance in Division I were insignificant, amounting to PLN 0.005 million in 2021 and PLN 0.013 million in 2022. In 2021 and 2022, no claims and benefits will be paid from active reinsurance. The share of reinsurers in gross premiums written (outward reinsurance) of Division I (life insurance) amounts to PLN 535.8 million in 2022, 8.8% more than in 2021. The share of reinsurers in Division I premiums will increase from 2.23% in 2021 to 2.49% in 2022. Reinsurers' share of gross claims and benefits will be PLN 258 million in 2022, 2.3% less than in the previous year. The reinsurers' share of claims was 1.37%, 0.6% lower than in the previous year. In 2022, gross premiums written from active reinsurance in Division II (non-life insurance) amounted to PLN 3,333 million, 0.2% more than in 2021. The share of active reinsurance in Division II premiums in 2022 was 6.56%. Gross claims and benefits paid by enterprises under active reinsurance amounted to PLN 1,526 million in 2022, 27.0% more than in the previous year. The share of active reinsurance in Division II claims was 5.98%. The share of reinsurers in gross premiums written (outward reinsurance) of Division II in 2022 was almost PLN 10.3 billion, 6.7% more than in 2021. The share of reinsurers in non-life insurance premiums in 2022 is 20.26%. Reinsurers' share of gross claims and benefits in 2022 will be PLN 4.3 billion, 25.5% more than in the previous year. The reinsurers' share of claims will increase by 1.85% to 16.7% in 2022.[45]

926. Reinsurance activity is regulated by the AIRA of 11 September 2015. Reinsurance activity may be conducted by an insurance company (which conducts both insurance and reinsurance activity) or by a reinsurance company (which conducts only reinsurance activity). In the latter case, the reinsurance activity is regulated by a separate section of the Act. These provisions were introduced into the Polish legal system as an implementation of the Reinsurance Directive (Directive 2005/68/EC of the European Parliament and of the Council of 16 November 2005 on reinsurance and amending Council Directives 73/239/EEC, 92/49/EEC, as well as Directives 98/78/EC and 2002/83/EC). Finally, they comply with the Solvency II regime.

927. The legal requirements for the conduct of reinsurance activities are almost identical to those for the conduct of insurance activities. It concerns the forms of conducting reinsurance activity, rules of conducting reinsurance activity in Poland by foreign reinsurers (from EU and non-EU countries), reporting, merger, liquidation, etc. The specific rules (which are similar to the rules for insurance activity) concern the financial aspects of reinsurers, i.e., the own funds of reinsurers, the assets for covering liabilities and the principles of their calculation.

928. Reinsurance contracts are not subject to specific provisions of the PCC or other regulations. Certain rules taken from various areas of civil law must be examined on a case-by-case basis in order to determine to what extent they apply to reinsurance. It is clear that the general provisions of the Code of Obligations, inserted in Title I of Book 3 of the Civil Code, are applicable when the ceding insurer demands payment from the reinsurer. However, it should be emphasised that reinsurance contracts are usually based on standard terms and are often governed by foreign law. However, even if Polish law is applicable, the agreements are based on standard market terms. In the case of compulsory insurance, reinsurance agreements are usually governed by the law applicable to the insurance contracts themselves.

45. Annual Report of the Polish Chamber of Commerce of 2022.

Part IX. Taxation of Insurance

929. With regard to insurance and distribution activities, corporate income tax, personal income tax and VAT should be mentioned. As a rule, the provisions of EU directives have been transposed into the Polish tax system.

§1. Income Tax

930. Activity in the insurance sector is recognised as a business activity. Insurance intermediaries, such as agents and brokers, as well as insurance companies, are recognised as entrepreneurs and are subject to taxation depending on the form of their activity.

931. Insurance companies, which by law are corporations, are obliged to pay corporate income tax on their taxable income, as are all business entities operating in Poland. The main rules of corporate income tax are set out in the Act of 15 February 1992 on Corporate Income Tax (as amended). The rules of corporate income tax apply to all companies having their registered office in the territory of Poland. There is no general income tax exemption for companies with foreign participation.

932. Polish tax law is strict and provides for few subsidies and incentives for legal entities. These mainly consist of tax exemptions, reliefs and deductions.

933. A company may deduct certain costs and expenses incurred to generate income and those necessary for its operation. The depreciation of fixed assets and the amortisation of intangible assets and legal rights are considered deductible revenue-generating costs.

934. The following costs should be mentioned among an insurance company's revenue-generating costs: technical provisions, deductions for the prevention fund and payments to insurance supervisory authorities.

935. The 19% corporate income tax is the basic corporate income tax.

936. In addition to insurance companies, which are generally subject to CIT, insurance intermediaries are subject to CIT: limited liability companies, joint-stock companies and other legal entities; companies in the process of being established;

limited partnerships with a registered office or management board in Poland; unincorporated companies with a registered office or management board in another state if, under the tax legislation of another state, they are treated as legal entities and are subject to taxation in that state on all their income, irrespective of where it is earned; organisational units without legal personality, with the exception of civil partnerships, general partnerships, professional partnerships and limited partnerships.

937. In the case of intermediaries carrying out intermediary activities in the form of a partnership (other than limited partnerships), no CIT is levied. Instead, partnership income is allocated to the partners and is subject to PIT together with other income.

938. Taxpayers with a place of business or management in Poland are subject to CIT in Poland on their total income. Taxpayers who do not have an office or management board in Poland are subject to CIT only on income earned in Poland. However, Poland has concluded several treaties for the avoidance of double taxation, which may provide for specific solutions depending on the nationality of the taxpayer.

939. It should be mentioned that indemnities and other benefits paid by insurers to policyholders or other beneficiaries are exempt from income tax.

940. Natural persons engaged in business activities are taxed according to the tax scale. Such individuals may, upon request, have their income taxed at a flat rate of 19%, taking into account restrictions on services provided to former/current employers and management services. Depending on the scope of the business activity carried out, the taxpayer may request the application of simplified tax forms if certain criteria are met.

§2. VAT

941. Polish regulations on Value Added Tax (VAT) are based on EU legislation, currently (UE) 2017/952 z 29 maja 2017 r. (ATAD 2). The VAT legislation follows the EU model.

942. The basic transactions subject to VAT are, *inter alia*, supplies of goods and services deemed to have been carried out in Poland. In some cases, the supply of goods or services free of charge may also be subject to VAT.

943. VAT is charged on the sale, export and import of goods and services in Poland. The basic rate is 23% and applies to most goods and services, with lower rates of 8% and 0%. Due to the financial crisis, the government increased the VAT rate in the period from 1 January 2011 to 21 December 2013 to 23% and 8%, respectively, and are still valid for 2021.

944. It should be noted that insurance services, which are a type of financial services, and insurance intermediation services are exempt from VAT. As a result, insurance companies and intermediaries cannot reduce the tax during the course of their business.

945. However, insurance companies and intermediaries are usually registered as VAT payers. It may be convenient for insurance companies to engage in other activities related to insurance but not exempt from VAT, such as trading in goods taken over from the insured in the course of claims settlement.

946. It should be noted that VAT taxation in the insurance sector is subject to the case law of the European Court of Justice (ECJ). The ECJ has again confirmed the need for a narrow interpretation of the exemption for insurance activities in the context of outsourced services. In particular, in the Polish case of *Minister Finansóww v. Aspiro* (ECJ, 17 March 2016), the ECJ confirmed that the VAT exemption does not apply to other services (even if they are insurance-related) if they do not form part of the insurance services as an indivisible whole. Thus, outsourced claims handling services cannot benefit from the exemption unless they are provided by an insurance broker or agent (which requires involvement in bringing together insurers and persons seeking insurance). In addition, the remuneration of insurance brokers or agents may be subject to VAT if it consists of services other than the mediation of the conclusion of an insurance contract (e.g., the provision of advice or assistance in the settlement of claims by insurance intermediaries may be subject to VAT).

947. The Polish rules on the place of supply of services are in line with similar rules applied in other EU Member States. In the case of services supplied between taxpayers (B2B basis) with their place of business/residence/permanent establishment in other countries, the primary place of taxation is the country where the place of business/residence/permanent establishment of the entity purchasing the service is located. The reverse is true for services supplied by a taxable person to a non-taxable person (B2C basis), in which case the place of the business establishment/residence/fixed establishment of the supplier is the primary place of taxation.

948. In the case of cross-border supplies of services, VAT may be payable in Poland if the place of supply is in Poland. As a result, according to the general rules, VAT is payable in Poland on service transactions between taxpayers from different countries only if the recipient of the service has its place of business, residence or permanent establishment in Poland. However, in the case of services provided by a Polish taxpayer to a non-taxpayer entity, VAT is payable in Poland if the service provider has its place of business, residence or permanent establishment in Poland. There are several exceptions to the above rules – for example, the place of taxation of services related to immovable property is always the place where the immovable property is located. The place of taxation of restaurant and catering services is the place (country) where they are actually provided.

949. First, we should underline here that Article 135(a) of the Council Directive 2006/112/EC of 28 November 2006 on the common system of Value Added Tax[46] (the 'VAT Directive') exempts, from VAT, 'insurance and reinsurance transactions, including related services performed by insurance brokers and insurance agents' and confirms the status set since 17 May 1977.[47] The exemptions provided for in favour of certain activities in the public interest including postal services, medical activities, welfare and social security activities, are listed in Chapter 2 of the Title IX of the VAT Directive, while Chapter 3 of the VAT Directive provides for the exemptions in respect of 'other activities', which include the exemption of 'insurance and reinsurance activities and other financial activities'.

950. Although exemptions for activities in the public interest are understandable, for a tax that claims to be neutral from the point of view of the entrepreneur, it seems difficult to understand why there are so many exceptions to the general rule. The 'other exemptions' were introduced because they were considered to be difficult activities to tax, in the sense that there were technical concerns about the application of VAT to such activities.[48]

951. Such exemptions may seem very favourable to industry. However, this is a misconception. A company benefiting from a VAT exemption does not have the right to deduct the input VAT on the services it outsources: the latter is a revenue-generating cost for these companies. In order to solve this problem, insurers have used cost-sharing arrangements to create cost-sharing groups. However, the Court of Justice of the EU recently ruled that insurers could not enter into such agreements because they were only open to bodies carrying out activities in the public interest.[49] The need to amend the current VAT rules applicable to the insurance industry is all the more pressing given that insurance companies also provide services that may potentially fall within the scope of VAT.

952. Since 2011, numerous exemptions have been called into question, as they run counter to the application of VAT, which results in a broad tax base. In one of its working documents accompanying the Green Paper on the future of VAT, the European Commission considered that 'there is a growing acceptance that the technical problems [which justified the VAT exemptions in 1977] can be overcome'.[50]

---

46. Council Directive 2006/112/EC of 28 Nov. 2006 on the common system of Value Added Tax (OJ L 347, 11.12.2006, pp. 1–118, as amended).
47. Article 13, B(a) of the Sixth Council Directive of May 1977 on the harmonisation of the laws of the Member States relating to turnover taxes – Common system of value added tax: uniform basis of assessment (77/388/EEC).
48. Piia Ahonen & Isabella Kartila, Will VAT Exemption of Financial and Insurance Services Become History?, 29 Oct. 2020, https://www.hannessnellman.com/news-views/blog/will-vat-exemption-of-financial-and-insurance-services-become-history/ .
49. CJEU, Judgment of 4 May 2017, *Commission v. Luxembourg*, C-274/15.
50. Commission Staff Working Document, Accompanying Document to the Green Paper on the Future of VAT – Towards a Simpler, More Robust and Efficient VAT System (COM (2010), 695 final) – of 1 Dec. 2010, p. 30.

953. In recent years, the questioning of these long-standing exemptions has been at the centre of further discussions. For example, in its position paper of 7 March 2018, Insurance Europe, the European insurance and reinsurance federation, called for the modernisation of the VAT rules applicable to financial services[51] as the current rules create an 'uneven playing field within the EU' and 'VAT is becoming a key factor affecting the EU's competitiveness'. At its 26th meeting on 5 April 2019, Insurance Europe's Group on the Future of VAT provided an update on the state of financial and insurance services and their VAT treatment. In its report, the Group noted that the existing exemptions are outdated in view of the development of new services in the financial sector. The position on reviewing the scope of VAT exemptions and clarifying the definitions of different insurance and financial services was presented on the REFIT platform.[52]

954. Given the concerns expressed by certain major players in the insurance sector, we can expect further developments regarding the VAT exemptions for insurance and financial activities.

955. These 'technical concerns' justifying the exemption of insurance services from VAT have not prevented EU Member States from introducing specific taxes exclusively applicable to insurance contracts, i.e., insurance premium taxes (the 'IPTs'), which are the main subject of this paper, or the so-called parafiscal charges.

§3. Withholding Tax

956. Dividends paid by companies resident in Poland are subject to withholding tax at a rate of 19%. The tax is payable directly by the company paying the dividend by deducting it from the payment made. Dividends paid between Polish companies are not subject to CIT at the shareholder level.

957. Tax treaties concluded by Poland with other countries may provide for a lower rate of withholding tax on dividends (5%, 10% and 15%) if certain conditions are met (e.g., the company paying the dividend should be in possession of the shareholder's tax residence certificate).

958. There is a possibility of exempting dividends if the company receiving the dividends is a company subject to taxation on its entire income in Poland or in another EU Member State, the Swiss Confederation or an EEA country.

959. The condition for exemption is continuous holding for two years by the company receiving the dividends of the required 10% (in the case of Switzerland –

51. Insurance Europe Comments on the Need to Modernize VAT Rules for Financial Services, 7 Mar. 2018, CO-TAX-18-012.
52. REFIT Platform Opinion on EU VAT Directive (2006/112/EC) Affecting Insurance and Financial Services by the Board of Swedish Industry and Commerce (NNR) on 14 Mar. 2019.

25%) of shares in the capital of the company paying the tax. The requirement is met even if this period expires after the date of receipt of the dividend.

§4. Insurance Premium Tax

960. There is no IPT in Poland. Instead, certain parafiscal charges apply, such as contributions to the Financial Supervision Authority (Komisja Nadzoru Finansowego), the Polish Insurance Chamber (Polska Izba Ubezpieczeń) or the Financial Ombudsman (Rzecznik Finansowy).

961. The lack of taxation concerns insurance contracts concluded in Poland. However, the IPT may apply to Polish insurers providing insurance services in other countries where the IPT is mandatory. The obligation to pay this tax depends on the country where the insurance risk arises. The subject of ambiguity is both the amount of the IPT and the existence of other fees and formalities that an insurer operating in a country other than Poland may be obliged to pay. The rate of IPT and other fees and formalities are regulated by the internal regulations of the respective country.

Part X. Risk Management and Prevention

§1. Risk Management in Insurance

962. Risk management has become a determinant and integral part of organisational culture, which means translating it into strategic, tactical and operational objectives, as well as strictly defining people's responsibilities on an individual, functional and territorial basis. An extremely important issue in this area is the adoption of common standards. Until 2009, many countries relied on standards developed by national standards bodies. Today, international ISO standards are being achieved, ensuring that concepts in this area are standardised internationally. According to ISO, risk management is a coordinated set of activities for managing and controlling an organisation's exposure to risk. In order to determine the meaning of risk management, the concept of risk should also be specified. Among many different definitions, the one based on ISO 3100 is the most popular. This recognises risk as a combination of the probability and impact (consequence) of a hazardous event on the organisation.

963. International standards, as well as European and national standards, can be divided into standards containing general requirements, certain principles and standards containing specific requirements. A characteristic of the so-called general standards is their flexibility, i.e., the possibility of applying the requirements they contain to organisations or systems with different characteristics. In other words, regardless of the type of business or services provided, organisations can apply the requirements of the same standard. Standards with specific requirements usually apply to specific groups of products, processes or systems. Both types of standards are used in different countries, depending on the stated purpose, technical conditions, climate, geography, infrastructure and safety requirements.

964. Introduced in 2009, ISO 31000 is primarily a set of frameworks, processes and principles to be followed when implementing a risk assessment process in any organisation. The main aim of ISO 31000 is to standardise risk management processes within organisations, regardless of sector or type of business. The recommendations contained in this standard can be used by companies of any type, associations and groups, and even individuals. In addition to the ISO standard, the most popular risk management standards used in Poland include the Risk Management Standard developed by the Federation of European Risk Management Associations (FERMA), Enterprise Risk Management – Integrated Framework developed by the Committee of Sponsoring Organisations of the Tradeway Commission (COSO II) – Australian and New Zealand Risk Management Standards AS/NZS 4360:2004. These risk management standards do not, of course, exhaust all possibilities. In addition to the solutions mentioned, there are also national or industry-specific standards.

965. The FEMA standard provides examples of how to describe identified risks and introduces a three-level scale of probability of occurrence of an event and its consequences. The consequences of an event are treated as both an opportunity (positive consequences) and a threat (negative consequences). In this way, risk is understood in its entirety and not, as is sometimes the case, only through the prism of its negative impact on the organisation. The standard also makes reference to the internal legislation of the organisation implementing a risk management system. The need for formal regulations is indicated, as is the definition of the role of the various bodies involved in the process: Board of Directors, Management, Risk Manager (Committee) and Internal Audit. The FEMA standard is very general and universal. It shows in an illustrative way what the components of the risk management process are and how to set sample benchmarks for estimating identified risks. On the one hand, this universality makes it possible to adapt the solution to almost any organisation and does not limit one's own inventiveness, but on the other hand, it requires a lot of knowledge and further search for detailed solutions to specific problems.

966. ISO 31000:20093 is a set of principles, frameworks and processes that can be applied to any organisation in the field of risk management and crisis management more broadly. It does not provide ready-made solutions, but rather risk management components to be incorporated into systems to improve their effectiveness. The implementation of these components does not complicate an organisation's operations but increases the chances of achieving its objective. It is emphasised that this requires the use of common, understandable terminology, transparent processes and sufficient information.

967. According to international standards, the risk management process consists of risk assessment – including risk identification, analysis and evaluation – decision making, risk management, monitoring and review. This process applies to every risk and must be an integral part of the organisation's activities in practice, with a contractor who can provide the right methods and tools for its implementation. Risk management is not just about compiling a list of risks and actions to be taken. It requires a serious approach to risk assessment, which is a set of many activities, including risk identification, analysis and evaluation. It is a systemic view of the whole business that requires a well-planned strategy. Risk management is a process that falls under the responsibility of the management, board of directors, managers and employees who are charged with identifying risks and dealing with the development of strategies for the organisation's activities that may have a positive or negative impact on the organisation's operating processes and, with a view to achieving the objective, protecting the organisation from risks that are higher than acceptable. Risk management is also the reduction of uncertainty and the ability to cope with it.

968. Risk management is the selection of risk-modifying actions and their rational implementation. The basic action is to control and mitigate risks while paying attention to avoidance and transfer. Modelling based on cost-benefit analysis is more favourable. The studies of the standard raise the problem of not fully defined risk financing, which results from a dual approach: (1) impact financing (insurance); or (2) allocation of funds for risk mitigation. Any action taken against a risk after its assessment should, as a minimum condition, guarantee: (1) effective and efficient functioning of the organisation; (2) effective internal controls; (3) compliance of actions with laws and other applicable regulations.

969. Risk management must have a legal basis, in particular internal control processes, which should be implemented and operated as transparently as possible. Without controls, it is difficult to talk about risk management. When the cost of mitigating risk is disproportionate to the risk itself, flexibility is recommended, but not when it comes to human health and life. In everyday life, methods of financial protection against the possible consequences of risks are used, for example, insurance.

970. Risk management has become an integral part of many areas of government activity. This is especially true for activities related to security in the broad sense (solutions for the entire sector) and in the narrow sense (solutions for individual institutions), as one can speak, for example, of the security of public finances, economic development or branches of state administration, on the one hand, and of flood security or the security of specific territorial units and entities, on the other. For the whole spectrum of risk management in Poland, the Polish legal system has introduced a systemic approach to risk management in the public finance sector. The Act on Public Finance has introduced solutions that strengthen the control over the disbursement of public funds and mandates numerous entities, i.e., ministries, central administration, banks and other public administration entities and institutions, to enforce such solutions.

971. Risk management at the national level in Poland is usually combined with a crisis management system. This system was the result of many years of discussion, and the first act introducing elements of the crisis management structure into the Polish legal system was the Decree of 3 December 2002 on the manner of establishing the Municipal, District and Voivodship Crisis Response Teams and the Government Crisis Coordination Team and their functioning, implementing the delegation from Article 12 of the Act on the State of Disaster. The system was established five years later when the Emergency Management Act came into force.

§2. INSURANCE PREVENTION

972. Insurance is traditionally a form of risk management, but its function has always gone beyond purely compensatory aspects. One of the subsidiary but important functions of insurance is undoubtedly risk prevention, which is considered the most rational method of loss control. The methodology of insurance even refers to two basic but equal functions of insurance – compensation and prevention. It is also argued that without prevention, the business of insurance would be unprofitable. Prevention can make an insurer's claims process more sustainable and sometimes even become a competitive factor in the insurance market. However, the importance of the preventive function is not only due to the competitive market factors mentioned above but also to the social role of insurance (including private insurance). In this context, it can complement the social and organisational role played by the state, especially in the area of catastrophic and health risks. Thus, although both doctrine and sometimes even legislation entrust insurers with a preventive function, the legal regulations in this respect don't go much beyond this general function (such as the financing of road safety campaigns or the financing of fire extinguishers, etc.) and are not expressed at the level of individual insurance relations.[53]

973. Risk prevention is directly related to the predictability of risk. A useful definition, therefore, is one that includes measures and actions taken in advance to prevent new risks from arising or to impede their development and intensification. Prevention should therefore include both measures aimed at preventing the risk from materialising – known as 'precautionary measures' – and those aimed at preventing [avoiding or reducing] the consequences of an accident that has already occurred, which can also be called 'mitigation'. If we consider the objective of preventive action, which is the ultimate reduction of costs, as well as the unavoidable nature of natural hazards such as earthquakes, volcanoes and hurricanes, it seems obvious that, from an economic and axiological point of view, all the above actions should be recognised as risk prevention. It is claimed that risk prevention aims to systematically reduce the likelihood of a risk occurring, although given the definition of risk, prevention can act on both elements, i.e., the likelihood and the impact of the event. Risk prevention methods include all techniques and management practices that help to avoid unnecessary or foreseeable risks.

974. The role of prevention in the insurance sector, although always present in some form, is growing. Strengthening the preventive role of insurance may have the effect of making many uninsurable risks insurable, thanks to the technical possibility of managing, controlling and preventing them. The importance of making inclusiveness more than a postulate is obvious. This applies both to health and home insurance (with the help of the Internet of Things and a wide range of available data) and to agricultural and other climate risks (with the help of geospatial data). Although home insurance and climate risks seem to be a quite natural trend, some

53. K. Malinowska, Risk Prevention and Insurance. Reaching or Trespassing the Insurance Boundaries?, Wiadomości Ubezpieczeniowe 4/2023/.

ethical questions can be raised in relation to health insurance – what kind of data and to what extent can be used, whether data can be cross-referenced and whether prevention plays a role as one of the ultimate goals. Nevertheless, this trend has started to become commonplace in various types of insurance and is claimed to be a new business model in insurance, based on new types of risk assessment and behaviour-based pricing. An equally important trend resulting from the capabilities of technology is the prevention of risk as part of a holistic approach to risk assessment by insurers. This holistic approach, known as the 'risk prevention framework', has the potential to transform risk management processes both within insurance organisations and within the organisations of the insured.

975. The role of law in relation to insurers' preventive capabilities is primarily sought in the regulation of insurance activities. Some analysis has been carried out on the basis of solvency regulations, in particular the Solvency II Directive. Solvency II states that 'In order to promote good risk management and to align regulatory capital requirements with industry practices, the Solvency Capital Requirement should be determined as the economic capital to be held by insurance and reinsurance undertakings' (…). That economic capital should be calculated on the basis of the true risk profile of those undertakings, taking into account the impact of possible risk mitigation techniques as well as diversification effects. In addition, 'risk mitigation techniques' have been defined as 'all techniques that enable insurance and reinsurance undertakings to transfer some or all of their risks to another party'. Risk mitigation techniques are part of the risk management system of insurance undertakings. However, this appears to be applied at a general level of management of the insurer and does not relate to actions concerning individual insurance contracts. It is therefore only regulated in the context of solvency requirements (*see* Articles 100 and 108 of the Solvency II Directive). Only a few examples of insurance legislation in Europe explicitly proclaim the preventive role of insurance. These include the Polish and Hungarian laws. The preamble to the Hungarian Insurance Act states: 'In order to protect the interests of policyholders, to promote self-sufficiency, to increase confidence in insurance and insurance companies, to strengthen the role of the insurance industry in general and of insurance companies in the national economy, to increase the viability and reliability of the insurance industry and the guarantees for insurance services, (…) to promote the role of insurance companies in preventing losses (…), Parliament has adopted the following act' (Hungarian Insurance Act; Act LXXXVIII of 2014). Another example is the Polish Insurance Act, which stipulates that activities directly related to reinsurance are, in particular, activities in the field of statistical consultancy, actuarial consultancy, risk analysis, research for the benefit of clients, investment of funds of the reinsurance company, as well as activities aimed at preventing the occurrence of an insured event or reducing its effects or financing such activities from a prevention fund (Polish Insurance and Reinsurance Act).

976. The modern premise of insurance, and indeed of an insurance contract, should be not only to compensate for the financial consequences of the insured event but also to support the insured in relation to the covered risk before it materialises. In fact, the inclusiveness approach to risk prevention should be applied as an inherent element of insurance coverage. Thus, the main challenge for insurers may be to move from a product-centric to a customer-centric approach and to offer not only products but also prevention and mitigation services as part of their promise. This seems possible, especially given that insurers have expertise that no one else has, making them valuable partners in the ecosystems that are developing to offer consumers both compensation for losses and risk prevention services. The absence of explicit regulatory obligations in this regard should not prevent us from applying the well-established principles of utmost good faith and reasonable expectations, which should serve the changing technological landscape.

977. The approach to risk management in this area is remarkable, as insurers have understood that the viability of these products and the effectiveness of risk management in general cannot be questioned without a proactive approach to risk prevention and participation in the de facto management of these risks with policyholders. Insurers must lead the way in developing the most effective techniques – from proactive monitoring to incident response – to combat cyber threats. By protecting their own assets and systems, insurers can build trust with consumers.

978. A similar approach should be taken in relation to health insurance, particularly in relation to genetic data or genetic research. The latter seems to be developing particularly rapidly. Although most legal systems prohibit insurers from requesting medical genetic data, the issues surrounding the reliability and safety of genetic data raise questions about insurance risks. This is a special category of insurance prevention. The increasing volume of these data and the possibility of their automatic processing and aggregation means that they can fulfil a special preventive function.

979. Loss prevention is an area where new technologies can play a significant and relatively uncontroversial role. It involves not only the identification of factors that increase the risk of loss events but also the ability to respond quickly when there is a chance of reducing their impact. Examples include the Internet of Things (IoT), advanced image analysis tools such as satellites and health insurance in relation to genetic data. As with underwriting, the potential of new technologies lies in the identification of risky behaviour on the part of the insured, but also in the post-contractual phase, in the stimulation of insured behaviour, by encouraging or imposing good practices on the insured in order to mitigate claims, and finally in the prediction of the outcome of insured behaviour, or even in the monitoring of insured behaviour through the use of connected devices. For example, the monitoring of driving behaviour by telematics devices not only serves to assess risk but also has a significant and ad hoc influence on the behaviour of a driver who is aware of the presence of such a device. This means that moral hazard can be reduced and can certainly be seen as one of the real benefits of using artificial intelligence in insurance. Data from new sources, better processed and in greater quantities, has the potential to facilitate the implementation of advanced risk management and early warning systems. These, in turn, allow timely intervention to reduce not only the frequency of insured events but also the severity of losses when risks materialise. The use of new technologies can therefore help to broaden the role of insurance, transforming it from a function of protecting against the consequences of an insured event to a function of predicting and preventing the materialisation of risks. As in other stages, the creation of models to predict the frequency and severity of claims is relevant to the entire insurance cycle and should definitely be linked to product design, distribution and marketing. Thus, it seems that risk prevention should also be recognised as an additional or enhanced insurance service.

Selected Bibliography

Brodecki, Z. (ed.). *Insurance Law*. Kluwer Warsaw, 2010.
Brodecki, Z. *Insurance Contract Law in Poland.* Gdańsk: Info Trade, 1993.
Fuchs, D., Malinowska, K. Maśniak, D. *Kontrakty na rynku Ubezpieczeń.* Wolters Kluwer, 2020.
Fras, M. Kucharski,B. Malinowska, K. Maśniak, D. Szaraniec, M., *Dystrybucja Ubezpieczeń.* Wolters Kluwer, 2020.
Gliniecka J. *Financial Law*. Wolters Kluwer, 2016.
Gnela, B. *Ubezpieczenia Gospodarcze, wybrane zagadnienia prawne*. Warsaw: Kluwer, 2011.
Konert, A. *Ubezpieczenia lotnicze.* Warsaw: Kluwer, 2014.
Krajewski, M. *Umowa ubezpieczenia według kodeksu cywilnego*. WKP, 2011.
Kucharski, B. *Świadczenie ubezpieczyciela w umowie ubezpieczenia*. Wolters Kluwer, 2019.
Malinowska K. *Customer's Best Interest as a Rule in Insurance Contracts, Considerations Against New Regulations on Insurance Distribution in: Insurance Challenges of Anno Domini*. Kozminski University, 2018.
Malinowska, K. *Dyrektywa w sprawie dystrybucji ubezpieczeń – krytyczne spojrzenie na metodę implementacji w kontekście systematyki polskiego prawa ubezpieczeń,* in: Nowak A., Nowak S. eds, *Jagodziński, Polski obszar Europejskich rynków finansowo ubezpieczeniowych.* Anno Domini, 2017.
Malinowska, K. *Insurance Contract in Europe Without Boundaries.* Branta, 2008.
Malinowska, K. Quo Vadis Collective Insurance, Observations on ECJ Rulings Affecting Group Insurance, Gdańskie Studia Prawnicze XXVII – No. 3 (60)/ 2023.
Malinowska, T. *Transparency in Insurance Contract of Poland*, in: P. Marano, Noussia K. eds, *Transparency in Insurance Contract Law.* Springer, 2019.
Malinowska-Kamińska, K. *Claims Made Policy According to the Polish Law.* PA 1/2001.
Malinowska-Kamińska, K. *Product Liability Insurance.* PA 1/2000.
Maśniak, D. *Ubezpieczenia ekologiczne*. Lex, 2003.
Orlicki, M. *Ubezpieczenia obowiązkowe*. Warsaw: Kluwer, 2011.
Sangowski, T. *Ubezpieczenia Gospodarcze*. Warsaw: Poltext, 1998.
Sangowski, T. *Vademecum Ubezpieczeń gospodarczych.* Saga Poznań, 1998.
Szczepańska, M. *Ubezpieczenia na życie z ubezpieczeniowym funduszem kapitałowym*. Lex, 2011.

Selected Bibliography

Tarasiuk, W. *Polish Market: Distribution of Life Insurance Products in the Polish Market*, in: Caldana M., Gouden M., Moran M. eds, *Private Life Insurance*.

Tereszkiewicz, P. *Obowiązki informacyjne w umowach o usługi finansowe*. Warsaw: Kluwer, 2015.

Index

The numbers here refer to paragraph numbers.

Index